The Way of the Fox

Painting by Lu Palmer   *Photo courtesy U.S. Army*

George Washington,
the Commander-in-Chief

Portraits of Washington made during the years he was commander-in-chief of the Continental army were for the most part too highly stylized to be considered accurate. Not until he was much older were the really fine paintings done. In this study, the artist has stripped the years from those later portraits to show him as he would have appeared early in the war.

The Way of the Fox

American Strategy in the War for America

1775-1783

Dave Richard Palmer

Contributions in Military History
Number 8

GREENWOOD PRESS
Westport, Connecticut ● London, England

Library of Congress Cataloging in Publication Data

Palmer, Dave Richard, 1934-
  The way of the fox.

  (Contributions in military history, no. 8)
  Bibliography: p.
  1. United States—History—Revolution, 1775-1783—
Campaigns and battles. 2. Strategy. I. Title.
II. Series.
E230.P24   973.3'3   74-5992
ISBN 0-8371-7531-3

Library of Congress Catalog Card Number: 74-5992
ISBN: 0-8371-7531-3

First published in 1975

Greenwood Press, a division of Williamhouse-Regency Inc.
51 Riverside Avenue, Westport, Connecticut 06880

Manufactured in the United States of America

To Lu—
For a Thousand Reasons

Contents

List of Illustrations

Acknowledgments

Standing at the head of the list of persons to whom I owe thanks for their contributions to this book is Theodore Ropp. He provided guidance and counsel and, most importantly, ideas. Jim Ransone, Ann Fisher, Sue Frazier, Win Holt, and Kenneth Pruett donated valuable service by reading parts of the manuscript and acting as a sounding board for many of the concepts. Tom Griess, from the United States Military Academy, and Jay Luvaas, from Allegheny College, read the manuscript and contributed scholarly, constructive criticism for which I am particularly grateful. The artwork in the maps is a measure of the talent and generosity of Edward Krasnoborski from the department of history at West Point. The Army War College and the army's Military History Research Collection, both located at Carlisle Barracks, Pennsylvania, gave me special assistance in the form of administrative support and official encouragement. Delorious Bailey did a fine job preparing the manuscript, while Alma Brown pitched in to help me meet deadlines. Through it all, Lu, Allison, and Kersten formed a much-appreciated rooting section.

Every author, once he expresses his gratitude for those who helped him, is bound to add that such errors as the book contains are his fault, not theirs. He is bound to because it is true.

DRP
Arlington, Virginia
1974

Introduction

The Revolutionary War was not a revolutionary war. Nor was it a war for independence. Our two most commonly used titles for that much-studied conflict are more than a little misleading. It fell rather short of being a revolution—and sought goals quite beyond independence. For their part, Englishmen have always been inclined to refer to it as the American war—a better label, perhaps, but one still not entirely descriptive.

The very word "revolution" implies a radical and fractious upending of society, a fundamental break in the political tradition of a people, the violent overthrow of one group or class by another. Such, clearly, was not the case in the American Revolutionary War. For the most part, power belonged to the same element of society before, during, and after the war. The fight began, it should be remembered, not so much because London had authority over the thirteen colonies but because royal ministers decided to try to exercise that authority. Long accustomed to de facto, if not de jure, independence, Americans stubbornly resisted Parliament's efforts to impose greater controls on them. Theirs was not a revolution to overthrow English government; it was a rebellion to retain American government. At best, though the words themselves fit together most uncomfortably, it might be called a conservative revolution.

As for independence, that word, too, can be misleading. For one thing, few civilized peoples in the world have ever enjoyed a greater degree of personal or political freedom than those eighteenth-century British subjects living in North America. They controlled their own individual destinies, and, hampered by remarkably little influence or interference from London, they ran affairs in their respective colonies as well. Colonial citizens were quite plainly Americans, not Englishmen. In the first months of the war, moreover, independence was not even a goal of the rebels. Redress of grievances was what patriots originally fought for, which is to say, for their rights as Englishmen. Then, when they saw no recourse but to separate from the mother country, a few pen strokes on parchment was all it took. Declaring it was doing it. The United States, a country long independent in virtually every way except form, came into being simply by announcing itself born. From then on, the struggle was essentially one to gain recognition and to settle the shape and expanse of the new nation. For Americans, it was a war for America.

That was not so for others, however. No one knows better than the British themselves that the American war was something more than that title suggests. Well before it had run its course, the conflict had spread to other powers and other theaters. France, Spain, and Holland eventually ended up in a state of declared war with England, while many other nations banded together in a League of Armed Neutrality, which was more anti-British than neutral. India, Africa, and Europe, in addition to the Americas and the high seas, provided varied settings for armed encounters. In a word, it was a worldwide war.

All of this is simply to say that one errs in viewing the American Revolutionary War as either a revolution or a fight for independence, or for that matter, as merely an American war. It contained elements of each, to be sure, but approaching it from any of those perspectives—or from a combination of all three—is probably too simplistic. The struggle our forebears found themselves engaged in some two centuries ago was rather more complex than military historians have since led us to believe.

It is not surprising that the wide-ranging war fought between 1775 and 1783 has proven elusive to label or difficult to understand. Its military aspects, in total, have yet to receive comprehensive study. Sandwiched tightly between the remarkable campaigns of Frederick the Great and the historical thunderclap of the Napoleonic era, and consequently dwarfed in military comparison, this clash of arms in America seemed relatively unimportant to military writers at the time—and since. In the main, historians have devoted their labors to the social, political, and economic ramifications of the struggle, or to biographical studies. Military works have tended toward the tactical; that is, they have been more or less limited to battles or, at best, to campaign studies. While some broader subjects, such as logistics and administration, have received limited attention, others, like command arrangements or the overall strategic framework, remain virtually untouched. Is it any wonder, then, that few Americans fully understand how patriots fought the war that established our nation? Nor should it be unexpected that of the various names by which the rebellion is remembered none is notably descriptive. A lack of crispness in its title generally mirrors a lack of comprehension of its conduct.

Apart from neglecting significant areas of the war, writers unfortunately are also guilty of clouding many of those very issues that they have attempted to describe. All in all, it is not too sweeping an indictment to say that, over the years, historians have handled few, if any, major events in our history quite as ineptly as they have the Revolutionary War.

Beginning with Parson Weems and others of his saccharine and chauvinistic ilk, generations of Americans were treated to a star-spangled collage of contrived images pasted on a Fourth of July poster—a picture having little more depth or dimension than the cardboard itself. It showed a chopped cherry tree and a dollar skimmed across a river, omnipotent frontiersmen standing beside embattled farmers, freezing huts at Valley Forge, laden boats wallowing amidst ice floes on the Delaware River, and, superimposed over it all, a determined trio of ragged bandsmen. The message was of the inevitable triumph of good over evil; the Deity marched alongside the patriots.

Then, rebelling against that teeth-curling diet of historical fudge, came the revisionists. In a spate of books written earlier in this century, they painted the military scenes somberly in black and gray, bleakness being the predominant theme. Washington was clearly a stumblebum general—impressive, to be sure, but a stumblebum nonetheless. His lieutenants were no better. Stubbornness was the greatest of the patriots' military virtues; they had simply hung on, had somehow muddled through to win. British leaders were even worse dolts who repeatedly snatched defeat from the jaws of victory. It was really more a case of Englishmen blundering the war away than of Americans winning it. In short, nothing in the *war* of the War of Independence merited scholarly attention or explanation.

Lately, as might be expected, the pendulum of perspective has swung back to center. Scholars have staked out a position somewhere in the middle ground, rejecting both extremes. The conduct of the struggle and the personalities of the participants have been depicted more objectively and have been generally described with commendable, if not remarkable, precision. Still, though, modern historians have persisted in selling short the military side of the war. Maybe, being preponderantly academicians, they do not have an intimate grasp of military factors, or consider such topics to be insignificant, or even harbor an aversion to subjects martial. There is even a school that considers the outcome of the revolution to have been predestined, much like a Greek tragedy. A residue of revisionist thinking, this line holds or implies that, since Washington and his lieutenants were utterly incompetent, they could have done nothing positive to influence the war's course. Thus, the generals are pictured merely as actors playing inflexible roles in a larger plot drawing unswervingly to a foreordained conclusion. For whatever reason or reasons, the fact remains that military aspects of the Revolutionary War have been particularly poorly portrayed. That should not be. It was, after all, a war.

Foremost among the considerations slighted by historians would have to be the strategic concepts under which the war was waged. (A startling omission, that, for without understanding the strategic framework on which *everything* else hangs, one may find it difficult to comprehend *anything* else.) If strategy is mentioned at all, it is likely to be couched in terms of the much ballyhooed —but possibly misconstrued—Fabian streak in George Washington and Nathanael Greene. (Fabius was a Roman general [275-203 B.C.] who believed the best way to defeat Hannibal was to avoid battle, letting time, attrition, and frustration wear the Carthaginians out.) The patriots get high marks for their adroitness at avoiding decisive battle, for their ability to wear down and outlast the British; they rarely receive even honorable mention for possessing or displaying any positive attributes of strategic skill.

Consider these evaluations of American strategy. John Alden, writing in the late 1960s: "The Americans had only to keep the field until Britain should tire of the struggle." From an edited volume published in 1965: "The plan of the Americans was the simple defensive—to oppose the British as best they could at every point, and to hold fast the line of the Hudson." Douglas Southall Freeman: "Washington's strategy had to be patiently defensive." North Callahan, in a brief biography of Washington published in 1972: "Washington did not really win the war but Britain lost it, mainly to circumstances rather than the American enemy." James Thomas Flexner, in what is probably the best biography yet of the American commander-in-chief, does credit him with creating an effective hit-and-run capability but clings to the traditional view that he was a Fabian strategist. Russell Weigley weighs in with a similar comment: "Since his army suffered from defects that might have made decisive contests fatal ones, Washington chose the methods of warfare that gave him his reputation as the American Fabius. . . . Unless he enjoyed unusual advantages of position, he believed he must evade direct tests of battle. But he had to try to wear down the enemy." Weigley says the patriot strategy was one of attrition, or, at best, erosion. The "necessary object" of the Continental army, wrote Thomas Frothingham in a study of Washington as commander-in-chief, was to conduct operations designed to bolster and embolden partisan fighters and to do "all that was possible to hold in check the superior main forces of the British."[1]

If it is ever safe to generalize, it is safe to say that historians today see American strategy in the Revolutionary War as being strictly one-dimensional: defensive. Moreover, they do not repudiate outright the concept of an inevitable outcome; overtones of the Greek tragedy persist.

The overall purpose of this book is to investigate and lay bare the war's strategic framework. Along the way, it might be shown that other dimensions existed as well and that the players had much to do with the way their drama ended.

What's more, with great good luck, we may also catch a fresh glimpse of the generalship of George Washington. Something new about Washington? How can it be, one might ask with pardonable incredulity, that with so many biographies of the general lining library shelves any aspect of his work could remain incompletely revealed? The answer is much the same as that given about strategy in the war: historians have talked *around* rather than *to* the subject. Indeed, Washington's generalship and the war's strategic framework are inextricably spliced together. As one biographer noted several decades ago, there are historians ''for every taste —those who treat Washington as a heaven-sent Messiah to those that treat him as a stupid old bore.'' The same is true today, although most reputable scholars have eliminated as definitely incorrect those judgments placing the Virginian at either extreme. He was neither a demigod nor a bumpkin.

Consider these contrasting evaluations of Washington's strategic ability. In the opinion of Thomas Jefferson, the military mind of the commander-in-chief was ''sure in conclusion'' but disappointingly ''slow in operation, being little aided by invention or imagination.'' John Marshall thought otherwise: ''[Washington executed] a series of judicious measures adapted to circumstances, which probably saved his country. . . . He has been termed the American Fabius; but those who compare his actions with his means will perceive as much of Marcellus as of Fabius in his character.'' Charles Stedman, a contemporary who fought on the other side, wrote admiringly of the American commander, ''who has been proverbially called a Fabius, but in whose character courage, in fact, was a feature still more predominant than prudence.'' Shifting to a modern writer, Russell Weigley thinks Washington's ''general military policy bespoke the caution of a man who could all too easily lose the war should he turn reckless.'' Douglas Southall Freeman seems to agree: ''If a choice had to be made, he preferred active risk to passive ruin, but in strategy as in land speculation, Washington was a bargain hunter. He always sought the largest gain for the least gore.'' Don Higginbotham sees him somewhat differently: "It is surprising that older histories depict him as a Fabius, a commander who preferred to retire instead of fight. . . . While Washington has been criticized for excessive caution, he was actually too impetuous." Marcus Cunliffe says flatly, "Grand strategy was not his forte"; Richard Ketchum writes that "he was less than a brilliant strategist. . . . his method can only be described as persistence"; and John Alden believes he was "not a consistently brilliant strategist or tactician." But Ernest and Trevor Dupuy emphatically state, "Washington was by far the most able military leader, strategically and tactically, on either side in the Revolution." There you have it. He was bold or cautious, brilliant or bumbling, judicious or just plain lucky. It depends on which author you choose to read.[2]

Obviously, American strategy in the war and the role of General Washington as a strategist are subjects quite open to interpretation and most demanding of further study. That is what this book is all about.

Strategy does not evolve in a vacuum. It is a derivative of such diverse considerations as contemporary tactics and technology, prevailing social and geographical conditions, enemy actions, governmental policies, and overall objectives. The first part of this book consists of several chapters in essay form. "To essay" means to make a beginning, to try to put to the test. That is the intent of these opening essays. Following an initial chapter on the general theory of strategy are five others exploring the various ingredients of strategy as they acted to shape the conduct of the Revolutionary War. With that as a base, a beginning, we will be set to study the actual planning and execution of American strategy.

The war itself passed through four more-or-less distinct phases, each presenting different situations and demanding different military responses. Those divisions—which, it must be emphasized, were consciously recognized at the time by patriot leaders—serve admirably as tools to help analyze the quality of George Washington's strategic ability. Four chapters, one devoted to each phase, comprise the book's second part.

When all is summarized, it may have been demonstrated that the strategic problems facing American leaders were in fact more complex than has been usually accepted, that Washington's strategic acuity existed at a level rather higher than has been normally granted, and that the astuteness and stupidity of the contending leadership groups did in fact affect the war's course and conclusion. If readers are prompted only to reexamine their thinking on the subject, I shall feel the book has succeeded. The strategic underpinnings of the war are much too important to escape critical analysis or to be glossed over. The truth of that point is obvious enough to avoid argument. I have written, then, in the spirit described by Justice Oliver Wendell Holmes when he said we need education in the obvious as much as we need investigation into the obscure.

Part One

Strategy Essayed

1

Strategy before

Clausewitz

"Strategy" was not a word George Washington used. It entered the language some years after his death, at about the same time that Napoleon's startling triumphs extended theorists' comprehension of warfare. The closest term listed in a military dictionary published in London in 1802 was "stratagem," but its meaning was clearly explained as a ruse, a gambit to gain surprise. A book published a year earlier in Paris used the word *Strategie*, which was described as the movement beyond the visual circle of the enemy or out of cannon shot. Not until a generation later, when Carl von Clausewitz wrote his landmark treatise, *On War*, did the world have a working definition of strategy. Only then did it become something quite distinct from tactics. But that does not mean strategy did not exist before Clausewitz any more than one could say there was no sex before Freud or seapower before Mahan. Although they didn't codify or articulate it, all the great captains of history—and probably all the near great—obviously understood and implemented the concept.[1]

If the theory of strategy suffered in the eighteenth century from a general lack of definition, it suffers in the twentieth from an excess of definition. The very term has expanded so in meaning that it has become impressively imprecise. Authors of the 1972 version of the Department of Defense's *Dictionary of Military and Associated Terms* felt obliged to differentiate between "tactics," "strategy," "military strategy," and "national strategy." But even that array of expression is apparently insufficient, for the Army War College also decided at about the same time to insert "higher tactics" between tactics and strategy so that its soldier-students could conceive of still more subtleties of intent. And in what may be the unexcelled example of obfuscation, the 23 June 1974 issue of *Newsday* used the phrase "strategic strategy." Verbiage has increased apace with the proliferation of meanings. Strategy, the *Dictionary of Military and Associated Terms* tells us, is "the art and science of developing and using political, economic, psychological, and military forces as necessary during peace and war, to afford the maximum support to policies, in order to increase the probabilities and favorable consequences of victory and to lessen the chances of defeat." It is debatable whether such a mouthful of jargon is useful in helping us comprehend warfare today; it almost surely is of no utility in trying to understand strategic concepts of a war two centuries in our past.

The problem is, strategy is dynamic. Warfare is a reflection of society; as societies have evolved, have grown incredibly complex, so too have the ways of waging war. We plainly cannot explore strategy in times before it was a term in the terms of our own time. There must first be a general understanding of what strategy is, how it developed, where it stood in the process of evolution when redcoats and minutemen began shooting at one another, and how it was viewed by those charged with implementing it. Then, and only then, will we be prepared to study and evaluate strategy as devised and executed by Americans in their struggle for independence.

Starting with the Greek word *strategos*, meaning "leader of troops," lexicographers coined our word "strategy." Its derivation from an ancient language is particularly fitting, for the concept spans all those centuries even though the term itself is relatively new. Modern warfare began with Napoleon, and modern strategy began with his interpreters, Jomini and Clausewitz, but neither war nor strategy is the sole possession of modern man. Both have been around at least since the beginning of recorded history.

Until the nineteenth century, war was the sport of kings, and strategy the rules of the game. Those rules were written largely in the form of maxims and were held rather tightly in the entourage of the sovereign. They were ''how to'' lists, and only that handful of men privy to the ruler's secrets needed to know how to use them. Sun Tzu, who may have been a committee rather than a person, provides the earliest and best single collection, but his works were not read in the West until 1772—and he does not mention strategy. Vegetius, another oft-quoted ancient, wrote of training, organization, dispositions, fortifications, and naval operations—but not of strategy. Others through the centuries added to that type of literature, but the fundamental concept of strategy remained hidden in histories, maxims, and memoirs. Strategy was a secret passed on from one prince to another. Gustavus learned from Maurice of Nassau and Frederick from Eugene of Savoy, just as Alexander had understudied Philip of Macedon, and Hannibal had been tutored by his own father and uncles. As a method to perpetuate the principles of war, it worked well so long as warfare remained relatively simple and the ruler himself served as his own first soldier. It flourished when the prince was a man of genius, faded when he possessed lesser talents. But, withal, it sufficed.

By the eighteenth century, however, warfare stood at the threshold of a new era. Gunpowder and other technological advances had restructured the battlefield; increases in wealth and population had made larger armies feasible; diminishing dynastic ambitions had tended to bestow more form and precision to the battle arena; intensifying national rivalries had widened the horizon of hostilities; and a series of successful navigators had extended the scene of conflict to shores beyond the oceans. The political leader who personally led troops in battle had become the exception rather than the rule; Frederick and Napoleon were the last of the great warring princes, and, at that, Napoleon won renown as a warrior before he crowned himself emperor. By the end of the Age of Reason, philosophers and soldiers were beginning to seek out the various rules of the art (or science?) of warfare. War had become too complicated to be left to kings and privy counsellors.

But how to begin? Where lay the key to the trunk of secrets? Napoleon believed the histories of seven great leaders

—Alexander, Hannibal, Caesar, Gustavus, Turenne, Eugene, and Frederick—would constitute "a complete treatise on the art of war." An aspiring soldier could only profit from a study of the exploits of the great captains, to be sure, but the campaigns of the past, even if other famous battle leaders were included, would hardly contain all the clues of combat, much less provide an elementary theory of warfare. Some better sort of synthesis was needed. Neither would a simple listing of maxims or principles be adequate. Some would prove to be universal (Napoleon's "mass multiplied by mobility" is the same as Nathan Forrest's "fustest with the mostest"); some would be jejune ("victory is the main object in war" by Sun Tzu is about as illuminating as Vegetius' "fleets are . . . for the protection of seas and rivers"); some would remain strictly local in time and place (Maurice de Saxe: "When you see the soldiers changing shirts, . . . you are going to be attacked because they put on all their shirts, . . . in order not to lose any"). Clearly, distilling all the maxims down to a few commandments, or principles, had both biblical precedent and the blessing of simplicity, but, like a study of the great captains, it was not the ultimate answer. A general who knew intimately, say, how Hannibal employed certain principles of war to win at Cannae might still be unable to relate that knowledge to operations in the age of gunpowder. What was missing was more basic yet. Somehow, the searchers had to get at the very essence of warfare itself; they had to break it down into its core components. Then they could see how to reassemble it. Only after that could they grasp its underlying theory.

No single figure in history owns a certain claim to have been the first to begin the process that led eventually to our modern understanding of the social phenomenon called war; many thinkers began grappling with the problem at about the same time. However, there are claimants to the laurels. Marshal of the Soviet Union, V. D. Sokolovsky, for one, alleges that the pioneering work was done on Russian soil:

> . . . the birth of scientific knowledge of war is usually
> attributed to the middle of the 18th century, when the En-

glishman Henry Lloyd, serving in Russia, in his introduction
to the history of the Seven Years' War, systematized and put
forth a number of general theoretical concepts and principles
of military strategy.[2]

That may be stretching the point to satisfy national pride, but it is
hardly worth arguing about. The truth is that many men, working
independently, were doing the kinds of thinking during the eighteenth century that would permit an intellectual breakthrough in the
nineteenth. Warfare had begun to take on its modern shape and
dimension by the time of the American Revolutionary War. The
terms "higher tactics" and "elementary tactics" had come into
usage, with the latter being understood as those formations taught
on the drill field and employed by units in battle. Higher tactics
was everything above that, such as selection of terrain or the
science of fortifications.

In his *Essai général de tactique*, published in 1772, the Comte
de Guibert lumped both those types of tactics under the heading of
the art of the general and proposed that raising and training troops
was the other essential aspect of warfare. But Guibert, Lloyd, and
others never quite found the combination. It was not until after
Napoleon had catapulted warfare into an entirely new epoch that a
Prussian professional soldier isolated and defined the basic elements of war. Born during the American Revolutionary War, Carl
von Clausewitz fought in the Napoleonic wars and wrote in the
years after Waterloo; his own life thus fittingly bridged the abrupt
chasm separating modern warfare from the old.

As the first to classify the primary components of warfare,
Clausewitz was not sure his ideas about strategy would be accepted. "No doubt there will be many readers," he wrote, "who
will consider superfluous this careful separation of two things
lying so close together as tactics and strategy." Accordingly, he
felt compelled to define the new term repeatedly: "Strategy fixes
the point where, the time when, and the numerical force with
which the battle is to be fought"; "Strategy is the employment of
the battle to gain the end of the war"; "Tactics is the theory of the
use of military forces in combat. Strategy is the theory of the use of

combats for the object of the war.'' In a word, Clausewitzian strategy was the assembly of forces in terms of time and space.[3]

Writing more than a century later, British historian and military theorist Sir Basil H. Liddell Hart took exception to Clausewitz, claiming the Prussian's definition of strategy was too narrow. He argued that it failed to separate governmental policy from military activities, hence implying ''the idea that battle is the only means to the strategical end.'' Sir Basil's criticism is somewhat unjust, as he himself obliquely admitted; nevertheless, he made a valid point that there is yet another dimension of warfare: higher, or grand, strategy. ''As tactics is an application of strategy on a lower plane,'' Liddell Hart explained, ''so strategy is an application on a lower plane of 'grand strategy.' '' Grand strategy is policy in execution. Its role is ''to co-ordinate and direct all the resources of a nation, or band of nations, towards the attainment of the political object of the war—the goal defined by fundamental policy.'' More recently, an American scholar, John M. Collins, said grand strategy ''looks beyond victory toward a lasting peace.''[4]

Thus, there are three levels of warfare: tactics, strategy, and grand strategy. The dividing lines between tactics and strategy, on one hand, and strategy and grand strategy, on the other, are by no means clear. Although separation is convenient for discussion, there has to be an influence of one on the other, as well as some degree of overlap. In the conduct of a campaign, one will always find tactics and strategy overlapping, while the initial planning for the operation will have been shaped by considerations of both strategy and grand strategy. In vastly oversimplified fashion, it can be said that grand strategy prescribes where and why to fight, strategy how to get there, and tactics what to do upon arrival.

At first glance, these distinctions might seem to be entirely academic; however, if we are to investigate the strategy of the Revolutionary War, we must know what meaning the term conveys, if for no other reason than to provide common ground for debate. Similarly, we must appreciate that, among those factors influencing strategy, tactics and grand strategy are far from least.

George Washington, who lived and led entirely in the eighteenth century, probably knew something of the era's intellectual ferment over the quest for the principal ingredients of warfare. But he almost certainly lost no sleep over such questions, which he perceived as being largely theoretical and of no immediate practical advantage. He was not a philosopher. Having had but an indifferent education, the Virginian's knowledge came not from books or formal military training but from common sense and uncommon wisdom—both sharpened on the stone of experience. When the Second Continental Congress appointed him commander-in-chief, neither he nor any of the other delegates could have defined strategy; nevertheless, it was a concept they could sense if not describe. And they must also have sensed that the outcome of the war would in large measure be influenced by how well the general would perform as a strategist.

Clausewitz, who was not born until after Washington had served five years as commander-in-chief, believed the ability to operate in the realm of strategy was a supreme talent reserved for only a few. To execute the correct strategy of a war, he wrote, "requires, besides great strength of character, great clearness and steadiness of mind; and out of a thousand men who are remarkable, some for mind, others for penetration, others again for boldness or strength of will, perhaps not one will combine in himself all those qualities which are required to raise a man above mediocrity in the career of a general."[5]

2

The Prussian Shadow

Soldiers of the 1770s and 1780s plied their trade in the awesome shadow of Frederick the Great. The warrior king's campaigns were widely acclaimed as classics, and he himself as a battle leader of the first order. His techniques were universally studied and openly copied. He had perfected the prevailing theory of tactical deployment, demonstrating to the wonder of all that it was possible to win decisive victories in the age of limited warfare. Ironically enough, the existing system of warfare—which had begun with Gustavus Adolphus and had been employed and improved upon by such outstanding soldiers as Marshal Turenne, Prince Eugene, and the Duke of Marlborough—was moribund even as it was brought by Frederick to the very pinnacle of its achievement. It was about to be swept aside by the military revolution Napoleon Bonaparte would ride to fame. But when British colonists ignited rebellion in America, the French Revolution still lay some fourteen years in the future. For George Washington and other generals of his generation, the only living oracle held court in Berlin.

The structure of warfare in any era is the sturdy offspring of the union of society and technology. It consequently acquires characteristics of both, usually the face of the former and the physique of the latter. In the eighteenth century, society was stratified and technology stagnant, a combination giving monster-birth to a deformed system of fighting. Linear tactics, epitomized by Frederick's marvelously rigid, precisely formed Prussian lines, were the battlefield embodiment of that defective system. Methods had become standardized, if not solidified, rules of conduct were well known, procedure was strictly followed, formations were highly stylized and completely structured. In a word, tactics were stereotyped. An inflexible system had evolved as a direct result of the technological standstill.

Not in the lifetime of any participant of the American Revolution had the weaponry of war changed. The last significant advance had taken place about a century before when someone had been shrewd enough to see that by fixing a long blade to the end of a musket, every soldier could in effect become both a musketeer and a pikeman. From then on, formations consisted of infantry armed with fusils and bayonets, artillery firing cumbrous and short-range pieces, and cavalry equipped with sabers and some form of light firearms. Changes were few and minor; those that did occur were merely improvements in existing arms rather than innovations of new ones. Perhaps the greatest development was the iron ramrod introduced by the Prussians; it replaced a wooden model, being better only in that it would not warp and was less likely to break.[1]

The primary weapon of all armies was the flintlock musket, a smooth-bore, muzzle-loading gun that threw a lead ball in unpredictable trajectories. Best known was the British "Brown Bess," dating back to the time of Marlborough in 1702 or so. Bess, a prototype for most other muskets then in use, had an unwieldy overall length of nearly five feet and weighed around fourteen pounds; a bayonet extended the length by more than a foot and added a pound in weight. She fired a slug roughly three-quarters of an inch in diameter and weighing a little over one ounce; it was a large projectile with the ability to smash as well as to penetrate. A musket could kill or maim at distances up to three hundred yards, but, because of inherent inaccuracy and erratic loading, its effective range was much less; fifty to eighty yards was considered to be maximum useful distance, while firing at anything beyond a hundred yards was simply wasting ammunition. It was generally accepted that "a soldier must be very unfortunate indeed who shall be wounded by a common musket at 150 yards, provided his antagonist aims at him." The order given at Bunker Hill—"Don't fire until you see the whites of their eyes!"—is often misconstrued as an inspirational and heroic gesture; actually, it was sage advice from a veteran who knew full well that his green men were likely to expend their precious ammunition too soon to be effective unless he gave them a practical yardstick.[2]

Because of the musket's length, loading could not normally be done in the prone position. A soldier who discharged his weapon in the open was therefore an inviting target until he went through the numerous steps required to reload. First, he had to bite open a cartridge of powder wrapped in paper, next pour some powder into the priming pan, then ram the cartridge down the muzzle, followed by the ball and wadding if it had not already been included in the cartridge, and before firing remember to close his cartridge box and replace the ramrod. Ordinary infantrymen could fire two or three times a minute, but the rate could be increased by intensive drilling. Prussians approached four or five rounds a minute. Aiming was not necessary; the firer merely leveled his musket, pointed it in the general direction of the opposing body of troops, and let fly.

Despite persistent myths to the contrary, the American rifle was not the dominant weapon in the War of Independence. Made in Pennsylvania by German immigrants, but in later years popularly called the "Kentucky" rifle, it was more accurate than a musket and had a longer range. A good rifleman could rather dependably hit individuals at two hundred yards and sometimes farther —which caused much indignant grumbling among British officers who, as special recipients of that selectivity, thought such treatment ungentlemanly. But the rifle was delicate, could not be reloaded rapidly, and had no bayonet. It was of considerable utility in special situations, particularly in backwoods clashes, but a rifle unit in the open could not stand up to one armed with muskets and bayonets. To their credit, Americans recognized that fact. When Maryland, in October 1776, proposed to raise another company of riflemen, a representative of Congress asked them to reconsider. "If muskets were given them instead of rifles the service would be more benefitted, as there is a superabundance of riflemen in the Army. Were it in the power of Congress to supply muskets they would speedily reduce the number of rifles and replace them with the former, as they are more easily kept in order, can be fired oftener and have the advantage of Bayonets.'' General Washington, when he formed Daniel Morgan's Corps of Rangers in 1777, was deeply concerned that the riflemen might be caught at a serious disadvantage without bayonets. He tried to compensate for that handicap. ''I have sent for spears,'' he told Morgan, ''as a defense against horse.'' Until the spears arrived, though, Morgan was to act with utmost caution. The British quickly lost their dread, if not their respect, for rifles: ''The riflemen, however dextrous in the use of their arm, were by no means the most formidable of the rebel troops; their not being armed with bayonets permitted their opponents to take liberties with them which otherwise would have been highly improper.'' Some German outfits and a few British units, especially those comprised of Loyalists, employed rifles, though never as extensively as did the Americans. All in all, the rifle remained an auxiliary weapon, useful but not decisive.[3]

Bayonets, as one can deduce from the comments of participants, were far more important in that war than most modern military men might imagine; the advent decades later of repeating rifles made the bayonet all but obsolete. But, so long as firearms had to be loaded one shot at a time through the muzzle end, the ''white weapon'' remained an absolute necessity. A force without bayonets would have been helpless should an opponent equipped with them ever close to within fifty yards, for the bayonetless soldiers could deliver at most one volley before finding themselves at close quarters with no means of defense, their discharged muskets good only as clubs. That is what happened at the battle of Bunker Hill when the British finally got to the top. Similarly, rain often rendered firearms inoperative, requiring recourse to cold steel. An English historian recorded how British soldiers, knowing that few American units initially had bayonets and that even fewer were adept in their use, ''prayed for rain so they could attack with bayonets without fear of enemy fire.'' Aware of the problem, Congress seriously considered providing spears to the entire Continental army as a stopgap measure until enough bayonets could be obtained. And, throughout the war, American officers went into battle armed with a short stabbing spear known as a spontoon. In fact, one could assert with some validity that thrusting arms were the single most decisive weapon in the Revolutionary War. Beyond doubt, they were quite important.

Field artillery pieces (as opposed to siege guns) were hardly more than big muskets. Smooth-bore tubes on wheels, they were also muzzle-loading, inaccurate, and short ranged. Gun crews could select solid shot or some kind of pellet ammunition, and, with an effective distance for shot of perhaps four hundred yards, they could out-range and overpower the musketeers. But the bulky guns were extremely difficult to maneuver in battle; crews usually emplaced them initially with horses and then moved them themselves during the course of combat using shoulder straps and lever bars. Moreover, a commander rarely had sufficient guns or suitable terrain to mass his fires, which further limited artillerists' influence in an actual engagement. Frederick had experimented with using horses to shift pieces in midst of battle and had found occasions to mass his batteries, but, for the most part, artillery still played a secondary role when two armies met in the field.

Cavalry had only a limited capability in the fray itself. Mounted warriors were at a distinct disadvantage in any exchange of fire. Not only were their weapons less effective, but horse and rider comprised a larger target than a man on foot. What's more, reloading on horseback was a real feat for even the most agile of troopers. A saber charge against unbroken infantry was ordinarily futile, if for no other reason than that horses had their own ideas about running into a prickly wall of bayonets. Nevertheless, horsemen possessed great capabilities which could not be dismissed out of hand. They could be devastating, for instance, if they could find an unprotected enemy flank. Washington, whose appreciation for cavalry grew as the war progressed, asked Congress to authorize him a larger mounted force in 1778, stating: "The benefits arising from a superiority in horses are obvious to those who have experienced them." Aside from providing added strength in battle, he explained, cavalry allowed one to inhibit minor movements of the enemy, to screen friendly movements, and to gather intelligence.[4]

The very limitations of the weaponry available to a field commander dictated the techniques he could employ during an encounter. When hostile forces met, the primary goal of each was to obtain a superiority of firepower in order to overwhelm the other. As one historian described it, "Infantry was not a thing that stood, but a thing that fired." Since both sides consisted mostly of infantry and were similarly armed, the one that could best mass its musketry would ordinarily have the edge. Therefore, officers placed individual soldiers elbow to elbow in order to concentrate fire better. For the same reason, they closed ranks, with the first kneeling, the second leaning, and the third upright. However, soldiers more than three ranks back could not shoot, so formations began to grow longer and thinner, developing into a line solid across the front but only three or four men deep. That line brought devastating power to bear straight ahead, but it was quite weak on the flanks—which did not matter much, because once forces were formed facing each other they were virtually unable to maneuver in order to envelop a flank. Frederick's famous oblique order was the exception that proved the rule. Any movement other than directly forward was perilous, for all was lost if the line should break. There was little or no depth to the battlefield, making the linear array dangerously brittle. Because of that, success in combat hinged on strict alignment, coordinated firing, and synchronized movement.

Commanders habitually sought flat, open fields for battle and avoided broken ground, darkness, woods, and winter. When armies collided in a set-piece battle, it was apt to be a memorable affair. At close range (with muskets, there was no other range), the two lines would blast each other to bits, continuing until one or the other could no longer take it. Then the stronger would close with the bayonet to secure victory. But, clearly, there could be no victory for either side in such an exchange. When armies grappled, it was with the clumsy embrace of inept wrestlers rather than with the slashing grace of skilled fencers. It was a muscular hug of death. No one has better described the fatal clash of lines in the eighteenth century than Winston Churchill:

[The Englishmen] and their brave, well trained opponents

marched up to each other shoulder to shoulder, three, four, or six ranks deep, and then slowly and mechanically fired volley after volley into each other at duelling distance until the weaker wavered and broke. . . . Keeping an exact, rigid formation under the utmost trial, filling promptly all the gaps which at every discharge opened in the ranks, repeating at command, platoon by platoon, or rank by rank, the numerous unhurried motions of loading and firing—these were the tests to which our forebears were not unequal. In prolonged severe fighting the survivors of a regiment often stood for hours knee-deep amid the bodies of comrades writhing or forever still. In their ears ranged the hideous chorus of the screams and groans of a pain which no anesthetic would ever soothe.[5]

Not all battles were such gruesome slugfests. Frederick and a few other leaders of genius found ways to avoid frontal clashes. But such improvements were merely incremental, for even the great king himself was hobbled by the same rules and tools holding back everyone else. Frederick's technique was to train and discipline his troops so thoroughly that they could perform in battle intricate evolutions allowing them sometimes to outflank an enemy's line without losing the cohesiveness of their own. Even so, losses were likely to be terribly high. Reflecting with both pride and sadness on the splendid exploits of his nation's soldiers, Frederick once remarked, ''With such troops one would defeat the whole world, were victories not as fatal to them as to their enemies.'' Technology had given rise to a tactical arrangement rendering decision by battle unlikely and the blood price of a stand-off exorbitant.[6]

Society, the other parent of eighteenth-century European warfare, acted also to shape a no-win tactical order. It did so by altering the normally accepted version of victory and by espousing a concept of limited warfare.

From the end of the Thirty Years War to the beginning of the Napoleonic wars—nearly a century and a half—European conflicts were noted for their extraordinarily reasonable nature. They were strictly limited in every way but one: frequency. There were plenty of them.[7]

Many factors contributed to limit the scope of hostilities. Among them, the horrible excesses of the Thirty Years War were not the least; monarchs and advisors had before them vivid and unforgettable evidence of what happens when armies run amok. A second reason was the mood of the period itself. Known as the Age of Reason, it was marked by an almost slavish devotion to reason and logic, to form and orderliness. It followed quite naturally that warfare, too, would be viewed in a detached, analytical, rational context. It was just another affair of state, nothing to get overly excited about; emotions had no place in such matters. And, in fact, it came to pass that wars actually involved very few people other than the soldiers themselves. Many citizens, unless they unluckily happened to live where armies clashed, were often unaware whether their country was at war or peace with its neighbors. Nor did they really care as a rule.

Still another consideration was a growing awareness that a nation's strength sprang from what modern economists call gross national product. Accordingly, establishing and maintaining the productive capacity of one's country became increasingly important; but, at the same time, states found it necessary to retain large military forces. Security demanded it. Because farmers and artisans could not grow crops or fabricate products if they had to leave field or factory to bear arms, the ranks could be filled only from the unproductive segments of society: officers from the idle aristocracy and soldiers from jails or gutters—the steeple and the mudsill of the social structure. But even vagabonds and criminals would not voluntarily flesh out Europe's swollen armies; by force or fraud, the shiftless and unfortunate had to be inducted. Press gangs roamed the Continent looking for recruits, paying scant heed to national boundaries. A foreign hireling was worth three men: one soldier more under arms, one less for some potential enemy, one native worker able to remain at his job and pay taxes. Voltaire penned a classic contemporary view of high-pressure recruiting in *Candide*:

He halted sadly at the door of an inn. Two men dressed in blue noticed him. . . . They went up to Candide and very civilly invited him to dinner. "Gentlemen," said Candide with charming modesty, "you do me a great honour, but I have no money to pay my share." "Ah, sir," said one of the men in blue, "Persons of your figure and merit never pay anything; are you not five feet tall?" "Yes, gentlemen," said he, bowing, "that is my height." "Ah, sir, come to table; we will not only pay your expenses, we will never allow a man like you to be short of money; men are only made to help each other. . . ."

"We were asking you if you do not tenderly love the King of the [Prussians]." "Not a bit," said he, "for I have never seen him." "What! He is the most charming of kings, and you must drink to his health." "Oh, gladly, gentlemen." And he drank. "That is sufficient," he was told, "You are now the support, the aid, the defender, the hero of the [Prussians]; your fortune is made and your glory assured."

They immediately put irons on his legs and took him to a regiment. He was made to turn to the right and left, to raise the ramrod and return the ramrod, to take aim, to fire, to double up, and he was given thirty strokes with a stick; the next day he drilled not quite so badly, and received only twenty strokes; the day after, he had only ten and was looked on as a prodigy by his comrades.[8]

That practice of raising armies from only those elements of society that could be spared was "selective service" in truth if not in name. Men thus attracted, however, were unlikely to find inspiration from motives higher than fear or to respond to discipline less than harsh. They deserted at every opportunity, compelling officers to keep them under tight control at all times. As a result, units lived, marched, and fought in herds. Commanders shied away from operations at night or in forested areas where desertion would have been easier. This necessity for ironclad control reinforced the acceptance of linear tactics and tended to limit warfare further.

It followed logically that soldiers became expensive. Armies, larger than ever and in being year round, were a heavy drain on a monarch's scarce resources. Equipment, training, and pay amounted to no insignificant investment. Casualties, then, equated directly to a loss of capital. Moreover, to produce a soldier completely skilled in the intricate evolutions required by the system of linear tactics consumed anywhere from two to five years. On top of the considerable monetary loss should a man be killed had to be added both the delay and expense in replacing him. Quite obviously, economic considerations inhibited rash inclinations to engage in set-piece encounters. A great victory could ruin a ruler whose finances were unable to recover from the shock of his success. Maneuver, therefore, largely replaced battle. A good commander did not fight to win so much as he fought not to lose. The definition of victory was turned inside out. That is what Maurice de Saxe had in mind when he said: ''I am not in favor of giving battle, especially at the outset of a war. I am even convinced that a clever general can live his whole life without being compelled to do so.''

The proliferation of fortifications also had a hand in limiting warfare. Every power worthy of that title blocked its borders with a belt of fortresses. Even if a general should have taken a notion to invade an enemy's land, he was obliged first to reduce his opponent's frontier defenses. Leaving hostile strongholds astride one's line of communications would have been folly, but to neutralize them normally required at least the first campaign, granting the foe time to react. Furthermore, even if the original barrier should be breached, penetration could not be rapid. The huge armies of the era consumed huge quantities of gunpowder, food, fodder, and other supplies. A good rule of thumb was that a force in the field had at most a five-day tether: it could march no more than five days from its source of supplies without incurring grave risks. Therefore, a commander had to advance in cautious stages, building, stocking, and securing depots as he went. Erecting those magazines enabled him to continue and provided a safe route of retreat, but it did not exactly lend itself to supporting a lightning advance. Historian Peter Paret called this proliferating network of magazines "the leg-irons of eighteenth century war." Commanders—at least the perceptive ones—recognized the limitations of the system. "It is not I who commands the army," Frederick complained, "but flour and forage who are the masters." But even the gifted generals had no solutions to propose. Roads remained primitive, of course, and transportation ponderous and uncertain. The number of horses required to move an army remained high. Proximity to rivers and access to crops were, therefore, primary logistical considerations—and key factors affecting mobility. Most wars, as a result, were confined principally to populated border areas, were rarely fought far from waterways, and consisted mainly of sieges.[9]

In keeping with the times, sieges became as extravagantly orchestrated as a stage production, as formalized as a parade-ground exercise. Since a siege was inevitably successful unless the defenders received outside help, officials decided it made very little sense to hold out to the death. Surrender in order to avoid needless bloodshed was rational, even respectable. Hence, mutually agreeable rules of conduct came into being to permit a defender to submit with honor at the proper moment. Capitulation became a rather complicated business, painstakingly learned by military engineers of the day. Some students complained that schools taught "not the art of defending strong places, but that of surrendering them honorably after certain conventional formalities." Should a fortress commander be so boorish as to refuse to surrender when properly summoned, attacking troops then had the right to put his garrison to the sword and sack the city. That did not happen often. Horace Walpole noted, "War has become so peaceful that when a city is besieged today and falls, the women inside can't even hope for the benefits of a good rape." Sieges were great shows resplendent with pomp and color and ceremony, especially after engineers gained enough skill to predict the climactic moment. Louis XIV, for instance, often made a social event of them, inviting courtiers and their ladies to partake of a banquet spread on a convenient hillock from where they could watch the spectacle. Final assaults were launched to the accompaniment of violins. Waltzes, one might surmise, were preferred.

Societal imperatives had combined to exert severe pressures obliging commanders to minimize casualties incurred in armed conflict, while, paradoxically, tactics and technology provided the commander no way to win a battle without absorbing intolerable losses in the process. For generals, it was an awkward dilemma. Nations could not abide costly battles, but they could not manage cheap ones. The sheer mass murder inherent in linear tactics proved of itself, therefore, to be a rather effective deterrent. Battle became rare. Positional war prevailed over mobile war; campaigns for cumulative minor advantages were considered to be more productive than attempts at annihilation, which were, more often than not, counterproductive. Armies fell into the habit of hibernating during winter and posturing during summer. Opposing generals shadowboxed with one another, seeking a decision on points rather than a win by knockout. Neither would submit to battle if the terrain and the time were not just right, and rarely could one bring about an encounter without the concurrence of the other. Most commanders, in fact, simply quit thinking in terms of destroying the enemy army.

Such was the atrophied condition of the art of war at the time of the American Revolutionary War. Of course, all generalizations are subject to exceptions. Some historians have contended, probably with accuracy, that European military thinking was not as ossified as it has usually been portrayed. Indeed, eighteenth-century military theorists were searching diligently for means to break out of the linear stranglehold. Various armies had been experimenting with different formations, trying out such concepts as rangers, skirmishers, and light infantry. The French had fielded *chasseurs* and the Germans *jägers*, both being a form of light, highly mobile, elite troops, "hardy and well made young lads, not less than 5 feet 4 inches high." There was even a growing realization of the potential of attacking in column. At Bunker Hill, for instance, the initial British attack was in column against the American left. Still, those were new ideas springing up for the very reason that a tactical stalemate existed. Moreover, they were by no means universally accepted. For the most part, military men believed Frederick the Great had arrived at the ultimate solution: perfection within the old system.[10]

Military thinking in America was at once similar and different. Colonists had read European works on war, which were mostly tracts explaining the techniques of marching and forming for battle, describing the necessity for discipline, detailing the manual of arms, and so forth. If one accepted the premise that linear tactics as executed by Frederick the Great were the last word in warfare, then he could find no fault with any of those instructional manuals. And Americans, like their English cousins, did accept that basic premise. When selecting their first batch of generals in 1775, the Continental Congress carefully included three ex-British officers in hopes they would be able to inject some European professionalism into patriot forces. Congressional commissioners went to Europe charged, among other things, with obtaining the services of foreign officers trained in the contemporary style of warfare. Washington's primary task, as both he and Congress saw it, was to create an American army patterned after those standing in Europe. When Congress debated the adoption of a stronger set of Articles of War in August and September 1776, John Adams led a successful fight for copying the British system: "It would be in vain for us to seek in our own inventions, or the records of warlike nations, for a more complete system of military discipline." Americans were, after all, European in origin. The prevailing philosophy of warfare flowed from east to west across the Atlantic. It did not spring up fresh and full-blown from American soil.[11]

On the other hand, conditions and concepts were different in the colonies, for society itself was different. In terms of experience, Americans were accustomed to smaller forces and greater distances; they were used to a looser style of fighting, with fewer controls and greater responsibilities placed upon individual officers and men. In the New World, too, because survival had demanded it, nearly every citizen, not just the shiftless and ne'er-do-wells, could be expected to wield a musket.

Writing in 1738, Reverend Ebenezer Gay had sounded a clear tocsin for universal military service. There were to be no exemptions, he said. Lest he be misunderstood, he had listed for clarity those who would serve: men and women, the righteous and the wicked, high and low, rich and poor, strong and weak, old and young, the lazy and the busy. To be absolutely sure no loopholes remained, he then added that neither the "new-married nor the faint-hearted" would be excused. One could suspect that any army raised in America would be mostly a citizen army of volunteers rather than a conglomeration of generally unwilling wretches serving no cause higher than regimental pride and discipline. In some ways, a citizen force would be much inferior, in others much superior. But, most importantly, it would be different.

English officers themselves perceived some years before the Revolution a contrast in the style of fighting in the colonies and on the Continent. Officers experienced in Europe were openly contemptuous of those trained in America. They looked down upon campaigns in the North American wilderness as being just colorful sideshows to the *real* war in Europe. The disdain was mutual. At Bunker Hill, General Thomas Gage, who had risen to high rank in America, declined what turned out to be the good advice of General Henry Clinton, a veteran of European fighting. Clinton later observed acidly, "Mr. Gage thought himself so well informed that he would not take any opinion of others, particularly of a man bred up in the German school, which that of America affects to despise."[12]

Clearly, then, in conducting a war in America, generals were bound to encounter some departures from the system in vogue in Europe. The unanswerable question was, how extensive would be the departures? For their part, leaders on both sides recognized that local conditions would inevitably exert an influence that could not prudently be ignored. Nevertheless, they saw such matters as being peripheral; neither Americans nor Englishmen anticipated any fundamental alterations in the system of warfare: they expected the war to be limited and the tactics to be linear. Both would be surprised somewhat from time to time as the war unfolded, but, all told, their early observations were correct. Traits typical of eighteenth-century European warfare—the rattle of musketry from opposing lines, a constant jockeying for position, extreme worry for the safety of lines of communication, overweening concern with avoiding casualties, an unwillingness to go for the jugular, fortifications and formal sieges, the flash of bayonets—quite accurately describe the greater part of the fighting in the American Revolutionary War.

Frederick the Great, who followed the contest closely from Berlin, saw nothing really novel in it. It looked like his kind of war, which, for the most part, it was. Only in the perspective of history can we appreciate the irony in the way it was waged. The modern world's first major revolutionary war was the last major conflict in which combatants met under dynastic rules of engagement.

3

The Meager Setting

So much for theoretical matters. To be sure, the broad implications of strategy and the narrower application of tactics, considered in the abstract, are indeed crucial to developing a fuller appreciation of military events occurring in the latter half of the eighteenth century. They provide an essential frame of reference. But it is time now to turn from general concepts to actual situations, from the academic point of view to the real. And the stage must be set with the geography of North America in 1775. The peculiar nature of any particular theater of war always affects the construction of campaigns waged there by prescribing and enforcing unique rules of tactical grammar and strategical logic. Therefore, it becomes exceedingly difficult to fathom more than the sketchiest details of what happened, virtually impossible to know why, without a clear glimpse of theater environment. Besides, in few conflicts was the setting more significant than in the American Revolutionary War. Its impact was all pervasive and evokes crucial questions. What was the colonial backdrop against which strategy would be devised? What was the social scene from which rebellion could spring and be sustained? What were the local conditions from which tactical adjustments would arise?

The forested wilderness that was colonial America some two hundred years ago eludes the imagination of most modern citizens. It was a wild, rough-and-tumble, primordial land, pricked ever so slightly by civilization. In point of time, today we are not far removed from the last quarter of the eighteenth century; in point of technology and development, though, we could as well be separated by millennia. In fact, a careful historian could build a good

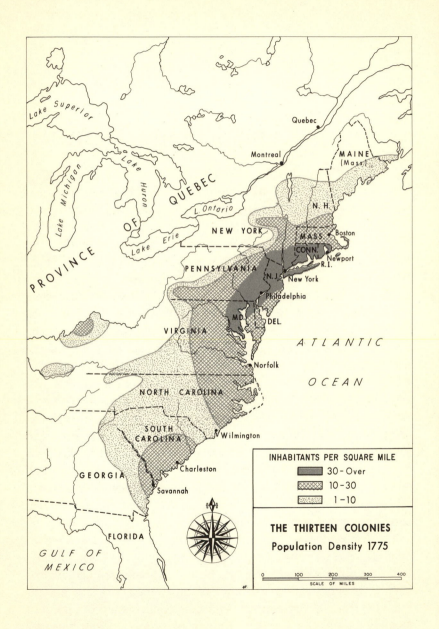

THE THIRTEEN COLONIES
Population Density 1775

INHABITANTS PER SQUARE MILE
30 - Over
10 - 30
1 - 10

case to defend the contention that people living in the thirteen colonies at the time of the Revolution had more in common with citizens of the Roman empire than with their own descendants in the United States of some two centuries later. To understand that statement, to *really* understand it, one must mentally cartwheel from the day of jet travel to the time of sailing ships, from the age of intercontinental ballistic missiles to the era of "the whites of their eyes." Nothing could be more misleading than to visualize the Revolutionary War being fought in an environment and countryside more than remotely similar to that existing today. It was an entirely different world.

Perhaps the single most significant geographical factor of George III's rebellious New World provinces was their extreme sparseness of population. Something over two and a half million inhabitants were scattered throughout an eleven-hundred mile arc stretching along the Atlantic coast from Boston to Savannah. Today, more people than that live just in the single borough of Brooklyn. Everywhere but inside the far-flung towns and villages themselves, loneliness—even isolation—was a fact of life. In most places, civilization ended just miles from the ocean. An American traveling from Boston through Maine to Quebec in 1775 wrote: "This is the first house I saw for 31 days, having been all that time in a rough, barren, and uninhabited wilderness, where we never saw a human being except our own men." A squirrel, it has been said, could have visited almost every square mile in the North American colonies without once touching ground, so few were the acres cleared for cultivation. The center of population stood somewhere in northern New Jersey, indicating that outside of New England and away from the ocean, human settlements were even fewer and distances between them even greater.[1]

Cities were small. When the war broke out, only four—Boston, New York, Philadelphia, and Charleston—had populations exceeding ten thousand. All the inhabitants of New York City would fit neatly into today's Madison Square Garden; the whole urban population of the colonies would fail to fill many modern football stadiums. Among the remaining centers, Newport alone could have been described as a city; others were at best large towns. All cities and most towns were seaports, standing at oceanside or not far inland alongside navigable rivers. Trade was their lifeblood. Some, like Philadelphia or Boston, were relatively cosmopolitan and sophisticated; others retained the crude and bumptious personality of frontier communities; all changed abruptly at the city limits into rough, rural countryside. Urban sprawl was a phenomenon reserved for a later age.

The people themselves were at once diverse and alike. Although most came from the British Isles or from Europe west of the Elbe and north of the Alps, they were certainly not cast in a common mold. Among those who made the long sea voyage voluntarily were rakes and adventurers, the politically persecuted and the politically ambitious, the well affected and the disaffected, the penniless and the pious. Not a few Americans began life in the New World as convicts. London sent maybe a thousand such men a year, a policy having the happy dual benefit of helping to people the provinces while relieving pressure on cramped prisons in the mother country. However, despite the diversity among immigrants, and dissimilarities between them and the old settlers, assimilation was rapid. In the vast new continent, where a man needed only a good axe and honest grit to chop out a home, the annual flow of newcomers blended smoothly with those folk already established. All, or nearly all, became united by the ties of English language, law, and culture. They came to share like values derived from similar colonial experiences and expectations. They had known common fears, had overcome common dangers. And, though the form and degree varied from colony to colony, most citizens enjoyed a long tradition of self-government. That was not true for everyone, of course. About one face in every five was black. Some Negroes were free, but most were slaves. Many whites, too, were bound in servitude, but their indentured obligations were to endure only for a set number of years, after which they were free to work for themselves. But, slave or settler, planter or preacher, the colonists proudly called themselves Americans. As historian John Alden has noted, they were "moving steadily in the latter part of the colonial period toward that community of sentiment which has been the basis of the modern national state."

In short, they were different from their European relatives—and they thought of themselves as different.[2]

The composition of the population was certain to have considerable impact on the type of army the rebels would be able to raise. As discussed in the previous chapter, armies of the eighteenth century, while officered by the aristocracy, filled their ranks by scouring the social gutters for human flotsam. Neither extreme of person existed in any significant number in America. There were neither blue bloods from which to recruit officers nor heaps of social sawdust from which to impress troops. That left room at the top for natural leadership to rise, while it meant that sons of guild members and landowners—men with a stake in victory—would comprise the bulk of the Continental army.

As for the provinces themselves, differences abounded from colony to colony. Varying accidents of size, government, climate, economics, and history left each distinct from its neighbor. Canada, the West Indies, and the two Floridas, having only recently been brought under the British flag, were understandably even more dissimilar than the thirteen older provinces. Between them all, old and new, there existed an evident degree of competition, of jealousy, even animosity. But there had also been occasions of cooperation. Common threats had provided impetus to lay aside internal disputes. The lines of unity had been drawn indelibly during the Stamp Act crisis of 1765 when several provinces had agreed to disagree with the ministry. With the exception of a few revenue stamps issued in Georgia, the thirteen old colonies had flatly refused to allow them to be sold. Canada, the Floridas, and the sugar islands, on the other hand, had gone along with the provisions of the Stamp Act, signifying their inability or unwillingness to disobey ministerial decrees. As war gradually approached throughout the succeeding decade, events had drawn those original thirteen protesting entities more and more into the loose confederation of interests, permitting them to be called the thirteen colonies—and ultimately the United States.

The sheer distances involved cannot be too greatly emphasized. Communications between colonial capitals and the colonial office in London rested on the skill of sea captains and the vagaries of weather. Even with the fastest of ships and the best of conditions, an official in America could hardly hope to get a response in much less than three months from the day he penned a query; it was usually nearer six months and often longer. That time lag would inevitably become a major consideration in the planning and execution of military operations.

Messages did not travel a great deal faster overland between colonies, either. Roads—the few there were—can only be described as exceedingly poor. Not until after the Revolution did engineers bridge the large rivers or lay down turnpikes and plank roads to link communities. Travelers depended on fords or ferries more or less joined by muddy, rutted, narrow roads, which were little better than wide paths cut through the forests. Eloquent testimony of the low quality of pioneer highways is found in a post-Revolution law requiring builders to remove from the roadway every stump over one foot high. Travel was time-consuming, exhausting, undependable, and dangerous. Coachmen calculated a trip by carriage from New York City to Baltimore in terms of days rather than hours. When Benjamin Franklin led a congressional committee on a hurried trip from Philadelphia to Montreal in spring 1776, he needed thirty-six days to get there. Sailing vessels putting to sea from Boston carried dispatches to Charleston faster and more surely than could couriers on horseback. Hard as it may be to believe, the mail really was slower two hundred years ago than it is today.

In such an undeveloped land, settlers were obliged to rely on rivers to move goods. It was no accident that the forward edge of civilization followed streams inland. Roads, too, followed rivers, at first leading from new settlements to the water and then winding along the river banks. Strategic maneuvers would inescapably be shaped—and often predicated—by considerations given to inland waterways. They were forbidding obstacles to forces faced with the necessity of crossing them and high-speed avenues of approach to elements moving parallel with them.

Economically, most Americans existed at little more than subsistence level. Though relatively wealthy in agricultural produce, they lacked manufactured items. In part, that was due to the very nature of the pioneers themselves; tending to view wealth in terms of acreage, they were more inclined to carve plantations from the wilderness than to establish manufacturing complexes. In part, too, it was due to the colonial policy of London, which saw America primarily as a source of raw materials for English factories and a market for English products. Even without such policies, American industrial growth likely would have been only slightly more rapid, but, still and all, those restrictions were factors negatively affecting the colonial economy. A good example is the Iron Act of 1750, which prohibited colonists from constructing any new foundries for producing finished iron; the act had the effect of holding down the development of most other industries. Policy and preference had together established an agricultural country. Thus, at the outset of the Revolution, the output of American factories was sorely limited in both quality and quantity, standing far below the level necessary to meet the minimum requirements of peaceful pursuits, much less the demands of rebellion. The country was patently incapable of supporting a war effort.

Trade was, of course, quite important. In return for manufactured goods, Europe obtained from America such items as tobacco, rice, flour, indigo, pelts, masts, and spars. Nevertheless, it is easy to place more emphasis on commerce than is warranted. Trade was not everything. Take, for instance, Connecticut on the eve of war. Comprising some two hundred thousand souls, that colony imported goods in 1774 amounting to £200,000. Exports were valued at the same amount, thereby pegging the annual per-capita level of foreign trade at about one pound sterling —hardly an impressive indicator of a trade-based economy. The truth is that while many businessmen saw trade as a primary economic necessity, the large majority of Americans got along mostly on what they themselves grew or constructed.[3]

Agriculture was America's strength. Rich soil, boundless land, and a favorable climate made the production of food rather easy. (Even in wartime, the problem would not be producing food but distributing it over the rudimentary transportation system.) The "granary" of the thirteen colonies extended generally from the

Connecticut River in the northeast to the Potomac in the south. Farmers in the Connecticut River valley exported wheat and corn, settlers in the Mohawk and Schoharie watersheds in upper-state New York raised surpluses of grain, Baltimore millers yearly processed more flour than local citizens could use, Quakers in Pennsylvania grew prosperous cultivating their rich fields of wheat, and Virginia planters produced such bountiful crops that Alexandria merchants asked for state controls. Farmers raised livestock throughout the colonies, of course, but in especially substantial quantities in New England. Connecticut's animal exports were considerable; horses, cattle, pigs, and sheep constituted the bulk of the province's peacetime out-of-state trade. Anyone analyzing the sources of food in 1775 would have seen right away that the Hudson River served as a rough dividing line: meat for the Continental army would come from lands east of it, bread from those to the west and south. That fact would become a key strategic consideration in the Revolution.[4]

The America that rose in rebellion in April 1775 was a raw and spartan land. Its separate provinces were not united politically, although officials widely understood the necessity for a common defense. Its few people, hardy and independent individuals, living in sparse settlements near rivers or beside the sea, subsisted mostly on what they alone could grow or make. Its ability to manufacture sufficient weaponry of war was virtually nonexistent. Its capacity to produce foodstuffs quite outstripped its potential for transporting them. Its poorly charted lands were as poorly served by inadequate roads. Its extensive forests and broad rivers loomed as imposing barriers to eighteenth-century armies. Altogether, it was a most meager setting for war.

Considering that setting in light of the established style of fighting, perhaps the most noteworthy point for the eighteenth-century strategist was the scarcity of positions from which to wage positional warfare, at least in comparison with the European environment. As events would demonstrate, there was in all the provinces only one strategic position whose occupation clearly might have been decisive—a mountainous choke point on the Hudson River some fifty miles north of New York City, the site where patriots would build Fortress West Point. All other centers were cities. Strategically, the New World was an all but barren area, a most menacing arena of war. Not only was the countryside manifestly inhospitable for formal military operations, it was a logistician's nightmare as well. Nevertheless, it was at the same time curiously enticing to military planners. The cities, which London assumed were focal points of rebellion, were practically defenseless against a strong amphibious force. A victory seemed very probable because those population centers seemed so very vulnerable. To the soldier, then, the setting was at once forbidding and alluring; it was the kind of dichotomy that would later ruin Napoleon in Spain and Russia, not to mention more modern examples.

4

The View from London

Three men directed the war effort from London: the king, the prime minister, and the secretary of state for the colonies. Not one of them stands charged at the bar of history for possession of any unusual degree of wisdom.

George III, although only thirty-seven years old when the American war opened, had already worn the crown for fifteen years. Coming to the throne in the midst of the Seven Years War, it was his unhappy lot to reign during both the American and French revolutions as well as the Napoleonic wars; it was as trying a half-century as any English monarch has ever known. The king's mind, mediocre at best, eventually snapped under the strain. He went mad in 1811, spending his final years "addressing imaginary parliaments, reviewing fancied troops, holding ghostly courts." His highness had been anything but promising as a child. "Had he been born in different circumstances it is unlikely that he could have earned a living except as an unskilled laborer," concluded one eminent British scholar. "He was lethargic, apathetic, childish, a clod of a boy whom no one could teach." He was eleven before he could read. The man showed no more brilliance than the boy. However, George III had a highly developed sense of responsibility and a strong will, owing perhaps to his German heritage. He was his own king, not a figurehead for Parliament.[1]

The prime minister was Sir Frederick North, more courteously than accurately called Lord North. He reached that office in 1770 at the age of thirty-eight, after having served some sixteen years in Parliament. He was a bulky man, bulbous-nosed and bug-eyed, indistinct of speech and weak of resolve, rather more amiable than able, but gracious and honest. Extraordinarily complaisant to the wishes of his monarch, the cabinet leader was loyal and hard working, a dedicated servant with whom the king felt comfortable. To his credit, Lord North did not share his monarch's confidence in his abilities, always feeling inadequate for the crushing task of leading a government in wartime, but his requests for permission to resign were repeatedly denied until 1782 when the government itself fell on the loss of the American war. Serving more as moderator than outright leader of the cabinet's weekly strategy sessions, North once confessed, "Upon military matters I speak ignorantly, and therefore without effect." It was his fate to oversee the destruction of Britain's first empire.

Ever since the early years of the seventeenth century, England had been the world's most successful colonizing nation. Students of modern bureaucracy might note with profit that for a century and a half London had managed quite well without benefit of a bureau exclusively responsible for colonial affairs. Only in 1768 did the office of secretary of state for colonies come into being —and then most gains made in the previous fifteen decades were promptly lost in the next fifteen years. At the outbreak of hostilities in America, the office was occupied by the Earl of Dartmouth, whose biggest drawback seems to have been a vast ignorance of America and Americans. His failure to recognize the extent of colonial unrest and his consistent underestimation of patriot strength helped bring on the war. Dartmouth did not have to face the full consequences of his errors, however, for Lord George Germain replaced him on 10 November 1775. Germain held that post until the North ministry dissolved in 1782.

No office in London had more to do with the direct control of the American war than Germain's, and no cabinet member was less suited for his duties than he. Sixty years old, a seasoned member of Parliament, haughty, opinionated, a man of many enemies, Germain was a staunch political supporter of George III and an avowed proponent of using force to put the colonists back in their places. Incredibly, this minister who was responsible for directing military operations in America was an ex-army officer convicted by a court-martial of malfeasance in the face of the enemy during the Battle of Minden in 1759. Members of the court had declared him "unfit to serve . . . in any military capacity whatever." So incensed at the failure of his general was King George II that he ordered the shameful verdict read to every regiment in the army. George III, however, considering Germain's partisan political beliefs of more consequence than his military reputation, thought the Minden affair unimportant. A cleverer monarch would have seen the absurdity in such a situation. J. W. Fortescue, the historian of the British army, quite bluntly wrote:

> In any case it was a disgraceful thing that one who had been publicly degraded for misconduct and struck off the list of the Privy Council should have been restored to high office; still more that he should have been appointed to a department which gave him control of the Army abroad, from which he had been expelled as unworthy to hold a commission. It was asking very much from the loyalty of brave officers that they should receive their orders from one whose name they could never hear without shame; and the evil of the appointment was not diminished by the fact that Germain nourished an old grudge against Carleton [commanding in Canada], and was not too well disposed toward Howe [commanding in the thirteen colonies].[2]

Had Germain possessed exceptional talents as a war minister, his selection still would have been highly questionable; as it was, he suffered serious shortcomings as either a strategist or a leader. The ghost of Minden would haunt British operations in America throughout the war.

No person holding high office in London had ever been to America. King and cabinet knew more about Madrid or Vienna than about Boston or Charleston. They had no firsthand knowledge of the colonies and, surprisingly, were disinclined to listen to the advice of those who did. Only too late did they ascertain that they had grievously misjudged the rebels. William Eden, a member of the futile peace commission that went to the United States in 1778, was astounded at the differences between what he had believed in London and what he found in America. He regretted "most heartily that our rulers instead of making a tour of Europe did not finish their education by a voyage around the coasts and rivers of the western side of the Atlantic." That widespread lack of understanding severely hampered England's early war efforts. Officials tended to think in terms of police actions rather than full-fledged military operations, of dispersing mobs of mutinous riffraff rather than warring with thirteen united colonies.

General Thomas Gage was not one who thought that way. He knew colonials; his wife was American, and he had served in North America for the past twenty years. The long-time commander of British forces in America, Gage became thoroughly alarmed upon taking station in Boston in 1774. Having fought at Culloden, he knew the ferocity of civil war; having marched with Braddock, he understood the difficulty of campaigning in North America; having lived so long in the colonies, he sensed the depth of patriot sentiment. Prepare for war before attempting to suppress the rebellion, he wisely told London. To take the field against the colonists, he reported, would require at least twenty thousand troops, including both cavalry and artillery. He had at hand no more than four thousand men. Moreover, the general warned, regaining control of New England would require up to two years.

His warnings went unheeded. George III ridiculed his pessimistic field commander, labeling him timid and incompetent. He decided to retire Gage gracefully at the end of 1774 and replace him with Sir Jeffery Amherst, but Amherst declined the appointment, so Gage stayed on. Feeling that an injection of vigor might improve the situation, Dartmouth ordered Gage early in 1775 to take forceful action to destroy rebel caches of war supplies. He received the order on 14 April and obediently marched to Concord five days later, igniting the revolution. In lieu of the tens of thousands of troops the commander in America had wanted, London sent a mere handful of soldiers and three major generals. Those three—John Burgoyne, Henry Clinton, and William Howe—had all been members of Parliament. They arrived after the sobering events of 19 April, but in time to participate in the battle of Bunker Hill. After that bloody clash, even the most chuckleheaded minister had to admit that a rap on the colonial knuckles would not suffice. The rebellious provinces would indeed have to be subdued by a large expeditionary force. Gage, on the scene, had better judged the temper of Americans than had men sitting in cozy offices in faraway Whitehall. For being correct, he was recalled to England. William Howe assumed command on 10 October 1775.

A month later, Germain replaced Dartmouth, and Great Britain's war team was complete: the king, North, and Germain in England; Generals Howe, Clinton, and Carleton in America. Clinton was fated to succeed Howe as commander and to be followed in turn by Carleton. Of the six, only Carleton would emerge from the war with his reputation intact.

All the English leaders agreed on the ultimate aim of the war. It was quite simple: to obtain some sort of settlement which would restore the rebellious colonies to their former status as subservient members of the British empire. Ministers never had any intent of annihilating the insurgents or of destroying their countryside; rather, they wanted to apply whatever degree of pressure might be required to return the provincials to their colonial status quo. However, while there was complete accord on the overall objective, there existed serious disagreement on how to achieve it, that is, over grand strategy. Many influential and vociferous Englishmen believed conciliation was the answer, splitting sharply from those who espoused coercion. That division lasted throughout the war, fostering vehement opposition to the government's policies and weakening the king's hand in conducting military operations. Nevertheless, a large majority in Parliament supported George III in his insistence that "blows must decide whether they are to be subject to this country or independent." The king's views prevailed. Americans were to be quelled by the sword.

As soon as it became evident to Englishmen in both London and Boston that conducting major military operations was in fact going to be necessary, officials scurried to open maps and memories of the vast land beyond the Atlantic. Clearly, some overall strategy had to be devised. Where was the strategic center of the colonies, a place to hold which would cause the revolt to fold? What action might lead to a collapse of patriot fervor? How could English generals best maneuver against the Continental army? Answers were not readily apparent. All the port cities were accessible, but the occupation of no single population center would assure victory. Boston was a painful case in point. Moreover, Americans had no seat of government in the European sense; Philadelphia was merely a convenient place where the Continental Congress happened to hold its meetings. To compound matters, marching into the interior out of reach of the Royal Navy would be an open invitation to disaster. The colonies were huge, England's army small. Besides, there were few obstacles inland against which to trap and smash the rebel forces. Actually, as dismayed officers quickly discovered, no more than a handful of options were feasible—in fact, there were only five. Those surfaced very early in the planning process and remained relatively unchanged for the duration of the war.

Foremost on the list of strategies, at least in the minds of some military men, was the classic, if uncommon one of seeking out and destroying the rebel army. Commendably straightforward, no quibbling, a decisive-sounding strategy. But not so easy to do. Until mid-1776, British forces were too weak to attempt a set-piece battle; after that, Washington proved too wily to catch. Furthermore, even if a battle could be arranged, the English general had always to concern himself with losses; his army was not replaceable. The "thin red line" was simply too thin. To man the outposts of empire, from Bombay to Boston, not more than fifty thousand men wore the king's red coat. A too-costly English victory could literally throw away the war, for Washington could always reconstitute his ranks, whereas the British expeditionary force, operating three thousand miles from its base, had scant elasticity. Nonetheless, English generals never quit looking for the decisive battle. "My opinion has always been that the defeat of the rebel regular army is the surest road to peace," General Howe testified after his return to England. "I invariably pursued the most probable means of forcing its commander to action." But Howe added a caveat to those bold words. Battle could only be accepted "under circumstances the least hazardous to the Royal Army; for even a victory, attended by a heavy loss of men on our part, would have given a fatal check to the progress of the war, and might have proved irreparable.'' A year after Howe published those remarks, General Cornwallis demonstrated their accuracy by abandoning caution in a vain effort to destroy Nathanael Greene in the Carolinas. Greene lost the battles, but Cornwallis lost his army.[3]

Next on the list, and actually the first strategy proposed, was blockade. Defeat the rebels by economic strangulation. Gage, for one, recommended this course in 1774 as a cheaper alternative to the massive invasion he envisioned. Sir Edward Harvey, the senior serving army officer in England in 1775, wondering aloud whether a British force could ever overcome the thirteen colonies, seconded the idea of a naval blockade. ''To attempt to conquer [America] internally by our land force is as wild an idea as ever controverted common sense,'' he said. Lord Barrington, the secretary at war, also supported an economic strategy. Warships could close every major patriot port, smiting the mutinous Americans in the purse. Backers of this theory saw the colonies, their trade cut off, pleading for peace in due time. The plan never got far. For one thing, war with America was unpopular in England; victory had to be achieved surely and swiftly. For another, England itself was deep in debt; loss of the lucrative New World trade would hurt merchants at home as well as colonists abroad. It just might have turned out that the colonies could have withstood a blockade longer than could the mother country. Naval officials, it must be noted, were themselves dubious. Given the seriously neglected state of the navy, they thought a blockade beyond their capability. Hindsight seems to indicate that a blockade would have been ineffective in the first place and insufficient to turn the tide of rebellion in the second. As it happened, interdicting American commerce by raids along the coast and sporadic occupation of port cities always remained an undertaking supplementary to other operations, but never, until too late, did it become the primary strategy. Which was a mistake, concluded Basil Liddell Hart, writing in retrospect. He felt England's ''deep-land'' strategy was an unnecessary abandonment of its historically successful naval strategy. ''If we had from the start,'' he reckoned, ''put the money into naval force that we wasted on continental effort—in America—we might have saved all." His conclusions must remain in doubt. Indeed, he seemed to contradict himself later, saying, "A navy is a shield and a saw—a fleet is not fitted to be a sword."[4]

Yet another option was what might be called a southern strategy. New England stood apart as the bedrock of rebellion; provinces farther south appeared easier to dissuade, causing some planners to suggest working on them first. Many factors favored this strategy: terrain south of the Potomac provided no significant barriers to shield rebel forces; the proximity of British bases in the Caribbean would permit more reliable logistical support; Loyalist strength was considerable everywhere outside of New England; the reconquest of sparsely settled southern states, especially distant Georgia and the Carolinas, would be relatively simple and inexpensive. In addition, according to General Gage, southern patriots could not become as intransigent as their Yankee brethren because "their numerous slaves in the bowells of their country, and the Indians at their backs will always keep them quiet." In short, the South was an inviting target for the simple reason that it was obtainable. But was it decisive? The heart of the Revolution beat in New England; it was unlikely that northern rebels would lose their will to resist because of British victories in southern states. What's more, although it was not a consideration at first, once France entered the war, posing a threat to Britain's absolute control of the sea, a southern strategy might be unwise. The possibility of forces ashore being isolated by a temporarily superior French fleet would be an ever-present danger.

Known as "the line of the Hudson" strategy, the fourth course probably had the best chance of being victorious. Every other alternative had severe limitations, wrote historian Sir John Fortescue, for "there was no stronghold inland which could command any great tract of country, and therefore no certain line of operations. The enemy had but to retire inland, if pressed, and the invader could not safely follow them, from the impossibility of maintaining his line of communications. *The one exception to the rule was the line of the Hudson.*" By controlling the Hudson

River, British forces would own an interior path to Canada, would have New England effectively surrounded, and would be able to operate away from the ocean without losing touch with the fleet. This scheme proposed a methodical reduction of the rebellion. First, seize the Hudson to cut off the Yankees. Then drive into New England from the west and south, tightening the vise until resistance should cease. Finally, turn on the colonies south of the Hudson. Another British historian, Piers Mackesy, writing long after Fortescue and with benefit of all the recently opened and published documentary sources, corroborates Fortescue's findings. Mackesy contends, without equivocation, "For the enemy, British control of the Hudson would have been disastrous."[5]

Such conclusions did not wait to be discovered by historians. Officials charged with fighting the war reached them at the time as well. Doubtlessly, the germ of the line of the Hudson strategy had been fermenting long before the Revolutionary War began. The Colonial wars had amply demonstrated the river's strategic worth; it was an obvious route from the Atlantic to Canada. Ministers who had never seen North America had read reports submitted as recently as 1773 spelling out the strategic position of the waterway. Only days before the fateful shot at Lexington, Lord Dartmouth had written to General Gage, telling him of the value in basing a large amphibious force at New York City from where it could block "any attempt to send succour to the New England people from the middle colonies." But Gage did not need prodding to see the significance of the Hudson. The very day he sent troops to Concord, he rushed word to Carleton in Canada telling him to bolster the forts on Lake Champlain. Those fortifications were the link between the Hudson and Canada. Hence, even before becoming convinced of the seriousness of American resistance, Englishmen had contemplated a general scheme to occupy a line extending from Canada south along the Hudson to New York City, then hooking eastward along the coast to Boston.[6]

In this instance, British generals and politicians were in agreement. On 2 August 1775, Dartmouth sent Gage four alternatives in the form of questions. First, should the British commit their entire force directly against New England? Or, "viewing the whole state of America," should they grab New York City and make the Hudson the seat of war? Or, third, should they use the fleet to conduct raids for food and livestock and to "make an impression on other places" along the coast? Or, if all else failed, should they withdraw to Halifax and Quebec? Gage, replying just days before he relinquished his command to Howe, thought withdrawal unnecessary but discouraged any thought of operations into New England. Redcoats could penetrate the countryside, but at what cost and for what cause? Raids, on the other hand, would be worthwhile whenever cruisers were available, but, alone, such incursions could not be decisive. The only proper strategy, in his view, was the line of the Hudson. "It has always appeared to me most advisable to make Hudson's River the seat of war; its situation between the eastern and western colonies is advantageous, besides being commodious in transporting the necessaries of an army." Elaborating, the general stated the requirement "to be in possession of some province where you can be secured and from whence you can draw provisions and forage," a requirement best met by New York City. "There the foundation of the war should be laid by having troops in force, large magazines of military stores of all kinds, and the whole well fortified and secured." Boston, he noted, was good as a diversion but required a large garrison. Rhode Island would be better than Boston as a second base for it controlled the southern coast of New England and could easily be defended with nominal naval assistance. As events developed, Gage's letter was an amazingly accurate forecast of British efforts in the years ahead.[7]

Other generals had similar ideas. Henry Clinton, who had lived in New York during his youth, prepared a detailed study in the autumn of 1775. The Hudson should be taken immediately, he advised. An offensive northward from New York, coordinated with a southward expedition from Canada, could be decisive. Knowing that the eastern states obtained bread from the middle colonies, while they in turn depended on the eastern ones for meat, Clinton predicted that both areas would "experience the greatest distresses" as a result of English control of the river. Depriving Washington of the capability to assemble or feed his troops would be a valuable benefit, while "a ready intercourse . . . with Canada by way of the lakes" would be an "obviously important" advantage. One of the first papers to cross Howe's desk after he replaced Gage was an urgent appeal for reinforcements from General Guy Carleton, who was then being hard pressed in Canada by the patriot invasion. Howe turned him down. Securing the line of the Hudson, he explained, would prove to be more decisive in the long run.[8]

Nearly everyone agreed. An English officer, captured in 1777, stated ruefully, "Had we kept possession of the [Hudson] River, the war would have been by this time nearly terminated in favor of Great Britain." Washington himself stated repeatedly that enemy occupation of the Hudson would be fatal to the patriot cause. British Brigadier General Benedict Arnold, writing shortly after switching sides, appended the weight of his word to the plan of seizing the Hudson. There were but two ways to win the war, the traitor emphatically told his new commander. The first was to "secure the posts which command the Hudson, which could be done in a few days by regular approaches, and cut off the Northern from the Southern Colonies. The supplies of meat for Washington's army are on the east side of the river and the supplies of bread on the west; were the [Hudson] in our possession, Washington would be obliged to fight or disband his army for want of provisions."[9]

Arnold's second choice, which was the fifth and final strategy open to the British, was to concentrate the entire army, except enough to hold New York City, in an all-out effort to overwhelm the middle colonies between Virginia and New Jersey. That plan, like the line-of-the-Hudson strategy, would have separated New England (and in this case New York) from the remaining colonies. It would also have isolated the southern states. Philadelphia, the second largest city in the British empire, was certainly a worthy prize. Apart from the psychological value to be gained by seizing the town harboring the Continental Congress, Philadelphia would be an excellent base of operations for the redcoats. But operations to where? Militarily, roads from the city led nowhere. An attack against the South could be better supported from more southerly cities; a westward strike would hit nothing but scattered frontier settlements; a push northward would be difficult in the extreme since Washington would have all the defensive advantages of broad rivers and rugged mountains, not to mention more than enough space to permit him to avoid conclusive engagement. And, as English generals had learned by the time Arnold turned his coat, British forces controlled only those locations they physically occupied. There was no way they could stretch enough to hold the entire middle part of the United States. Invading the central states was quite likely the least promising option of all.

During the war's long course the British eventually tried all five strategies, sometimes separately, sometimes in combination. Some they attempted more than once. None worked.

Why, if the line-of-the-Hudson strategy was recognized as being the most opportune, did the king's commanders not pursue it forcefully, determinedly? Why had Howe, after having driven Washington from New York in 1776, followed the retreating Continental army into New Jersey instead of pushing up the virtually defenseless Hudson valley? What possessed him to march on Philadelphia in 1777, rather than to strike up the Hudson to join Burgoyne? What objective in 1781 brought Cornwallis to strategically unimportant Yorktown in Virginia when his commander, Henry Clinton, feared for the safety of the vital English base at the Hudson's mouth? In large part, those questions are unanswerable. But at least some of the reasons are known, while others can be surmised.

To begin with, Britain had no established system for strategy formulation. There was no great general staff, nor was the army staffed by great generals. The position of commander-in-chief was vacant. Individuals contemplated strategic matters without complete knowledge of the situation and in isolation from one another. Even good ideas had no assured way of being heard or acted upon. The only central point for strategic direction was the hip pocket of Lord Germain, a most unsuitable location. Moreover, the English command system was divided between a general in Canada and one in the thirteen colonies, a very serious mistake insofar as executing the line-of-the-Hudson strategy was concerned. Worse yet was the fact that Germain wrote directly to subordinate generals and they to him, bypassing theater commanders. Had an abler man than Germain occupied the colonial office, such blatant disregard of the chain of command would still have been an egregious error; with Germain there, it was fatal. He changed strategies in midcourse, issued instructions to subordinates without informing their superiors, and sent conflicting directives, leaving field commanders in doubt as to their missions. Combine that kind of faulty top leadership with slow and unreliable communications via sailing ship across the Atlantic, and you begin to see why English strategy in the American war has led many historians to conclude that British blunders alone brought about American victory.[10]

Nor was that all. Englishmen roundly misjudged their American cousins, causing royal generals often to select false courses that led time and again to grief. London consistently undervalued the strength of patriots while overestimating the strength of Loyalists.

From the start, ministers looked upon the rebels as merely an aggressive and vocal minority. Buttressed in that belief by wildly misleading reports from ousted colonial governors, British officials envisioned masses of loyal Americans rising to welcome and support redcoats wherever they might march outside of New England. Several expeditions were launched on that slender supposition. "Of all foundations whereon to build the conduct of a campaign this is the loosest, the most treacherous, the fullest of peril and delusion," wrote a British historian later. Sadly, and much too late, George III, Germain, and the British generals in America discovered the bitter truth in that statement. William Howe very early suspected that "almost all the people of parts and spirit were in the rebellion," but he and others nevertheless continued to chase the will-o'-the-wisp of a Loyalist counterrevolution. It was a futile quest. The Loyalists were just not there, either in numbers or will. Even when large pockets were found, few would take up arms to fight for their beliefs. Estimates vary widely, and any specific figures are highly suspect, but it appears probable that total Loyalist strength could not have been beyond 35 percent of the population and was more nearly 20 or 25 percent. At the same time, estimates of patriot adherents range between 35 and 55 percent, while those uncommitted persons, who mostly wanted no part at all of either side, made up from 15 to 30 percent. Loyalists, of course, were more numerous in some places than in others, but nowhere, it now seems certain, did they constitute a majority. Unaided, they could not seize or control any single province.[11]

Arrogance accounts for London's second gross mistake in judgment. Englishmen widely ridiculed colonials for their backwardness, their lack of sophistication, their disdain for discipline. Americans were contemptuously scorned as second-rate fighters, unworthy opponents for his majesty's professional soldiers. General Gage, some years before the war started, predicted that Bostonians would never resort to force because "they are a people who have ever been bold in council, but never remarkable for their feats in action." Just before the outbreak of fighting in 1775, Benjamin Franklin reported from London the comment of a British general. Given a thousand grenadiers, the officer had boasted, he would "undertake to go from one end of America to the other, and geld all the males, partly by force and partly by a little coaxing." A major who fought at Lexington and Concord believed "one active campaign, a smart action, and burning two or three of their towns, will set everything to rights." He died at Bunker Hill, perhaps holding a different opinion. But, as late as 1777, an English general could still write with apparent sincerity, "The native American is an effeminate thing, very unfit for and very impatient of war." Nor were disparaging thoughts limited to Britons. A Hessian officer, in a critical appraisal of William Howe, said Sir William was certainly no Caesar, nor even the best commander of the day, "but, for an American War, he is a good enough general." Such cavalier lack of respect for one's opponent does not predispose one to worry overly much with the choice of a strategy, for it would seem that any old idea ought to work.

Those notions changed as the war progressed, but the damage had already been done. In warfare, the time to give the devil his due is beforehand. Afterward is too late. King and cabinet had ignored General Gage in 1774 when he had reckoned twenty thousand troops would be required to subdue the insurgents. When he upped his estimate to thirty-two thousand in summer 1775, they were more inclined to listen, but they still expected a fairly easy time of it. After all, the rebellion originated in the cities, they thought, and the cities were vulnerable. Not until the disastrous campaign of 1777 did the ministry begin seriously to consider the specter of eventual defeat. Even Germain must have pondered words roared in Parliament by the ailing Lord Chatham, who, as William Pitt, the Great Commoner, had put together the British empire: "I know that the conquest of English America *is an impossibility*. You cannot, I venture to say it, *you cannot* conquer America. . . . If I were an American, as I am an Englishman, while a foreign troop was landed in my country, I would never lay down my arms—never—never—never!" A month later, when news of Burgoyne's capture at Saratoga reached London, Pitt rose again: "My lords, I contend that we have not, nor can procure, any force to subdue America. It is monstrous to think of it." But Pitt was dying, and the country was committed; it was too late to reconsider. France joined the United States early in 1778, and the entire situation shifted dramatically.

No longer was the strategic question merely how to beat down a colonial rebellion. The American war had turned into a worldwide war; strategic considerations in America became secondary to the needs of waging the broader and more dangerous conflict.

Panic overcame Lord North. He tried once more to resign. The king held firm, however, and girded the country for war closer to home. Challenged by their ancient French foe, Englishmen rallied around their monarch. They might dissent over using arms against fellow Englishmen in America, but war with France was an altogether different matter. For the moment, at least, George III enjoyed the support of a united populace.

Sir Jeffery Amherst, who had declined to command the military effort against the colonies, accepted nomination to the long-vacant position of commander-in-chief to defend Britain against Frenchmen. He quickly decided to limit operations in America while assuming a defensive attitude toward France. Against the United States, Amherst said, "future operations must be principally naval, to distress their trade and prevent their supplies from Europe,'' and they should be supplemented by a series of amphibious raids ''on every part of the American coast that is assailable.'' Appropriate orders went out under the king's personal signature. Philadelphia was to be evacuated, British forces were to concentrate in New York City or Halifax, and Henry Clinton was to ravage ports in the southern states and raid French-held Caribbean islands. It was essentially the naval strategy recommended some three years earlier but never adopted. The big difference, of course, was that now the French fleet was a factor unbalancing the equation.

For a while the new strategy worked. Americans and Frenchmen spent three frustrating years trying vainly to coordinate their efforts. The revolution sank to its low point in the black year of 1780. Paris began to tire of the effort, and patriots watched their own spirits flag. But the allies roused themselves for one great effort, and, fortuitously, Germain and Clinton played right into their hands. Deviating from Amherst's overall strategy, they committed British forces first to a campaign in Georgia and the Carolinas and then to an invasion of Virginia, the latter apparently on the advice of Benedict Arnold, who commanded it initially. The surrender of Cornwallis and his army at Yorktown was the disastrous outcome.

After that searing blow, the North ministry fell and the new government decided to write off the thirteen colonies. But, otherwise, London followed a naval strategy doggedly for two more years, reversing many previous misfortunes by victories in theaters other than America. As a result, observed military analyst Basil Liddell Hart, ''We had lost the American colonies, but we had preserved the Empire.''[12]

5

The Eternal Question

"One eternal question of modern history has been where do governments of free men draw the line between the civil and military branches in formulating *strategy*, which involves the planning and executing of operations consistent with the purposes of the war." So states a modern historian in a book about the War of Independence. Then, surprisingly, with just one long sentence and a rather cryptic paragraph, he dismissed the "eternal question" as it pertains to the Revolutionary War.[1]

The question is a burning one today; it was no less significant two centuries ago. Who made strategy for the thirteen colonies? Did the Continental Congress or the commander-in-chief plan operations? Washington or one of the other military men invariably executed American campaigns, but from whence came instructions—the State House in Philadelphia or the general's headquarters in the field? Was the course of war plotted by a civil or a military navigator?

One might surmise without probing deeper that both Washington and Congress had a hand in policy formulation, that the derivation of strategy was necessarily a cooperative affair. And such was the case. But it was not all that simple, nor was the arrangement between the first soldier and the central government either stated or stable. It changed as the war progressed.

Implicit in the "eternal question" is fear. Civil authorities have remained always fearful of the threat military forces pose to their continued existence—often with very good reason. Rare is the state that at one time or another has not succumbed to the unconstrained power of its own soldiery, has not known the nailed boot of military dictatorship. England, perhaps more than any other nation in the eighteenth century, dreaded the possibility. One Cromwell was enough. Americans, being essentially Englishmen, shared that dread in full measure. A standing army was a standing invitation for a man on horseback to overthrow constituted government. Thus, at the very outset Congress inherently grudged the powers it would necessarily be obliged to bestow on the bearer of its sword. "A standing army is always dangerous to the liberties of the people," harped revolutionary activist Samuel Adams: "Such a power should be watched with a jealous eye." This traditional fear alone assured a relationship marked by at least some tension and marred by more than a modicum of inefficiency. Lynn Montross, a modern historian of the Continental Congress, saw clearly the negative impact of the legacy of Oliver Cromwell: "The very name of the Lord Protector and his New Model [Army] was enough to arouse a shudder, and many blunders of the assembly can be charged to a fear of tyranny."[2]

But Americans had even more reason than did their British brethren to suspect and detest a standing army: it had been just such a force that had in large measure brought about the revolution.

In 1763, at the end of the Seven Years War, Britain stood as the preeminent nation in the Western world. Royal warships had swept the seas of hostile sail while royal regiments had wrested from European foes a splendid empire, especially in North America. Every settlement east of the Mississippi River paid homage to George III. The thirteen old colonies along the Atlantic coast were loyal and comfortable members of the empire, while Canada and the Floridas accepted the change of allegiance meekly enough, leaving only disgruntled tribes living in the wilderness beyond the Appalachian barrier to disrupt the quiet of his majesty's extended domain. Not unreasonably, ministers in London decided to station a large fraction of the Royal Army in America to keep the peace on the frontier. Though it may be argued that regular troops were not the most effective of forces to fight Indians, and though not a few colonists believed the numbers of redcoats to be excessive, the king's men earned their keep right away in the bloody flare-up known as Pontiac's War. Soon, however, it became apparent that an army with a mission of maintaining peace between savages and settlers might have to operate against both. When pioneers encroached on lands reserved for Indians, British soldiers forcibly ejected them, burning their new cabins and escorting them out of the forbidden hunting grounds. The peace-keeping army no longer looked so friendly.

Moreover, Americans soon learned that Parliament thought it no more than equitable that the colonies should help offset the financial burden of their own defense. That meant taxation. "Taxation without representation," the colonists retorted—and refused to pay. London responded by reinforcing its fleet and land forces in America. Thus began a decade of mounting frustration and confrontation over constitutional and economical questions, resulting eventually in outright warfare between the provinces and the mother country.

In April 1768, seven years before the war actually opened, the king's cabinet decided to evacuate interior posts in America and to consolidate its regiments along the coast. English settlers had become a more menacing threat to peace than frontier Indians. The arrival of troops and the implementation of the Mutiny Act—a bill requiring the colonists to quarter troops and to provide certain support for them—further bruised relations. Soldiers and civilians were put in direct opposition. Tension grew. Emotions boiled most dangerously in Boston, where four regiments were quartered by late 1768. Tempers did not abate with the passage of time. On 5 March 1770, a mob confronted a squad of soldiers, taunting and frightening them to the point that the harried redcoats opened fire. When the stunned crowd fell back, five bodies lay crumpled on the cobblestones. Martyrs were made. Each year thereafter, patriots (as they were coming to be called) held propaganda rallies on the anniversary of the "massacre" to praise the honored dead and revile the hated "bloodybacks." Finally, as things went from bad to worse—the last straw being Boston's famous tea party in December 1773—the cabinet clamped a stringent military occupation upon the city and appointed General Thomas Gage, the commander of all royal forces in North America, as governor of Massachusetts.

Gage moved from New York to Boston, assuming his new duties in May 1774. Later that year, the First Continental Congress met in Philadelphia. The delegates, not unnaturally, deplored both the martial law in Boston and the affront to Massachusetts comprised in the appointment of an active military officer as the chief executive of the colony. That was an intolerable blow to the cherished concept of civilian supremacy. When that first Congress adjourned, it called for another to convene on 10 May 1775. Before that date, of course, the War of Independence was fated to begin when Gage sent a column of soldiers out of Boston to destroy rebel supplies at Concord. It is hardly surprising that the Second Continental Congress, when it ultimately announced the separation of the United States from Britain, should devote about a third of its Declaration of Independence to a catalog of grievances touching on the militarism of George III.

Gage's men marching to Concord on 19 April bumped into a veritable hornets' nest of angry patriots, who swarmed so quickly and thickly that they very nearly annihilated the startled redcoats. From all over New England, aroused minutemen streamed to Boston, forming there a clamorous army of individuals, all hoping for a chance to shoot a "lobsterback." Promptly penning the shaken and greatly outnumbered royal forces in the city, the Yankees nestled down in motley array to await developments. Most of them were still there when the new Continental Congress met.

Delegates gathering in Philadelphia during the early days of May 1775 were sorely perplexed. New England members openly planned to seek approval from other colonies for their aggressive actions. They were expected to propose that Congress, in the name of all the provinces, accept the mantle of leadership in the current crisis. That presented a dilemma. Representatives had no authority from their own colonies to assume responsibility for the mob in Massachusetts nor did they possess a mandate to wage war. Legally, they could not act. Yet the exigencies (and the opportunities) of the situation demanded the exercise of some sort of central control. Anyway, doubts were soon overtaken by events.

On the very day Congress opened for business, a blustering

band of patriots seized Fort Ticonderoga. It was somewhat fortunate that the blow was even launched, much less that it succeeded,
for the effort enjoyed no unity other than agreement on what the
objectives should be. Benedict Arnold, a Connecticut officer bearing a Massachusetts commission, vied with Ethan Allen, a New
Hampshire man employed by Connecticut, for command of a force
attacking a British fort in the colony of New York. (Actually,
Allen was from Vermont, which was at that time disputed territory
between the province of New York and New Hampshire.) It was
all most confusing and proof aplenty of the crying need for central
direction. New York further prodded the reluctant assembly by
asking for military guidance, thereby implying the existence of a
continental authority which Congress itself was loathe to accept.
As anticipated, too, New Englanders did request the Continental
Congress to assume overall direction. Interestingly enough, Massachusetts' Provincial Congress raised the theme of civil supremacy in its plea, writing, "We tremble at having an army (although consisting of our own countrymen) established here, without a civil power to provide for and control them." So, by default
more than design, and somewhat less than wholeheartedly, Congress grabbed the flapping reins of rebellion.[3]

Although tacitly accepting a leadership role, the men meeting in
Philadelphia's State House experienced difficulty in defining a
proper line of action. Should they support and augment the armed
resistance being offered by the Yankees or attempt primarily to
mediate a reconciliation between the northern colonies and the
mother country? New Englanders argued that the time for talking
was past; American blood had already been spilled. But other
provinces, less directly threatened, were not about to be stam-
peded into joining the faraway fracas with General Gage. Congress proceeded cautiously. It sent an equivocal answer to New
York's request for defense advice. Should British troops disem-
bark in the city, the message said, they ought to be housed and
supplied so long as they acted peacefully; however, it would be
proper to "repel force by force." Then Congress appointed its first
committee to study a military matter: "To consider what posts are
necessary to be occupied in the Colony of New York, and by what

number of troops it will be necessary they should be guarded.''
Delegates selected as chairman the quiet but impressive member
wearing the uniform of a Virginia militia officer—Colonel George
Washington.[4]

Spurred by the startling news of the successful attack on Fort
Ticonderoga, the Virginian and his committee worked diligently,
their sessions lasting late into the May nights. The final report
urged vigorous action to secure strategically important New York,
a manifestly warlike recommendation. Essentially, the Hudson
was to be closed to British shipping. Washington's aggressive
proposal plainly obliged delegates to choose between appeasement
or force. After days of intense debate, Congress adopted the plan
on 25 May, thus taking its first outright decision to wage war in the
name of thirteen colonies in order to obtain redress from a
''wicked'' Parliament.[5]

The first bellicose step was the hard one. After it, the busy men
in the state house needed only three more weeks to establish
Congress' own army. The spontaneous incidents in Massachusetts
had blossomed into full rebellion.

By adopting the throng besieging Boston, and adding to it ten
companies of riflemen from Pennsylvania, Maryland, and Virginia, the Continental Congress created the Continental army. An
army needs rules and leaders; Congress provided both. Congressman George Washington helped draft the army's regulations, and
then congressmen drafted George Washington to be the army's
commander. He was to lead ''all the forces now raised, or to be
raised.''

Delegates were most judicious in their selection of general
officers. Their final choices represented considerations for sec-
tional jealousies, military abilities, the enemy threat, continental
unity, and—congressional control. New England, having fielded
the bulk of the soldiers, received most of the general officer
positions: two major generals and seven brigadiers. All nine of
them were already in command of troops at Boston; Congress'
action merely formalized their positions. New York then got one
major general, Philip Schuyler, and one brigadier. Schuyler, the
most influential landowner in the strategically vital Hudson valley,

was a logical selection to command forces near Albany, which, after Boston, was the only other area of conflict. The fourth major general and the adjutant general were Virginians, but those two, Charles Lee and Horatio Gates, had been born in England and were only recent immigrants, as was Richard Montgomery, the Irish brigadier from New York. Those three foreign-born Americans, having been career officers in the British army, were selected largely to inject some professional leavening into the Continental army. Of the thirteen subordinate generals, then, nine were Yankees, one was a New Yorker, and three were European professionals.

The key selection, of course, was that of commander-in-chief. Washington was a southerner, a native American, as experienced at war as anyone born in the colonies, a wealthy man of the soil, a natural leader who inspired confidence, an imposing person who even looked like a soldier. He was also a member of Congress, he and Schuyler being the only two among the fourteen original continental generals.

The tall, stately Virginian had been a prominent member of both the First and Second Continental Congresses. Delegates knew and respected and trusted him. He was, his colleagues reckoned, "discreet and virtuous, no harum starum ranting swearing fellow but sober, steady, and calm." Though Washington was qualified in so many other ways to head the Continental army, there was more than pure chance in Congress' choice of one of its own to that powerful position. (With Washington at Boston and Schuyler in northern New York, senior officers at both of the likely locations of hostilities would be ex-congressmen. Mere coincidence?) As a member of the very body which appointed him, the general, it could be hoped, would remain subservient to that body. If such a thought, conscious or subconscious, cruised through delegates' heads—and surely, given their fear of a standing army, it must have—they displayed exemplary wisdom in their choice. Their trust was well placed. General Washington never forgot that he was first Congressman Washington.

Lest there be any doubt as to the intent of Congress to exercise control over its field commander, representatives inserted this paragraph in his commission:

> And you are to regulate your conduct in every respect by the rules and discipline of war, (as herewith given you) and punctually to observe and follow such orders and directions, from time to time, as you shall receive from this, or a future Congress of these United Colonies, or committee of Congress.

Further, the delegates informed him, his commission would "continue in force, until revoked by this, or a future Congress." From the outset, then, the commander-in-chief was put on blunt notice that he served at the pleasure of Congress and that he was bound to follow its direction. At the same time, Congress did not intend to tie his hands. His commission vested him with "full power and authority to act as you shall think for the good and welfare of the services." The commission was issued on 17 June 1775, the same day patriots and Englishmen met in the battle of Bunker Hill.[6]

Congress amplified its guidance to the commander-in-chief with further instructions, including a parenthetical requirement to consider the advice of a council of war before maneuvering the army. The delegates, knowing Washington was not experienced at commanding large numbers of troops, apparently felt he should act with prudence. That limitation—which was later to be the cause of considerable criticism leveled at Washington's generalship—may have been added as a result of his own self-effacing attitude. He had not hesitated to make his colleagues aware of his sincere "conviction of my own incapacity and want of experience in the conduct of so momentous a concern."[7]

Time passed rapidly during the week between Washington's selection on 15 June and his departure on 23 June. It was an emotional and busy period. There were ceremonies to perform and farewells to make and discussions to attend and equipment to buy and instructions to receive. When formally presenting him his commission, the assembly concluded the ritual by stating: "This Congress doth now declare, that they will maintain and assist him, and adhere to him, the said George Washington, Esqr., with their lives and fortune in the same cause." For his part, the new commanding general thanked the members for their faith in him and solemnly vowed to "exert every power I possess in their service." Members of Congress hosted a dinner in Washington's honor at Peg Mullen's Beefsteak House, after which they excitedly toasted "the Commander-in-Chief of the American armies!" He responded in a touchingly awkward and humble manner. The relationship between the general and the Congress began with mutual respect and a clear sense of military subordination.[8]

Despite all the conferences, instructions, and assurances, neither Washington nor members of Congress possessed a precise understanding of the delineation of responsibilities relating to strategy making. As a matter of fact, it would be hard to show the existence of even a vague understanding. Congress obviously had retained certain military functions—the most notable examples being providing funds, procuring supplies, promoting and appointing general officers, and giving "orders and directions" to Washington himself—but the general had been handed "full power and authority to act" as he thought best. The truth of the matter seems to be that none of those involved in forming an army in those hectic June days had much time to ponder strategic concepts. Indeed, the evidence suggests that they never even thought in such terms. Certainly there was no overall plan. Like everything else in those feverish early months of the Revolutionary War, strategy would emerge piecemeal and spontaneously. Congress and commander cannot be faulted for failing clearly to divide that which did not clearly exist.

As might be expected, a period followed during which strategic thought and direction flowed uncoordinated from two sources, with, as might also be expected, a degree of duplication and inefficiency.

Congress had, of course, been involved in making strategic decisions long before Washington had even thought of becoming the commanding general. In fact, some delegates had dabbled in strategy before Congress itself had convened. On their way to Philadelphia, members of the Massachusetts delegation had stopped in Hartford, where Governor Jonathan Trumbull of Connecticut quizzed them on their views of the contemplated attack of Fort Ticonderoga. Defending New York City, closing the Hudson River, and garrisoning forts on Lake Champlain were among other early strategic matters handled by the representatives. Then, just days after General Schuyler left Philadelphia to take command of forces in northern New York, Congress ordered him to invade Canada in an effort to turn that immense province into the "14th Colony." That, certainly, was a strategic decision of the first magnitude. The assembly, among a host of other details, also concerned itself with the fine points of erecting defensive fortifications at strategically vulnerable places about the country, most notably in the Hudson Highlands fifty miles or so north of New York City. In short, members were up to their collective ears in military affairs during the opening months of the war.

For that matter, not a few delegates had difficulty in those early days sorting out the differences between raising an army and running one. The initial impulse to get closer to the fighting was powerful. On 5 June 1775, Joseph Hewes, a representative from North Carolina, proposed moving Congress to Connecticut so "that we might be near the seat of action." When the assembly adjourned briefly in August that year, many congressmen made their way to Massachusetts to visit the army rather than return home. Often expressed in Philadelphia taverns and drawing rooms was the desire to drop deliberations and take up a musket to fight as militiamen. Indeed, one delegate did later participate in the battle of Brandywine, though more in the role of observer than weapon wielder. Fortunately, political instinct prevailed over martial spirit. Congress remained a legislative body, to which role it was better suited than that of a glorified general staff. Nevertheless, the excitement of campaigning contrasted sharply with the tedium of enacting legislation. John Adams probably spoke for most of his cohorts when he bemoaned, after enviously watching Washington and the other generals ride off to join the army, "I, poor creature, worn out with scribbling . . . must leave others to wear the laurels which I have sown."[9]

Meanwhile, after instilling some order in his restless, makeshift army, General Washington, too, turned his thought to strategic considerations. Unable to muster the combat power needed to root Gage out of Boston, he began to look around for other objectives. Although aware of Schuyler's congressionally ordered invasion of Canada, the general sent a column of his own thrashing through the Maine woods toward Quebec, apparently without conferring first with Congress. Rapid perusal of a map convinced him that ships would be needed in order to strike at other English possessions as well as to interfere with enemy shipping. Forthwith, he armed several vessels, forming a small commerce raiding force known to history as "Washington's Navy." (Shortly afterward, Congress formally established a Continental navy and marine corps.) He dealt with Indians and worried about frontier settlements; he prodded New Yorkers to hasten their efforts toward erecting defenses along the Hudson River; he moved artillery pieces from Fort Ticonderoga to Boston for a siege there.

Gradually, as the months passed, Congress acted less and less in the strategic sphere, Washington more and more. The reasons were several. First, Congress simply had too many other matters competing for its attention. For instance, financing the war was proving to be just as trying a task as fighting it, and that was but one of Congress' chores. Attempting to handle a myriad of details without benefit of constituted bureaus was creating a sticky morass of administrative trivia into which delegates were slowly sinking. A fear of "executism" hampered them. An ad hoc committee was the inadequate method employed to process virtually every problem; members saw their hours devoured in an endless series of meetings. Striving to do everything was a sure way to accomplish nothing. Moreover, as the mood of the country drifted farther from reconciliation and closer to independence, purely political responsibilities burgeoned beyond what any delegate could have imagined in the summer of 1775. As confidence in Washington grew, weary and overburdened representatives became only too happy to shift military considerations progressively to his broad shoulders.

Second, the general and his ex-associates thought alike; they quite agreed on the ends for which they were struggling. What is more, a steady stream of correspondence from the constantly respectful commander-in-chief kept the assembly informed, while uniformly favorable comments from numerous congressional committees returning from visiting his headquarters left delegates satisfied with their top general. All told, they were pleased with his performance and increasingly disinclined to watch him with wary eye.

Finally, bitter experience had demonstrated the folly of operating with two heads, while highlighting the efficacy of unity of command. Washington's brilliant feat in forcing the British from Boston contrasted all too starkly with the crushing failure of the Canadian campaign, a failure which could be laid only at Congress' door.

Accordingly, after the victory at Boston and with a British invasion of New York imminent, a somewhat chagrined Congress ordered a gold medal struck in Washington's honor and, in effect, abdicated its role in strategy making. The general journeyed to Philadelphia in May 1776 to discuss the war with delegates, but there were no deep differences to debate. As American defenders prepared to meet the British thrust into New York, the assembly resolved "that General Washington be informed that Congress have such an entire confidence in his judgment, that they will give him no particular directions about the dispositions of the troops, but desire that he will dispose [them] as to him shall seem most conducive to the public good."[10]

At that point, coinciding roughly with the announcement of the Declaration of Independence, Congress had of its own volition delegated to the commander-in-chief virtually unlimited authority to make and execute strategy. In the name of efficiency—and after some prodding from Washington—members further decided to divest themselves of the daily chore of coping with most of their remaining military functions, which were largely routine in nature anyway. On 12 June 1776, they established "A Board of War and Ordnance," a standing committee to watch over matters pertaining to the administration of the army. By accepted practice, then, if not by actual charter, George Washington had emerged as the country's executive authority for waging the war, so extensive were the powers informally vested in him.[11]

Not that investiture assured victory. As a matter of fact, Washington's most serious reverses came just at that time. Full authority to conduct the war and full ability to succeed in combat were hardly one and the same thing. Through late summer and fall 1776, General William Howe methodically wrested New York City and its environs from the Continental army, pushed Washington around with apparent ease, and leisurely followed the beaten patriots across New Jersey to the banks of the Delaware.

Still, Congress did not question the general's supreme authority. As English and Hessian columns approached the Delaware, rumors raced through Philadelphia, many indicating the momentary departure of Congress. Wanting to quash such talk, Congress resolved on 11 December to have the commander-in-chief publicly contradict the rumor. Politely, but firmly, he refused. Instead, he told the delegates they should indeed consider displacing. Without a murmur of protest, the representatives obediently packed up and moved to Baltimore. That exchange, contends historian Lynn Montross, amounted to tacit recognition by the Congress of Washington's executive position. Nor was that all. "Desperate diseases require desperate remedies," wrote the general on 20 December. The assembly responded a week later by granting him special emergency powers afterward described as "dictatorial." The term may have been too strong, but the fact remains that Congress looked to the commander with complete—or at least desperate—confidence. Immediately thereafter, his remarkable feats in the ten-day Christmas campaign turned the war around, injecting new life into the rebellion and fully justifying Congress' faith in him.[12]

Those halcyon days did not, indeed, could not, endure unchallenged. Both the ever-present specter of a man on horseback and war's shifting fortunes operated to cause Congress to reassert itself. The inevitable confrontation took a year and a half in ripening, but it blossomed early.

Soon after declaring independence, Congress began to prepare revised articles of war. The original articles, drafted in part by delegate George Washington and approved by Congress on 30 June 1775, had proven to be inadequate to the needs of a long war. The new articles of war, adopted on 20 September 1776, gave Washington the increased disciplinary power he wanted but also spelled out the relationship of officers to Congress. The earlier articles made no provision requiring fealty of officers, but the latest version clearly delineated their duty to country, placing it just behind duty to God. The first article of Section II stipulated: "Whatsoever officer . . . shall presume to use traitorous or disrespectful words against the authority of the United States in Congress assembled . . . shall be cashiered." Plainly enough, Congress planned to retain its preeminence.[13]

Washington's lackluster performance in New York had raised some questions in Congress concerning his generalship, nagging questions which the resounding successes at Trenton and Princeton had not entirely erased. Nor had the indignity of flight from Philadelphia to Baltimore better disposed delegates to judge their field commander kindly. What was more, his soaring fame was beginning to produce both jealousy and fright among some members. Washington was becoming too big. The child was outstripping the parent. The public had already begun the process of elevating to demigod status the very human head of the Continental army. And, while American parents named their children after the Virginian, European princes marveled at his accomplishments. No less a light than Frederick the Great was quoted as describing the Christmas campaign as being "the most brilliant of any recorded in the annals of military achievement." The officer whom Congress saw as less than perfect was growing uncomfortably grand; that was good, in a way, but worrisome too. John Adams grumpily told other delegates that they should avoid the tendency to idolize the general. Benjamin Rush recorded Adams' warning:

I have been distressed to see some members of this house disposed to idolise an image which their own hands have molten. I speak here of the superstitious veneration that is sometimes paid to General Washington. Altho' I honour him for his good qualities, yet in this house I feel myself his Superior. In private life I shall always acknowledge that he is mine. It becomes us to attend early to the restraining our army.[14]

In all marriages, sooner or later, the honeymoon glow fades and the partners become aware of each other's uglier traits. By mid-1777, Congress and its officer corps had reached that point. Politically motivated promotions and the elevation of foreign adventurers over the heads of deserving Americans had precipitated a flood of protest from patriot officers. Congress, smarting from the resulting criticism—which was no less galling for being largely correct—reacted more with anger than wisdom. "I am wearied to death with the wrangles between military officers, high and low," wrote one delegate. "They quarrel like cats and dogs. They worry one another like mastiffs, scrambling for rank and pay like apes for nuts." Several officers resigned, and even such stalwarts as Benedict Arnold, John Sullivan, Nathanael Greene, and Henry Knox angrily threatened to quit, which shook Washington and sobered Congress but failed to smooth the strained relations. General Schuyler, himself a former member of Congress, dashed off an insulting letter to Philadelphia, which indignant delegates labeled "ill-advised and highly indecent." Washington and Congress argued stubbornly over the handling of prisoners, with the assembly for once overriding the general's objections. Congress even needled the commander-in-chief, implying he was not being aggressive enough. "Could I accomplish the important objects so eagerly wished by Congress," he snapped back, "I should be happy indeed." He might be better able to act, he pointedly let the lawmakers know, if they would get their own work done. "There are several matters also, which I referred to Congress some time since, and upon which I have not received the result of their deliberations."[15]

When Robert Morris, a delegate from Pennsylvania, suggested confidentially to Washington that Congress was being progressively weakened by the departures of its great members "without any proper appointments to fill their places," the general wrote right back in agreement: "Indeed, sir, your observations on the want of many capital characters in that senate are but too just." (The composition of Congress was, in fact, changing in a fashion assuring the diminution of regard for Washington; by year's end, only two of the group which had unanimously chosen him commander-in-chief would remain.) It was quite beyond his power, the Virginian stated acidly, "to make Congress fully sensible of the real situation of our affairs. . . . In a word, when they are at a distance, they think it is but to say Presto begone, and everything is done." At his bleak post in the cold New Jersey hills, exerting his every fiber to achieve the seemingly impossible task of putting together an army for the coming campaign, Washington resented those in Congress who "seem not to have any conception of the difficulty and perplexity attending those who are to exe- cute." The threat of England's 1777 offensive obliged patriots to close their ruffled ranks, but the rift was only set aside, not settled.[16]

During the year, Congress gingerly reinserted itself into the role of strategy maker, although, with the initiative belonging to the British, there was not much the assembly could do. As the cam- paigning season approached, Congress suggested gathering the Continental army near Philadelphia. Washington flatly refused. He stuck to his previous rendezvous point near the Hudson River. Then the delegates told him to take more care to assure the safety of that vital riverway. He complied, but not before angrily lecturing the lawmakers: "War in theory and the modes of defence are obvious and easy, but in practice they are more difficult." Later, on 16 August, members cautiously resolved to *inform* Washington that it was the "opinion of Congress" that five hundred riflemen, under "an active and spirited officer" should go to reinforce the northern department against Burgoyne's advance. Though hard pressed for men himself, the general complied, sending Daniel Morgan northward. Emboldened, Congress four days later *directed* Washington to send a thousand New Jersey militiamen to the Hudson River fortifications in order to free New York militiamen to oppose Burgoyne. Then, with Washington preoccupied by General Howe's approach to Philadelphia, Congress busied itself considering a complex scheme to attack Pensacola on the Gulf coast. An incredulous Henry Laurens, just arrived to represent South Carolina, helped defeat that untimely proposal, but informed Governor John Rutledge, "I can hardly forbear concluding that a great assembly is in its dotage." That proved to be Congress' final thrust into strategy before it had to demonstrate again its own strategic mobility by displacing to York, Pennsylvania, when Howe moved into Philadelphia and converted the State House into a hospital.[17]

Besides dabbling in strategy, Congress worked in 1777 to increase its organizational leverage over the army. The Articles of Confederation, passed by Congress in late 1777 (the states would not ratify them for more than three years), reserved for Congress "the sole and exclusive right and power of determining on peace and war." The Articles prescribed that Congress alone would have authority for "making rules for the government and regulation of the said land and naval forces, and *directing their operations.*" That last phrase was not an afterthought. Delegates also altered the concept of the board of war, changing it from a standing committee of Congress to an executive agency run by men not members of that body but obedient to it. Although ostensibly its charter made it wholly administrative, the board had the power to act in any way Congress wanted. Yet another means of control was the authority to investigate. On 28 November 1777, the assembly resolved that, whenever any expedition failed or any post fell, "it be an established rule in Congress to institute an inquiry into the causes of the failure . . . and into the conduct of the principal officer or officers." In every way they could, the lawyers were buttressing their legal case for civilian supremacy.[18]

When 1777 was over, it turned out that the year's armed clashes had achieved precious little to enhance cooperation, much to abet acrimony. Things had not gone well from the very first, leaving more blame than praise to be passed around. When General St. Clair had evacuated Fort Ticonderoga without a struggle, delegates were patently flabbergasted. It looked like Congress would have to shoot some generals to encourage the others, one representative had tartly suggested, an attitude hardly conducive to restoring good relations. Washington's setbacks around Philadelphia, so reminiscent of his reverses a year earlier in New York, had not improved his stock in the State House. Nor had other generals in that theater covered themselves with glory. Philadelphia surgeon Benjamin Rush, an ex-member of Congress, had condemned them all as a drunken lot of cowards and incompetents. Congress ought to establish unflinching rules, he had declared, requiring censure for any general who, in any twenty-four-hour period, should drink more than a quart of whiskey or who found time to get drunk more than once. Moreover, they should be ordered to sleep with their boots on and remain not more than five hundred yards to the rear in battle. His comments may have been a little extreme, but as congressmen once again fled Philadelphia to avoid capture, they must have felt disappointment, if not outright displeasure, with Washington's performance. Word of Horatio Gates' astounding capture of Burgoyne's entire army at Saratoga had given Americans a great and needed lift—and had provided unfavorable comparison with the losing efforts of the commander-in-chief. John Adams had not missed the chance to twist his quill in the Virginian's ribs. Had Washington rather than Gates gained the splendid victory, he confided to Abigail, "idolatry and adulation would have been unbounded; so excessive as to endanger our liberties, for what I know. Now, we can allow a certain citizen to be wise, virtuous and good without thinking him a deity or a saviour."[19]

When fault-finders cast about for a scapegoat, Washington was the immediate candidate. Having puffed up his own strength figures for propaganda purposes, his setbacks appeared to be worse than they actually were. Why had he not fought like Gates? With such large forces, why had he achieved so little? Those questions were posed often by members of the board of war, meeting in York in the crowded law offices of James Smith, a delegate from that little town where Congress had sought refuge.

Those opposed to Washington sensed his vulnerability. They grew bolder. Horatio Gates, who was dead wrong in both his high opinion of himself and his low opinion of Washington, became all at once aloof, virtually ignoring the commander-in-chief. The conqueror of Burgoyne began corresponding directly with Congress, arrogantly bypassing the man who had been unable to defeat Howe. Worse, he insubordinately refused to respond to Washington's orders to send Continentals from the northern department, where they were no longer needed, to the central where their timely arrival might make another American victory possible. Congress, too, took a swipe at the Virginian, telling him that his serious shortages of supplies were due not so much to any failure of Congress as to his own "too great delicacy in exerting military authority." James Lovell, a known congressional foe of Washington, chortled at the wording of that resolution. It was, he said, plainly "meant to rap a demi-G—— on the knuckles." The stage was thus set for the climactic encounter between the Continental Congress and the commanding general of the Continental army. Ironically, the young republic's first crisis in civil-military relations took its title from a French soldier of fortune, Thomas Conway.

The Conway cabal was not led by the man it was named after. And, according to generally accepted historical judgment, it was not a cabal; however, probably because of its alliterative and sinister sound, the term became a convenient label for the collision in the winter of 1777-1778 between pro-Washington and anti-Washington forces.

A clash of some sort was all but inevitable; it had been building too long to be averted. Moreover, the political structure of the United States actually pushed Washington and Congress into adversary roles. Congress clearly owned legislative powers, and the commander-in-chief as clearly had complete freedom to exercise command in the field. But there was no executive authority, leaving a crucial void in the country's war making powers. In politics as in physics, a vacuum is abhorrent. Both Washington and Congress tried to fill it.

Sticking his oar into those already roiling waters was Thomas Conway, an Irish-born French army officer who had managed to wangle a brigadier general's commission from Congress. His real role may never be known, but he was the catalyst (or at least the vehicle) which precipitated the clash bearing his name. That he was too loose with his tongue is sure; that he actually advocated and plotted for Washington's replacement is uncertain; that he was despised by Washington and his adherents is known; that he had the active support of any member of Congress is unconfirmed; that he was unwise is beyond doubt. All in all, whether guilty of conspiring against Washington or not, he was a minor character, at most a tool used by others and of no real significance to the story.

The important thing is that Washington and his supporters at headquarters *thought* there was a move afoot in Congress to supplant him with Horatio Gates, the celebrated victor of Saratoga. Aides had not failed to note the rising level of resentment within Congress, caused for the most part by jealousy of the power wielded by the commander-in-chief, nor had they missed the significance of actions aimed at lessening that power. Even if George Washington had not been as politically astute as he was, he would still have seen the confrontation coming. Friends within the Congress and about the country provided him ample warning. He was not caught by surprise. When men at least partly inimical to Washington gained appointment to the board of war, with Gates being named as its president, the conspiracy theory being tossed about during discussions at headquarters in Valley Forge gained credence. When Congress promoted Conway to major general —over Washington's strong objections—and exacerbated the insult by making him inspector general of the Continental army, Washington became incensed and even more convinced of the existence of a plot against him. The last straw was Congress' resolution on 22 January 1778 "that an irruption be made into Canada, and that the Board of War be authorized to take every necessary measure for the execution of the business, under such general officers as Congress shall appoint." The delegates, perhaps recalling a proposal of John Adams that all general officers ought to be elected annually, selected the commanders by ballot. Only then did anyone inform the commander-in-chief.[20]

It would make fascinating reading had Washington met what he saw as action against him by direct counteraction, but that was not his way: he was both too shrewd and too straight. He held his temper (though not all his lieutenants did) and awaited an opening. It came rather quickly. When he struck, it appeared to be done passively, but the effect was to scatter his opponents as a sudden cloudburst would chase Sunday picnickers. By simply refusing to deal with Conway, Washington rendered him impotent as inspector general. Releasing selected details of incriminating correspondence between Conway, Gates, and others, the general exposed many of his foes to ridicule, sending them scurrying for cover and causing them to turn angrily on one another. As for the Canadian venture, he merely remained quiet, letting Congress' own chickens come home embarrassingly to roost. Even with Washington's all-out backing, mounting an invasion at that particular moment—in the dead of winter with a supply system so rickety it could not even support the wretched troops trying to survive in Valley Forge—would have been highly impractical, if not impossible. As it was, the campaign never so much as got started, earning supreme scorn and criticism for the board of war, which is to say, for Congress. Not many weeks passed before it became apparent that a move to unseat General Washington could not succeed. The "cabal" collapsed abruptly.[21]

Therein lies what might well be the most significant point to the whole affair: its sudden collapse. Despite all the noise, no serious opposition to Washington existed. Only a handful of anti-Washington men ever surfaced, then or later, either in Congress or the army. Fear of a man on horseback and the all-too-human struggle to gain or maintain power had inflated the bubble of opposition beyond all proportion, and it had burst at the first prick. To one and all, the move to replace the commander-in-chief had posed the startling question: if not Washington, who? It was unanswerable. Indeed, it was unthinkable. "The toast among the soldiers," Congress learned, was "Washington or no army." The confrontation had confirmed the Virginian's unique position. Cause and commander were one and the same. No one could take his place. Close scrutiny of his actions and comparison with his competitors had redounded solely to Washington's credit. As it turned out, the affair consolidated and increased his power. His host of adherents admired him even more (if that were possible);

his handful of enemies stood largely cowed and discredited; those who had been in the middle shifted for the most part to become ardent supporters after the fright of trying to imagine the revolution without George Washington at the helm. The lasting result was that the commander-in-chief was left unchallenged as the executive authority in the country's defense establishment.

Events in spring 1778 soon confirmed his newly accepted eminence. On 10 April, when an action of the assembly ran contrary to a view Washington expressed, the members labored until late at night, painstakingly choosing words that would not antagonize the general, assuring him that they would "wish to preserve that harmony with you, which is so essential to the general weal." Gates was reassigned to the northern department, with his subordination to the commander-in-chief set down in no uncertain terms. When some officers known to have been anti-Washington submitted resignations, a routine method of protest, Congress shocked them by accepting at once, a policy rarely pursued before. Then, in a series of actions, the lawmakers clipped the wings of the board of war, leaving no doubt that its status was beneath that of Washington. Finally, they renewed and extended his special powers, which amounted to a permanently declared state of martial law wherever he went. Congressmen had learned their lesson, and probably found superfluous Washington's admonition against displaying in the future any distrust of his army which they might harbor. It would be best all around, he warned, to avoid making such sentiments public. While many governments feared a standing army in peacetime, Washington noted wryly, only that of the United States had such a concern in time of war. That must not be, he wrote. "We should all be considered—Congress, Army, etc.—as one people, embarked in one cause, one interest; acting on the same principle and to the same end."[22]

Congress established four executive departments in February 1781: finance, foreign affairs, marine, and war (although the Marine Department remained inactive). Robert Morris, the first superintendent of finance, handled marine (naval) matters as an extra duty. As for secretary at war, that sensitive position remained vacant until the end of October when General Benjamin Lincoln got the nod. Lincoln, fat, gouty, and lethargic, had previously distinguished himself in only two ways: leading his men into the worst American defeat of the war at Charleston in 1780 and becoming afflicted with an unusual sickness that caused him to doze off at the most unlikely times, a syndrome which medical researchers have since named after him. He was an administrator, not an intriguer. Furthermore, as a thorough-going backer of General Washington, Lincoln was sure to support him always, to compete with him never. Unambitious, he was not dangerous —which Congressmen appreciated. They wanted to keep relations smooth.

Significantly, Congress did not specify the relationship between Lincoln and Washington. Theoretically, the secretary at war headed the country's military establishment, but, practically, Washington remained the acknowledged leader. Delegates even gave the commander-in-chief full power to concert military moves with French and Spanish commanders beyond America's shores. For his part, Lincoln was content to leave field operations to the field commanders, while Washington was happy to work through an agency responsible solely for military affairs. It was a good arrangement, maintaining the façade of civil supremacy and retaining the efficiency of a powerful commander-in-chief.

All of which is not to say that Congress completely abrogated its responsibilities or interests in formulating strategy, or even that lawmakers refrained completely from interfering in the process. To the contrary, they constantly kept a finger in the pie. The best-known example is their decision to place Gates in command of the southern department in 1780 rather than an officer of Washington's choosing. However, when Gates promptly encountered disaster at Camden—when his "northern laurels turned to southern willows"—Congress meekly asked Washington to appoint a replacement. And, even when Congress acted, it was more often than not in complete deference to Washington's wishes. For instance, when delegates resurrected the idea of an invasion of Canada in winter 1778-1779, Washington resisted, spiking the proposal quite easily. Typical, too, was a committee Congress sent to camp in spring 1780: it was strictly instructed to avoid doing or ordering anything of any sort with which Washington did not concur. The committee was a symbol of congressional supremacy, the hobbling instructions an admission of Washington's primacy.

As the months and years passed, ordeal in the crucible of war progressively strengthened the power of the commander-in-chief while eroding that of the Continental Congress. Helped by the lessons of experience and the advice of foreign officers, Washington finally converted his tatterdemalion army into a respected and efficient fighting organization. He himself expanded in ability and confidence, and the participation of allied forces, particularly the French navy, added an altogether new dimension to his reach. Success, too, enriched his reputation. Congress, meanwhile, becalmed by the departure of so many men of genius who had made it such a brilliant senate in 1775 and 1776, foundered on the rocks of states' rights and sank in a sea of its own worthless paper money. Washington became loved if not worshipped, Congress disliked if not despised. Even a Hessian officer noted the eclipse, reporting late in the war that Washington's presence near the seat of government "is lending some dignity and respect to the declining Congress." After the war a participant recalled: "A governor of a state was beneath the dignity of a Commander-in Chief, and a President of Congress was still more contemptible."[23]

Derided by the enemy, rebuffed by the states, insulted by citizens, threatened by its own soldiers (Congress quit Philadelphia a third time when embittered troops sought redress at bayonet point in 1783), and even self-castigated by many of its own members, the assembly ended the war with but a shade of its onetime strength. No one called it King Congress anymore. However, not a few once-fervent republicans began to envision Washington wearing a crown. The general promptly quashed such talk; he had no interest in becoming King George I of America. Instead, he continued to support Congress wholeheartedly.

Few observers failed to note the phenomenon—Frenchmen found it especially incredible—of a general with the power to do about as he wished but who wished no power. Late in the war, a Frenchman of letters traveling through America, the Chevalier de Chastellux, marveled at Washington's restraint: "This is the seventh year that he has commanded the army and he has obeyed Congress: more need not be said."

As a matter of fact, the very weakness of Congress caused great concern at headquarters. Washington was no Cromwell. He never forgot that he was a congressman before he was a general, that his commission was from Congress, that his ultimate loyalty was to that body. He earnestly desired a strong central government and personally worked hard for ratification of the Articles of Confederation. A weak government in time of war was a poor one. Unless the states vested Congress "with absolute powers in all matters relative to the great purposes of war," he wrote in 1780, "we are attempting an impossibility, and very soon shall become (if it is not already the case) a many headed monster, a heterogeneous mass, that never will or can steer to the same point." However, when the Articles finally were adopted in 1781, few improvements resulted. They gave Congress authority only to do those things it had been doing all along. The Continental Congress, an inefficient and extralegal legislative body, became "the United States in Congress Assembled," an inefficient and *legal* legislative body. The Articles provided Congress the "privilege of asking everything and reserved for the states the prerogative of granting nothing," observed Robert Morris. "If you know of a compliance with one requisition of Congress, *in time* and quantity," James Lovell asked a Massachusetts friend, "do let me have it that I may show it to the delegates of the [other] 12 states who cannot produce a single instance." Alexander Hamilton, commenting on the absence of provisions in the Articles for a constituted executive, said the new government would be "neither fit for war or peace." He was right, as it turned out, but so long as George Washington continued to serve as the de facto executive authority for conducting the war, the weakness was not fatal.[24]

That situation brought about one of the most remarkable ironies of the revolution: the Congress which had begun the war with such a dread of a military takeover was at the end of the war saved by the very general it feared. And—this is the crux of the irony—it was protected largely from itself.

When peace negotiations opened in 1782, most Americans,

realizing the end of the long war was at last in sight, began preparing for the future. Until then, the external threat had bound the different states and factions together; they had understood well that they would either hang together or hang separately. Now, with peace around the corner, the binding started to unravel. Inevitably, political forces coalesced, competing for the support of various sources of power. And nothing else in the United States had as much self-evident power as the Continental army. Congress approached its army in two-headed fashion: certain factions tried to involve it in the political process (the very antithesis of the traditional Anglo-American urge to keep the military out of politics!) while others wanted to disband it hastily. Either course could have spelled disaster, could have caused a military coup. In the first instance, the disparity between political and military strengths would have made it highly unlikely that politicians would have been able to manipulate the generals. In the second, Congress apparently was unaware of the fact that Oliver Cromwell and his New Model Army had remained wholly loyal until Parliament had unwisely attempted to dismiss them without pay or proper recognition. While standing at the very edge of victory, the American Revolution was in danger of destroying itself.

Fortunately, General Washington resisted both courses. He forcefully held the army aloof from the political arena and fought staunchly to win just treatment for his officers and men. The former was the easier task; without Washington's personal participation or approval, the army itself possessed very little political clout. The latter was not so simple; in many ways, disbanding an army proved to be a more difficult job than raising one. It is quite likely that only Washington, with his great prestige and sense of duty, could have pulled it off without serious conflict between the civil and military sectors. The details of how the general held the army and the nation together in those dangerous days, though fascinating, are not pertinent to the question of who made American strategy in the War of Independence. But the broad facts are. They have been mentioned because they point out as perhaps nothing else can the relationship, as perceived by Washington himself, between Congress and the commander-in-chief.[25]

In answering the eternal question about the division of the process of strategy formulation between civil and military sectors during the Revolutionary War, one must recognize that there existed between the two branches an overlapping zone of constantly shifting width. For the first year or so, both Washington and Congress devised strategy, but with the assembly gradually backing off to hand the entire responsibility to the general. That arrangement remained more or less in effect until the confrontation in the winter of 1777-1778. From then until the war ended, the commander-in-chief possessed the primary responsibility. It is fair to conclude, then, that George Washington's voice was predominant in articulating patriot strategy. Therefore, when we speak of American strategy, we mean, in the main, Washington's strategy. It was he who executed it and, in most instances, planned it. It is he, therefore, who should receive credit or criticism.

When delegates met in Philadelphia in 1787 to write a constitution to replace the moribund Articles of Confederation, they specifically addressed the division of war-making powers. Being mostly men who had served in Congress and the army during the revolution, they recognized the need to have a constituted executive authority. Drawing on their successful wartime experiences, they not surprisingly formally incorporated into the new constitution the informal but effective relationship developed in that war. Congress would have the power to declare war, to raise armies and a navy, and to provide for them. The President would make strategy. His would be the power to direct the armed forces. In that capacity, his title would be the same that the Continental Congress had given twelve years earlier to George Washington: the commander-in-chief.

6

Beyond the Horizon

Grand strategy prescribes a war's ultimate aims. It is the underlying policy from which everything else is derived. "Furthermore," wrote military theorist Basil Liddell Hart, "while the horizon of strategy is bounded by the war, grand strategy looks beyond the war to the subsequent peace." As has been amply demonstrated in the twentieth century, proper strategy coupled with faulty grand strategy can lead to futile, frustrating victories; we have more than once witnessed the unhappy anomaly of winning the war only to lose the peace.[1]

The patriots had two basic war aims. First, they fought to gain and retain their independence. That goal is self-evident, although Americans stood in arms for more than a year before they articulated their claim to independence in a unanimous declaration. The second objective was territorial aggrandizement. An aim neither so well known nor so generally accepted as independence, nor ever formally announced, it was nonetheless an acknowledged objective even before hostilities began. The drive to expand preceded the desire for independence. Together they formed a concise statement of the goal of grand strategy in the Revolutionary War: a United States unencumbered by European control and preeminent on the North American continent.

Confusion shrouded the goal of independence for nearly fifteen months. When fighting began in 1775, few Americans envisioned splitting away from the mother country; they clamored instead for their rights as Englishmen, asking only to be treated as loyal subjects of His Majesty George III. Fort Constitution on the Hudson River, erected as a result of Congress' first warlike act,

77

took its name not from the American document, which at that moment was not even dreamed of, but from the British "Constitution." When Congress learned of the unplanned patriot takeover of Fort Ticonderoga, delegates prudently resolved that captured equipment be carefully inventoried so that it could be returned intact to English officers after "restoration of the former harmony between Great Britain and these colonies so ardently wished for by the latter." Through most of 1775, George Washington drank toasts to the health of George III; the fighting cry was raised not against the king but against a "wicked Parliament." However, as the war dragged on and casualties mounted, feelings gradually hardened. Discussions in the American camp turned more and more to independence; interest in obtaining a redress of grievances waned. Toward the end of 1775, congressmen cautiously began to ponder the delicate problem of leading "the public mind" to accept the radical goal of independence.[2]

Events outpaced Congress. The movement took form and momentum with the publication in January 1776 of a blockbuster pamphlet. Written in simple yet stirring prose, Thomas Paine's *Common Sense* struck a responsive chord in the breasts of Americans. It became an overnight sensation, the country's first bestseller. Paine jabbed directly and tellingly at the institution of monarchy, putting boldly into print what many patriots had secretly believed but had been hesitant to admit. "One of the strongest natural proofs of the folly of hereditary rights in kings," he wrote, "is that nature disapproves it, otherwise she would not frequently turn it into ridicule by giving mankind an *ass for a lion.*" Paine put flame to the fuse. In April, North Carolina authorized its congressional delegates to join other colonies in voting for independence if the matter should come up. A month later, Virginia instructed her representatives to initiate such a movement. Other provinces fell quickly into line. Despite impassioned resistance from some members who thought the step was premature, by the end of June 1776 Congress had rather easily concluded to proclaim independence. Closing ranks after their debates, delegates published a unanimous declaration. The war's primary objective was at last firmly established and announced.

After having evolved so slowly, the aim of achieving independence became an unswerving, unshakable goal. For Americans,
conciliation was no longer either permissible or practical. Nothing
in the remaining years of the war would be able to diminish or
cloud the soaring vision of an independent United States of
America.

On the other hand, territorial appetite had been a recognized
force motivating colonists almost from the very first founding of
settlements in the New World. Individuals, land speculation companies, separate provinces, various combinations of colonies, and,
of course, European kingdoms themselves all pursued the quest of
conquering those invitingly vast territories in North America.
Generation after generation dreamed of and worked at rolling back
the frontier. Young George Washington, to pick just one famous
example, had been deeply involved in speculation in western
lands. That expansionist trait remained firmly implanted in the
American psyche for decades after the Revolution was won, causing pioneers to push on to the Pacific and eventually achieving the
title of Manifest Destiny. In *Common Sense*, Thomas Paine had
not thought only of independence. He wrote also of an American
empire: " 'Tis not the affair of a city, a county, a province, or a
kingdom; but of a continent—of at least one-eighth part of the
habitable globe." However, at the time of the Revolution a policy
of territorial aggrandizement could not be proudly or even openly
proclaimed. It had to remain unspoken. Lacking the moral suasion
and philosophical inspiration of an ideal like independence, and
carrying certain political liabilities, expansion was a goal best not
advertised; nonetheless, it was present, a powerful imperative
shaping the very course of the conflict.

American leaders never once left any doubt concerning their
intense dedication toward ending the war in possession of a greatly
enlarged domain. A perusal of their domestic and diplomatic
endeavors vividly reveals just how strong that drive was. Congress' declarations during the initial year or so of the war, though
often muted by the sobering reflection that the course of rebellion
was not yet firmly set—and the outcome far from certain—were
clearly expansionistic. Only four days after General Washington

left Philadelphia to take command of the newly designated Continental army, Congress passed a resolution directing the commander of forces in northern New York, General Philip Schuyler, to "take possession of St. Johns, Montreal, and any other parts of the country, and pursue any other measure in Canada which may have a tendency to promote the peace and security of these colonies." In addition to Canada, covetous congressional glances fell early on the Floridas, Nova Scotia, English-owned islands in nearby waters, and woodlands west of the Appalachian watershed. A French scholar, writing two centuries after the Revolutionary War, concluded that the colonists' goal all along had been "to occupy, populate, and exploit the territory of North America and to maintain a unified sovereignty over it in order to avoid the perpetual rivalries characteristic of power politics—the curse of Old Europe." [3]

Not until after signing the Declaration of Independence, however, did the delegates actually announce any territorial ambitions, and then they restricted themselves largely to secret instructions given to American diplomats abroad.

The first such written evidence appeared in late 1776 in instructions prepared for commissioners going to Europe in hopes of obtaining aid and finding allies. France and Spain were seen as the best bets for assistance, France being the more likely of the two to help. As a carrot to Paris, commissioners were authorized to offer a share of the fishing rights on the Grand Banks as well as "half the island of Newfoundland," so long as "the province of Nova Scotia, island of Cape Breton, and the remaining part of Newfoundland be annexed to the territory and government of the United States." Should Louis XVI still waver, the commissioners could sweeten the deal by throwing in permission for the French to retain any British islands they could capture. As for Madrid, commissioners traveling to that capital could promise American cooperation with any Spanish attempt to seize Pensacola, "provided the citizens and inhabitants of the United States shall have the free and uninterrupted navigation of the Mississippi and use of the harbor of Pensacola." Thus, at that early date, Americans had set their minimum territorial goals quite high: Canada and the entire area east of the Mississippi, fishing rights in the western Atlantic, navigation of the Mississippi, and a port on the Gulf coast. Their audacity appears all the more remarkable when one recalls that, at the very moment those instructions were being penned, British forces seemingly stood on the verge of destroying the rebellion. General William Howe had overrun much of New York and New Jersey. His green-coated Hessians were camped along the Delaware preparing to celebrate Christmas. Congress had to flee an endangered Philadelphia.[4]

A bit more than a year later, on 6 February 1778, American envoys signed a treaty of alliance with France. In it, they gained an ally, recognition of independence, and those territorial concessions they had wanted. A key article stipulated that Bermuda and any lands north of the thirteen original states, if they should be captured, would become the property of the United States. France renounced all past claims to possessions on the continent itself but retained the right to keep any seized islands ''situated in the Gulph of Mexico, or near that Gulph.'' While Washington was desperately trying to keep his starving army alive in Valley Forge, and while British officers dallied with Tory belles in Philadelphia, diplomats in Paris congratulated themselves on the signing of a document recognizing American claims to northern and western lands.

Another year passed before Spain entered the war, but Madrid was to become an ally only to France, refusing to recognize the United States. Charles III found the thought of rebellion against another monarch to be quite distasteful, even though that monarch happened to be George III, whom he so heartily disliked. Madrid feared American republicanism. That was not the only reason Spain held back from an alliance with the Americans; Charles III suspected them of harboring designs on the Floridas, which he intended to restore to his own empire.[5] Nevertheless, neither Congress nor Paris could have foreseen that the Spaniards would refuse to side with the United States. Both governments worked earnestly if unproductively at creating an alliance.

Conrad Alexandre Gérard, the French ambassador to America, asked for a special audience with Congress on 15 February 1779.

With Spain about to enter the war, he suggested, it was time for the United States to specify its minimum war aims in order to be in a position to negotiate a treaty of alliance with Madrid. Congress agreed. Delegates forthwith ordered a committee to prepare two lists, one containing basic goals on which there could be no bending and the other outlining several that could be used as bargaining chips. A week later, the committee returned its report, specifying only two matters that Spain would be obliged to accept to obtain a treaty: recognition of the independence of the United States and guarantees of certain territorial rights. No one argued with the former, but an eight-month-long debate flared over the composition of the latter. The original committee report had set down six firm proposals and six negotiable ones. For the first time, congressmen were forced to come to grips with the necessity of stating just how much and precisely where they were willing to compromise. Ideally, they preferred to have all of Canada and Florida, but, practically, they realized something less was more likely to be their lot. For one thing, Gérard pushed hard to get them to lower their sights in order to facilitate future peace negotiations with England. France could not be expected to support American claims to territory beyond the original thirteen provinces, the Frenchman informed Congress on 22 May, unless Continental troops were in actual possession of the claimed lands when peace talks started. Very early in the debate, representatives reduced their six nonnegotiable demands to four: postwar boundaries, evacuation of all British troops from American soil, fishing rights on the Grand Banks, and free navigation of the Mississippi. Central and southern states questioned the need to insert fishing rights, but New Englanders refused to concede the point. The real argument, which was never satisfactorily settled, concerned the setting of boundaries. In the end, after an excess of acrimony, delegates agreed to accept a southern border running along the latitude line at 31 degrees above the equator (roughly the top of Florida today), a western edge following the middle of the Mississippi River, and a northern boundary taking in as much of Canada as possible, but in no case falling any farther south than a line drawn at 45 degrees latitude (which is today's demarcation between Vermont and Canada). That left Florida and the northern-most reaches of Canada in the negotiable category. Congress was never happy with the specifics, but it had at last laid out the details of four demands beyond which it would not give. It would deal with England only on the basis of London's recognition of American independence and acceptance of those four territorial demands. Moreover, Spain would also have to accept that position to make an alliance with the United States.[6]

To some extent, effort expended in the long argument was wasted because Madrid had no intention of entering into an agreement with the rebel Congress, especially not on rebel terms. Charles III, as Spanish envoys confided to French ministers, wanted the Floridas, Jamaica, fishing rights in the rich northern waters, and a belt of land east of the Mississippi. After Spain declared war on Great Britain, Paris instructed its new minister to the United States, the Chevalier de la Luzerne, to press for American acceptance of Madrid's goals. Congressmen had no serious qualms with any Spanish claim except that to both banks of the Mississippi. There they balked. However, 1780 was a particularly black year for the patriot cause. In desperate need of assistance from any quarter, delegates wavered. Their choice appeared to be an agonizing one between future expansion or present victory. Without victory, there could be no future—but, without assuring a proper future, victory would be hollow. Overwhelmed for the moment by bleak prospects of success, they reluctantly authorized John Jay, who was conducting the negotiations in Madrid, to withdraw insistence on free navigation of the Mississippi. In 1781, Jay did so momentarily, but, when the Spaniards did not immediately take advantage of his offer, he had second thoughts and quickly retracted it. The sacrifice was not worth any gain he could imagine. Benjamin Franklin, serving at the time in Paris, was adamantly opposed to Congress' weakened position. "Poor as we are, yet, as I know we shall be rich, I would rather agree with [the Spaniards] to buy at a great price the whole of their right on the Mississippi, than sell a drop of its water. A neighbor might as well ask me to sell my street door." As was his wont and genius, the wise old man had once more illuminated the key issue. America's front door, her future, opened on the West. The aspiring new nation could compromise with the Floridas, the West Indies, even with Canada, but not the western lands.[7]

It approaches triteness to attribute vision to the founding fathers. We are repeatedly reminded of the magnificent wisdom they displayed in launching our country; the Declaration of Independence and the Constitution, for example, are cited as irrefutable evidence of genius. Not so often, however, does one hear of their prescience as it existed during the actual unfolding of the fighting. Nevertheless, a strong sense of the future must have been present. The spirit that forged the United States could not have simply burst into being at the signing of an armistice. And what, if not a view of a better tomorrow, a concept of a grander country, could have sustained the will to endure for eight long years? They had a dream: an American empire stretching far into the still unknown interior.

Seven of the thirteen states professed ownership of western lands. Citing original charters or subsequent agreements, many of those, considering themselves to be "three-sided," claimed borders extending from sea to sea—or at least to the Mississippi River. Emotion ran strong on the subject. The future disposition of that huge hinterland was a matter of urgent concern, consuming a great proportion of the time and energy of patriot politicians. The six "four-sided" states, on the other hand, were reluctant to back claims that might give their seven neighbors inordinate power. Indeed, the debate between "landed" and "landless" states delayed the ratification of the Articles of Confederation for years. The impasse persisted until the dreary outlook for victory in the nadir year of 1780 compelled cooperation. Though there was animosity among Americans over ownership of lands beyond the Appalachians, there was unanimity among them that England should have no portion of the key area. Connecticut offered to cede its claims in October that year; Virginia followed suit three months later, and the Articles came into force on 1 March 1781. Having agreed on the redistribution of the western domain, the several states were finally able, five years after the Declaration of Independence, to promulgate a legal government, becoming in fact as

well as name the United States of America. Congress saluted its
newly found legitimacy. Thirteen cannons fired ceremoniously
from a hilltop in Philadelphia, answered by thirteen more from
John Paul Jones' frigate at anchor in the river. Jubilant delegates
"waited on the President of Congress . . . and partook of a
collation prepared at his house for that purpose." The evening was
loud with fireworks and the river front brilliant from lanterns
hanging by the hundreds in the rigging of ships. The air was filled
with renewed hope for the future.

Patriots often expressed their view of a future nation centered
more to the west. Not a year into the war, Henry Knox, the Continental army's artillery chief, visited Albany. Noting the town's
strategic location with respect to both Canada and the western lands, he predicted that it "must one day be, if not the
capital of America, yet nearly to it." A detailed study of the
campaign against the Indians in 1779 strikes the same theme:

> Washington and other leaders saw independence with a mere
> fringe of land along the seacoast would scarcely be worth the
> cost of the struggle if the rest of the continent to the westward
> and northward remained in the hands of the motherland.
> Washington knew by actual experience the potential wealth
> of the fertile regions of the interior of the continent. He
> realized that when the time came to discuss terms of peace
> that rich area could be secured for the young nation only if it
> was in the possession of the Americans. The conquest of
> western New York, the capture of Oswego and Niagara and
> the seizure of posts farther west would assure American
> possession at the end of the war. Hence in the Sullivan-
> Clinton Expedition *an inland empire was the stake for which
> Washington was playing* [emphasis added] and not merely the
> punishment of dusky foes on our border.[8]

Virginia politicians, led by Governor Patrick Henry, eagerly
encouraged George Rogers Clark to push to Detroit in an effort to
win the Old Northwest for the Old Dominion, a well-known
example of state interest in the future, interest by no means limited

to Virginia. Westward migration continued during the war despite the increased hazards. Frontier communities gained votes and representation as a result of an increasing population and the impact of new state constitutions which extended greater recognition to interior counties. The Tennessee town of Nashville was settled in 1779, one of several areas opened in midwar. Thomas Jefferson, after the Articles of Confederation were ratified, foresaw ten states being carved out of the Old Northwest alone. He even suggested names for them: Sylvania, Cherronesus, Michigania, Assenisipia, Metropotamia, Illinoia, Polypotamia, Pelisipia, Saratoga, and Washington. Congressmen, in the final year of the war, while meeting in Princeton and angry with their recent treatment in Philadelphia, considered shifting the seat of government to Fort Pitt in the forests of Pennsylvania as a way of showing their faith in the future of the West. It was only a thought, petulant at that, but it revealed something of the expansionist drift in the American consciousness. The future, with its glittering promise of fortunes untold, stood beyond the mountains.

But wealth was not everything. It would be unduly hasty to dismiss patriot expansionist aspirations as being motivated solely or even primarily by greed. Thought of profit was not unknown in America and speculation in land was widespread, but simple economic determinism fails to explain the passion and fascination with which colonists regarded the frontier. Upon a moment's reflection, one begins to sense something more complex, a motive transcending money. The western wilderness had quite evidently etched itself indelibly on American minds long before the rebellion erupted. It was the traditional source of danger as well as promise, of horror as much as hope. Americans were attracted to it like a moth to flame—except that they knew full well it could burn.

Picturing enraged patriots rushing to defend their seashores against British depredations is a common oversimplification ignoring the reality of life in eighteenth-century America. Historically, the ocean link with England had been the maternal tie, while the North and West had been the fount of sudden terror and violent death. Danger had heretofore lurked in the inland forests; the Atlantic had been the source of succor and friendship. Within the lifetime of all—and in the vivid memory of rebel leaders—had occurred the French and Indian War and Indian atrocities too numerous to recount. The constant, forbidding, harsh reality of a hostile backcountry was a fact of life (and death) not to be ignored. It is hardly plausible, then, to expect the colonists, even in their most violent opposition to the British, to have lost an older fear of an older enemy. The feud with Parliament was, after all, a relatively recent one grown intransigent only after undergoing a test by fire. Dislike of the king was a new emotion; it did not supplant fear of the frontier. Rather, it was superimposed on the older dread. General Washington could not simply square off to face an English enemy from the east; he was, in essence, surrounded before he could begin to fight. British control of the St. Lawrence, Ohio, and Mississippi rivers meant hostile encirclement. And, by virtue of their personal, bitter experiences, Americans of that era must surely have ascribed to the frontier a more sinister aspect than we normally attribute to it.[9]

Foremost among their worries were Indians, and for very good reason: savages and settlers were natural and implacable foes. Most vividly do documents of the revolutionary era dramatize patriot foreboding over the imminence of Indian war. It can be argued that no other single matter, in relation to its deep and painful impression on the people, has been so underplayed in the various accounts of the War of Independence. Quite beyond argument is the very real anxiety American leaders felt and the constantly tormenting sense of danger those citizens unfortunate enough to live within reach of marauding war parties experienced. Such apprehension was perpetuated by reports of actual events —which were awful enough—and magnified by the exaggerated manner so often used in describing Indian atrocities. One widely read poem, for instance, written to relate the wanton murder of a young woman, depicts painted savages slinking through the forest "like beasts of prey in quest of human blood" to slaughter an aged man, a mother with suckling child, and a maiden on her way to be married.

Congress acted early to neutralize the Indian nations. Smoke from the battle of Bunker Hill had hardly cleared before delegates in Philadelphia resolved to make overtures to the ''several tribes of Indians, for engaging the continuance of their friendship to us, and neutrality in our unhappy dispute with Great Britain.'' The next day, they decided to attempt forming an alliance with the tribes, but only if English agents approached the chiefs first. Letters signed by the president of Congress went to the forest nations, exhorting them to stay out of the fight. Washington personally received Indian delegations, gave presents to the leaders, and attempted to impress all the tribes with the strength of Continental forces. Hopes for winning Indian neutrality lingered through 1775, but, early in the next year, it became evident that the Indians would not remain impartial. Moreover, they gave vague indications that they would fight for whichever side appeared to have the better chance of winning, and English agents were actively courting them. General Washington, no lover of the noble savage, did not want to use them in the war at all. But, as their entry seemed unavoidable anyway, he finally recommended to Congress that they be employed by the United States, if only to keep them out of British ranks. In June 1776, Congress authorized General Schuyler to engage two thousand Indians in the upper reaches of New York State. Representatives from the Six Nations, a coalition of Iroquois tribes, visited Congress, where they were cordially greeted and entertained but were not swayed. Even a promised bounty of a hundred dollars for each captured British officer and thirty dollars for each enemy soldier failed to attract Indian recruits. The Indians saw in the arrival of large British forces in spring and summer 1776 a long-awaited opportunity to throw the hated settlers out of tribal hunting grounds—and maybe into the sea. A few tribes joined the Americans and some maintained a shaky neutrality, but most of the ferocious northern and northwest nations—particularly the feared Iroquois—sided with the British. So, too, did Cherokees and Creeks in the South. Patriots had no alternative but to fight them.[10]

The Cherokees went on the warpath in 1776, Iroquois and others a year later. From then on, even after the English themselves had conceded defeat and sailed home, the frontier, the ''dark and bloody ground,'' was ablaze with burning white settlements and flaming Indian villages. Raid followed raid, reprisal pursued reprisal. To keep the redskins at arm's length, frontiersmen constructed and manned stockade forts, while infuriated state governments, acting alone or in concert with Continental forces, mounted several expeditions against the marauders' bases. Just as Indians had viewed the Americans' rebellion against England as an opportunity to push back the forward edge of white encroachment, many Americans saw the war as a golden chance to rid themselves once and for all of the Indian problem. Both sides fought brutally. Quarter was neither asked nor given. Massacres were gruesome both in detail and frequency. Scalp belts grew heavy, and birds of carrion grew fat. The continuous killing, at a time when few Americans lived far enough from the forests to be absolutely sure of never hearing a war whoop, kept everyone's attention focused nervously on the Indian menace.

In addition to the two-century-old clash between aborigine and European, English-speaking colonists had also participated in the several wars fought between Great Britain and France. Americans, distant from the sources of antagonism and often ignorant of the origins of the fighting, supported their monarch nonetheless, but they insisted on naming the conflicts as they saw them. The war of the League of Augsburg they called King William's War; Queen Anne's War was the colonial title for the War of the Spanish Succession; the War of the Austrian Succession was known on this side of the Atlantic as King George's War; the New World name for the Seven Years War was the French and Indian War. In those American labels might reside a clue to American attitudes: all earlier clashes were fought in the name of the ruler of Great Britain; the final colonial war took the title of the colonists' actual enemies. Prophetically, it now seems, the last war finding England and her colonies on the same side began, unlike all former ones, in North America and spread to Europe. It was triggered by a rash, twenty-two-year-old militia colonel from Virginia. The young officer, leading an expedition against French forces operating on the frontiers of his colony, was George Washington.

So far as Americans were concerned, all the colonial wars were oriented against a major threat from French forces stationed to the north and northwest and against a minor one to the south where Spaniards held sway. Militiamen marched to do battle with Frenchmen at Fort Duquesne (now Pittsburgh), at forts around Lake Champlain, at Louisburg, at Quebec, at a hundred other remote sites; they fought Spanish soldiers at faraway and disease-ridden places like Cartegena and St. Augustine. Such martial adventures amplified in the colonial mind the importance of interior lands. Territory worth warring for, important enough to make men willing to die in its defense or for its capture, plainly had to have at least a perceived strategic significance.

As if past French and Spanish and Indian clashes were not enough to keep Americans keenly aware of the danger of hostile possession of the backwoods, English officialdom made it a burning issue by unwise policies enunciated right after the final colonial conflict. For the first time in anyone's memory, Frenchmen were ousted from Canada and Spaniards from Florida. A great and ancient danger was thereby removed. Peace along the bloody borders seemed possible. Settlers sensed a new promise of security beyond the western ridges, but those expectations were quickly dashed. The Proclamation of 1763 established four new colonies (Quebec, Nova Scotia, East Florida, and West Florida) and prohibited white expansion beyond the Appalachian divide, reserving lands between the mountains and the Mississippi for Indians. Squatters and speculators alike resisted, but English soldiers bodily removed homesteaders, burning their cabins in the process. A later minor adjustment of the no-settlement line to the western slopes of the mountains failed to satisfy either Indians or settlers. Nor was the outcry among Americans quieted when colonial agents in London reported that at least one of the reasons behind the proclamation had been to keep citizens of the old thirteen colonies locked along the Atlantic seaboard. Should the Yankees be permitted to cross the mountains, some Englishmen thought, they would inevitably begin to manufacture for themselves, thereby robbing the English factories of a market.[11]

Indeed, many farsighted Englishmen were growing increasingly concerned over the independent bent long in evidence in the several American colonies. Robust, blessed with a bountiful land, hard working, unusually prolific, and too far away to be closely watched, Americans possessed the potential to outstrip the mother country in time. They had to be handled with care. Finding royal forces in control of Canada after the Seven Years War, British officials were not unanimous in their decision to retain the huge province. That frigid land was worth little in itself, one faction argued, but so long as the French occupied Canada they were a threat to American colonists, which would help keep them in line. Those arguments, though unsuccessful, did not pass unnoticed on the western side of the Atlantic. Such attitudes aimed at limiting the expansion of the colonies may not have been official or even widely held, but Americans were naturally sensitive to them, especially when they seemed to be formalized in the Proclamation of 1763.

Then, close on the heels of a decade-long series of unpopular parliamentary revenue-raising schemes, came the Quebec Act of 1774. It extended the borders of Quebec to the Ohio River, biting deep into woodlands several other colonies claimed. It also established Catholicism as the official religion of the area. Americans were outraged. A Catholic Quebec was anathema to New England Protestants, while the threat of losing cherished claims to western stretches raised the nettle of most colonists. A body of embittered men met in Massachusetts shortly after learning of the Quebec Act. Publicly, they proclaimed:

> The late act of Parliament for establishing the Roman Catholic religion and the French laws in that extensive country, now called Quebec, is dangerous in an extreme degree to the Protestant religion and to the civil rights of all America; and therefore, as men and Protestant Christians, we are indispensably obliged to take all proper measures for our security.

On 20 October 1774, the first Continental Congress resolved that the Quebec Act violated the rights of Americans. Establishing French law and the Catholic church in Quebec was "to the great danger of the neighboring British colonies." A week later Congress issued an "Association" detailing all the American grievances. Prominent among them was the Quebec Act. Delegates feared that the extension of Quebec to the western borders of their own provinces would eliminate westward migration and could create an antagonistic country in the hinterland "whenever a wicked ministry shall chuse to direct." They saw themselves encircled. For many reasons, and not at all surprisingly, Americans felt impelled to extend their own influence westward and northward. Their very security required expansion.[12]

In sum, revolutionary America aspired to greater physical security and to enhanced future prospects. Attaining either generated irresistible pressures to spread beyond the limits of the thirteen original colonies along the Atlantic. Expansion was a deeply felt urge of the people, and one finding vigorous expression in the actions of public leaders. It was a fundamental aim of the revolution.

Territorial aggrandizement and independence together formed a tandem of goals prescribing the nation's grand strategy. To win the war—which is to say, to achieve the objectives of the war—patriots had to reach out, to be aggressive, to attack. To be sure, strategic defense was necessary from time to time but not at the exclusion of strategic offense. Saying that Washington had only to defend is patently incorrect; there were occasions when he had to pass over to the offensive. Attack and defense were both necessary. Independence had to be protected—but first won. Territory had to be defended—but first conquered.

The view beyond the horizon of the war showed a United States independent of Europe and dominant in North America. Any military strategy selected by General Washington had to keep that view in focus or it would, by definition, be faulty strategy. Success or failure in winning the peace would depend upon whether patriot aims achieved the dual objectives of the revolution. We know, of course, that the two aims were ultimately won. It is useful, then, in order to evaluate American strategy, to measure it against the demands of grand strategy. Did the new nation emerge free and enlarged because of or in spite of the strategy pursued? Did Americans shape their own destiny, or did it just happen?

Part Two

Strategy Executed

7

Run All Risques:

April 1775-June 1776

The war's first phase, more than fourteen months long, could be called "toward independence." It opened with that reverberating musket shot on Lexington Green and closed with Congress preparing to declare the United States a nation free of allegiance to the British monarch and independent of the British empire. When it began, royal governors, judges, and generals ruled the colonies —or at least regulated them. When it ended, rebels were in firm control of every English province in North America except those in Canada and Florida; not a single enemy soldier patrolled a single square foot of the soil of the United States.

It was the revolutionary period of the Revolutionary War, and it was marked by patriot aggressiveness. Virtually by definition, an insurgency or revolutionary movement is required to assume the offensive. Its very purpose is to grab control by destroying or ejecting those authorities and institutions which happen to possess at that moment the power it covets. The revolutionaries, standing on the outside trying to break in, must take the initiative and assault the established order. They are the ones who must overcome, and that is precisely what the Americans did, at first more or less by instinct, later by intention.

Word of the fatal English incursion to Lexington and Concord spread on the wind. Colonial reaction was of the knee-jerk variety. Infuriated New Englanders took arms and flocked to Boston by the thousands; it was a spontaneous uprising surprising even to the most ardent of American agitators, astounding to incredulous

British officials. It was a mass movement transcending the borders of Massachusetts and spilling over into other colonies, a movement, moreover, which snatched the initiative from General Gage on the war's very first day. However, inactivity can rapidly transform initiative to stalemate, a point becoming evident right away to those patriots outside Boston. The milling horde of New Englanders presented a sight awesome enough to discourage British thoughts of lashing out from behind their lines across Boston Neck, but neither could the unorganized Americans seriously contemplate assaulting those forbidding barricades. Unable to break into the city and disinterested in merely besieging the Britons, insurgent leaders eagerly looked around for other objectives.

Fort Ticonderoga, the renowned old French fortress on Lake Champlain, held the nearest known nest of enemy soldiers. The instinctive offensive bent of the rebels is perhaps nowhere better displayed than in their rapid decision to seize Ticonderoga. Several groups, in fact, seem to have thought of the fortress at about the same time, and a race developed to see who could get there first. With a handful of men and a great amount of bravado, Ethan Allen and Benedict Arnold overpowered not only Fort Ticonderoga but other British posts on the lake as well. The war was not a month old.

By the middle of June, the Continental Congress had taken the undeniably warlike step of creating the Continental army, lending legality of sorts to the hostile acts of hot heads. But before George Washington could reach Boston to assume command of forces there, enthusiastic and impatient local leaders precipitated yet another battle between patriots and redcoats by occupying Charlestown peninsula, which overlooked Boston. General Gage chased them off the spit of land but not before absorbing grievous losses in what became known as the battle of Bunker Hill. It was the third clash in as many months between Old World professionals and New World amateurs. On the whole, the pugnacious, impulsive revolutionaries had come out on top in the exchanges, winning two and conceding the British a Pyrrhic victory in the third. Momentum was clearly on the side of the rebels. At that juncture General

Washington arrived and took the helm. His job was to maintain the initiative.

At the outset, he did not see his task quite that way. Congress, unable to embrace revolution or to consider independence so soon, clung to the vain hope of reconciliation, of "restoration of the former harmony between Great Britain and these colonies so ardently wished for by the latter." Fresh from Congress himself, Washington shared that view. He intended only to contain the British in Boston. "To prevent them from penetrating into the country with fire and sword, and to harass them if they do," he told his brother, "is all that is expected of me." Just days after arriving, the new commander-in-chief held a council of war with senior commanders to discuss means of defense, steps to strengthen the army, and a contingency plan to reassemble the soldiers behind the "Welch Mountains near Cambridge and in the rear of the Roxbury lines" should the British sally out and scatter them. When some Massachusetts leaders proposed sending a thousand men and a dozen ships to raid towns in Nova Scotia and to destroy the British naval base at Halifax, the general applauded their "spirit and zeal" but rejected their plan. The people of Nova Scotia had done no harm to the Americans, he explained: "To attack *them*, therefore, is a measure of conquest rather than defense" and would be "inconsistent with the general principal upon which the Colonies have proceeded."[1]

But neither Congress nor commander-in-chief long entertained such false hopes or such careful scruples. Sooner or later, all revolutionaries attempt to export their product; with the patriots, it was sooner. Even before Washington had reached Boston, Congress had changed its collective mind and was contemplating a campaign of conquest into Canada. For his part, Washington was not in command a month before he began looking for ways to carry the battle to the enemy, for means to act aggressively rather than passively.

Sometime that summer, most (if not all) of the rebellious Americans came to recognize the overriding imperative of retaining the offensive. They realized they could not improve their position by waiting; indeed, delay could only worsen it. Logic stood on the side of accomplishing as much as possible before the king could send reinforcements. Washington dared not wait; time would surely work against him, for London could bolster its strength in America much faster than he could build a truly able fighting force. The men of the Continental army were inadequately trained and equipped, the officers inexperienced, the war chest empty. But, for the time being, the enemy was also weak—and the opportunities were marvelous. They could not be passed up. Boldness would have to do for experience, élan for knowledge, spirit for money. British regulars would have to be overcome with a people's army. In such a case, audacity becomes a virtue. On 4 August 1775, only weeks after reaching Boston, Washington wrote perceptively, "We are in a situation which requires us to run all risques."[2]

In addition to those redcoats besieged in Boston, royal forces still occupied the immense region of Quebec, a few bases in the Floridas, several forts scattered throughout the western lands, the maritime province of Nova Scotia, the Bermudas, and numerous other islands in the West Indies. There were also thousands of loyal Americans and a sprinkling of British officials residing in the thirteen colonies themselves. For the remainder of the opening act of the conflict, General Washington searched his meager bag of means for ways to get at his foe in every one of those locations.

A perusal of the commander-in-chief's correspondence during any given period of the war's first phase will paint a vivid picture of his overweeningly aggressive attitude. Take the last five months of 1775, for instance. During those weeks, he organized an expedition to Bermuda to capture gunpowder and seek support; he toyed with the idea of attacking Nova Scotia despite the presence of a British fleet in American waters; he recommended a campaign against St. Augustine; he made overtures to Indian tribes, hoping to secure their help against posts in the West; he tried to persuade citizens of the West Indies to join the fight against the mother country; he encouraged and supported rebel assemblies in the thirteen coastal colonies in purging their provinces of persons loyal to the king; he organized a "navy" of privateers to strike at

English shipping on the high seas; he sent an invasion force into Canada; and he constantly harassed the Boston garrison while looking for a way to assail the barricades there.[3]

Canada and Boston were his primary concerns, with Canada perhaps being the foremost. There, along the St. Lawrence, greater gains were possible than existed anywhere else: a large territory awaited conquering, a "14th colony" might be acquired, the western posts would be cut off if the St. Lawrence were taken, and the enemy would be deprived of a dangerous strategic salient threatening the patriot rear. Moreover, Boston was defended strongly, Canada weakly.

Even before taking command in New England, Washington had ordered preparations begun to "facilitate any future operation" into Canada. Shortly afterward, he exhorted General Schuyler, who was already proving dilatory, to "expedite every movement" aimed at bringing Canada into the Continental fold. When August came and Schuyler still had made no progress, Washington decided to launch an invasion of his own up the Kennebec River to Quebec. The project "has engaged my thoughts for several days," he wrote Schuyler, and it would be ordered into execution the moment the New Yorker agreed to kick off his overdue campaign to capture Montreal. Quebec would fall easily, the commander-in-chief thought, unless troops from Montreal rushed downriver to strengthen the citadel's defenses, in which case Montreal itself would be left unprotected. Schuyler finally responded to the prodding (rather, his deputy, General Richard Montgomery, did), and Washington started a force headed by Benedict Arnold hurrying up the Kennebec. Boldness, the Virginian had written shortly before, could bring success even to "enterprises which appear chimerical." Perhaps feeling his aggressive act might have seemed too rash to congressmen, he delayed a week after Arnold's departure before he sat down to report it. Knowing his message would reach Philadelphia much too late for Congress to countermand his orders, the field commander carefully assured the delegates that the decision had "met with very general approbation from all whom I consulted upon it."[4]

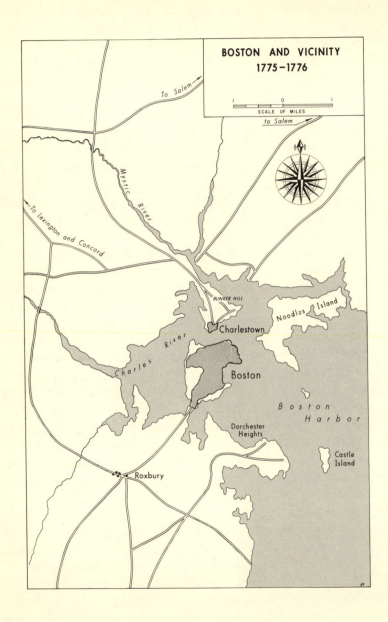

BOSTON AND VICINITY
1775–1776

SCALE OF MILES

To Salem

to Salem

To Lexington and Concord

Mystic River

BUNKER HILL

Charlestown

Noodles Island

Charles River

Boston

Boston Harbor

Dorchester Heights

Roxbury

Castle Island

In the meantime, Washington puzzled over the tricky problem of what to do about the enemy in Boston. He began to worry that the British were simply waiting for winter or boredom to dissolve the Continental army, both of which were very real possibilities. He was resolved not to remain inactive, but with scarcely enough powder for three cartridges per man and with an army unreliably responsive to command, his options were few. Putting his carpenters to work "building a kind of floating battery," he personally reconnoitered the bay area looking for a way to use it, all the time trying to devise a scheme to bring about a battle. He recognized in retrospect that Bunker Hill was a victory. Could General Gage be goaded again into attacking entrenched patriots? Hearing that the English commander was growing restive in his galling confinement, Washington decided to try to lure him out. In late August, Americans pushed forward to occupy Ploughed Hill, a cleared hump of ground standing close to British positions in the vicinity of Bunker Hill. The position invited attack. Washington recorded that by taking "a hill within point blank (cannon) shott of the enemy's lines on Charles Town Neck we expected to bring on a general action." Thinking his arrogant move gave his old friend Gage a "fair challenge to dispute it," the American commander was disappointed when that officer contented himself with merely shelling the new rebel positions. Gage saw nothing to be gained by rising to the rather obvious bait.[5]

September opened with the general chafing. "The inactive state we lie in is exceedingly disagreeable," he confided to his brother. On 11 September, he called a council of war to consider a plan he had worked up for making an outright attack of Boston. He would use boats for a flanking move in support of a frontal attempt to breach the lines at Roxbury. There were three reasons justifying an assault, the restless commander told the council of three major generals and five brigadiers: winter's imminent onset meant the army would soon need barracks, fuel, and clothing; stocks of powder were in dire shortage and probably would not increase; and enlistments were nearing their end. If the war were to be ended before first frost, some offensive blow would be necessary. After careful study based on his own reconnaissance and augmented by reports from secret agents, the Virginian concluded that an attack, if aided by surprise, "did not appear impractable, though hazardous." His generals unanimously disagreed. They thought the untrained army unequal to the task. Besides, many still hoped against hope that the next packet from England would bring word of the king's reconsideration, of his acquiescence to colonial demands. Why risk a bloody repulse when hostilities might already be over? The vote was no.[6]

Despondently, Washington informed Congress of his inability to strike Boston. It was, after all, Congress which had directed him to adhere to the guidance of a council of war. "The state of inactivity in which this army has lain for some time past by no means corresponds with my wishes by some decisive stroke to relieve my country from the heavy expenses its subsistence must create," he told the delegates. He had not changed his opinion recorded weeks earlier: "No danger is to be considered when put in competition with the magnitude of the Cause."[7]

The commander-in-chief found unanticipated support in Congress for his offensive spirit and promptly summoned another council of war on 18 October. Except for one change among the brigadier generals, the composition of the council was the same. This time, only five of the eight thought the project was totally impractical. Of the other three, Charles Lee demurred, saying he was not sure enough of the men, while Nathanael Greene voted yes if no fewer than ten thousand troops could be employed, and John Sullivan thought the plan could work, but only in winter. Part of the problem was the all but total lack of artillery to support any patriot assault. Washington sent fat Henry Knox, his youthful chief of artillery, racing off to Fort Ticonderoga to get the pieces captured there by Allen and Arnold months before. Then he sat down anxiously to await the arrival of snows, which would permit the movement by sled of Knox's artillery, and the advent of freezing weather, which would permit the movement of troops over ice to Boston.[8]

But the season that brought the needed snowfall and low temperatures also brought the end of enlistments. One army went home, and a new one arrived to replace it. All thought of attacking

Boston had to be postponed. The pages of history, Washington marveled, would likely reveal no other case of anyone keeping a post within musket shot of an enemy while disbanding one army and recruiting another. Just remaining in place during those delicate weeks was itself an act of rashness; attack was wholly out of the question. Nevertheless, the general announced, he was determined to strike the British as soon as his new soldiers were assimilated. Toward that end, just three days before Christmas, Congress pointedly absolved the field commander of any blame for possible damages to the enemy-occupied city, resolving "that if General Washington and his council of war should be of opinion that a successful attack may be made on the troops in Boston, he do it in any manner he may think expedient, notwithstanding the town and the property in it may thereby be destroyed." Clearly, lawmakers were encouraging him to risk an assault. Their fiery stance had been ignited by George III himself. The king's response to Congress's plea for reconciliation had reached America; the monarch was not about to forgive rebels or to permit them to establish "an independent empire." His remarks, issued on 23 August but not read in Congress until November, were titled "A Proclamation for Suppressing Rebellion and Sedition." They amounted to a royal declaration of war. Plainly, the armed confrontation would continue into 1776.[9]

Meanwhile, in Canada, Arnold had missed success by the narrowest of margins, and a tragedy was in the making.

In terms of human perseverence and suffering, no saga in the war surpasses that of Benedict Arnold and his band of eleven hundred patriots. The difficulties and hazards of making a winter march through the Maine woods to Quebec had been completely underestimated. Boats, made hurriedly of green wood, sprang leaks, ruining food and gunpowder. Portages were numerous and arduous. Repeated immersion in icy waters and constant exposure to chilling weather soon began to take a toll of men and morale. Summer soldiers faltered; the rear guard commander deserted, taking some three hundred men with him. Arnold grimly continued. For six weeks, he pushed his ever-thinning column through swamps, around rapids, along white-foamed streams. It rained

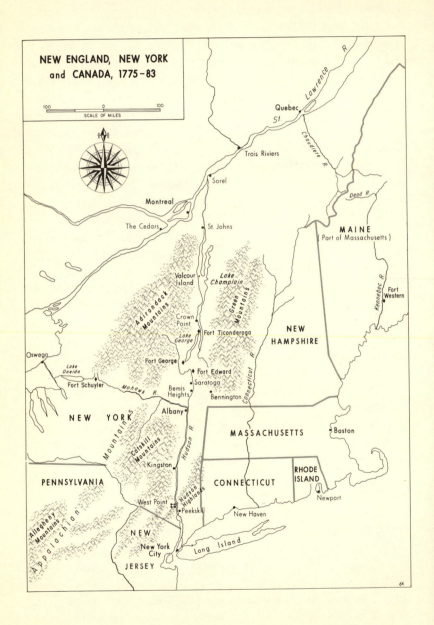

NEW ENGLAND, NEW YORK and CANADA, 1775-83

SCALE OF MILES
100   0   100

St. Lawrence R.

Quebec

Trois Riviers

Chaudiere R.

Sorel

Dead R.

Montreal

The Cedars

St. Johns

MAINE
(Part of Massachusetts)

Valcour Island

Lake Champlain

Green Mountains

Kennebec R.

Fort Western

Adirondack Mountains

Crown Point

Lake George

Fort Ticonderoga

NEW HAMPSHIRE

Oswego

Lake Oneida

Fort Schuyler

Mohawk R.

Fort George

Fort Edward

Saratoga

Bemis Heights

Bennington

Connecticut R.

Albany

NEW YORK

Catskill Mountains

Kingston

Hudson R.

MASSACHUSETTS

Boston

Mountains

PENNSYLVANIA

CONNECTICUT

RHODE ISLAND

Newport

West Point

Hudson Highlands

Peekskill

New Haven

Allegheny Mountains

Appalachian

NEW
New York City

JERSEY

Long Island

most of the time, turning to sleet and snow more often than the gaunt scarecrows could recollect. Food reserves were all consumed or lost. On the last days, meals consisted of boiled moccasin. Finally, on 2 November, the bedraggled column staggered numbly back into civilization, reaching a French farming community not far from Quebec. Perhaps half the original number had survived.

On that same day, Montgomery's column captured the strongly held British outpost at St. Johns, opening the road to Montreal. When patriot patrols reached that city on 11 November, General Carleton decided not to make a stand. As Washington had suspected, the British in Canada were too weak to defend both bastions on the St. Lawrence. Americans occupied Montreal on 13 November 1775. If the citadel of Quebec, too, should fall, the invasion would be an unqualified success: Canada would become the fourteenth state.

Arnold, after permitting his wretched men a short period of recuperation, shoved on to the St. Lawrence, reaching its banks opposite Quebec on 9 November. Within a day the energetic officer had gathered enough boats to ferry his force across for an assault, but a violent wind delayed him for two days, the first of two such storms that winter which would shake, if not shape, the course of history. When he was able to shuttle his troops across the wide waterway, Arnold discovered that a reinforcement of redcoats, racing frantically downriver from Montreal, had reached the citadel only hours ahead of him. Quebec, a plum which had until that moment hung all but defenseless, was now too strongly garrisoned for the little patriot band to attack. Washington's audacious plan had failed by a single day.

Nevertheless, all Canada save Quebec lay in American hands, and no British reinforcements could be anticipated until spring. Montgomery, having joined Arnold, assumed command of the combined forces. On the face of it, the Americans had only to bide their time, letting weather, hunger, and disease deliver Quebec to them.

But wait was the one thing they could not do; enlistments were nearly over, and the men made clear their firm intention of going home when their time was up. Montgomery, like Washington at Boston, decided he had no alternative but to stake everything on one all-or-nothing assault. "No danger is to be considered when put in competition with the magnitude of the Cause," Washington had proclaimed. Unlike the commander-in-chief, though, Montgomery was not bound by a council of war, and, in his principal deputies, Benedict Arnold and Daniel Morgan, he had two warriors who itched for a fight. He deployed his men for attack.

In a blinding snowstorm late on the last day of 1775, Montgomery gave the order to go. He led one column, Arnold the other. But Carleton was ready, and luck that night did not ride with the bold. A blast of grapeshot killed Montgomery in the first rush, and a musket ball smashed into Arnold's left leg, leaving the American troops leaderless and confused. The attack sputtered out. Morgan and a few stalwarts got into the city, but they were captured when the others withdrew.

General Washington did not learn of the repulse for nearly three weeks. All previous news from Canada had been good, so he was more worried in the early days of 1776 about Boston and New York. When a British expeditionary force dropped out of Boston harbor, the Americans felt sure New York City was their target. Washington sent General Charles Lee to coordinate the defenses at the Hudson's mouth, while he continued preparations for an assault of Boston. When a courier galloped in with grim dispatches from Quebec, the shocked Virginian took stock of the desperate situation there. It was far worse than earlier reports had prepared him to believe, but not hopeless. Though departures and casualties had left Arnold's army actually less numerous than Carleton's, and despite a smallpox epidemic raging through patriot ranks, the American leader continued stubbornly from his hospital cot to lead the investment of the city. Timely reinforcements might allow him to persevere after all. Although a more prudent move would have been to order a withdrawal to Montreal in order to consolidate and salvage at least a partial success, Washington wanted the whole prize. He immediately ordered northward those units that could be spared, the tribulations of making the long trek in January notwithstanding. Only afterward did he inform Congress of his decision to continue pressing the campaign. Congressmen agreed wholeheartedly. They, too, wanted all of Canada.[10]

Ice began to form along the shores of the bay around Boston. Washington, concerned over events at Quebec and knowing the British were contemplating a raid somewhere to the south, watched impatiently as the brittle, white sheet slowly spread. Now, more than ever, he burned to attack. But he needed artillery. Where was Knox?

That obese but industrious twenty-five-year old colonel had reached Fort Ticonderoga early in December. After selecting the cannon and mortars he would need to bombard Boston, Knox put carpenters to work building some forty-two sleds. Hastily gathering eighty yoke of oxen to pull them, the big artilleryman wasted no time starting his epic journey through the deep snows of northern New York and New England. All told, he transported fifty-nine weapons, with the largest mortars weighing in at something close to a ton each. At the end of January, he proudly dragged his "noble train of artillery" into the patriot camp at Cambridge. Washington had the weapons to support an assault. And the ice was thickening.

By mid-February, everything was ready. Recently arrived replacements were about as trained as they could expect to become that winter; Knox had drilled his novice crews to man the new artillery; and approaches to Boston were solid with ice. Washington convened a council of war to consider a third time the question of storming the defended city. American strength was nearly nine thousand men, exclusive of officers, and there were about fourteen hundred other soldiers who could be called in from detached duty. The British had fewer than five thousand fit to fight. The ice would not last much longer, enemy reinforcements were anticipated soon, and patriot powder reserves were spoiling faster than they could be accumulated. Now was the time, the commander-in-chief implored. He stood "not only ready, but willing and desirous of making the assault." But the vote was once more in the negative. The generals, who probably knew the weaknesses of their units better than Washington could have, believed the green Americans, having a mere two-to-one numerical superiority, were incapable of overrunning British regulars protected by fortifications. Moreover, with the bay frozen, Howe was bound to be more watchful than ever, diminishing chances of gaining surprise. Washington admitted, reluctantly, that he was perhaps inclined "to put more to the hazard than was consistent with prudence."[11]

Instead of dropping the matter there, however, the general kept the council in session until his hesitant officers adopted a positive course of action. Inaction was no longer tolerable. Impressed by their commander's insistence, they agreed that placing field pieces on Dorchester Heights, "with a view of drawing out the enemy," might cause a fight on grounds favorable to Americans. Dorchester Heights, looming above Boston and within cannon range of vessels riding at anchor, dominated the harbor; General William Howe, who had succeeded to the command upon Gage's departure in October, would be obliged either to counter the threat or quit the town. Dorchester Heights could become another Bunker Hill. Washington eagerly expected his occupation of that key terrain to "bring on a rumpus between us and the enemy." But, for reasons that would soon become obvious, he waited for the ice in the bay to break up.[12]

The ground along the top of Dorchester Heights was frozen too hard to dig into, so Continentals prefabricated their defenses and carried them to the crest of the ridge during the night of 4-5 March 1776. "[We are] obliged to depend entirely upon chandeliers, fascines, and screwed hay for our redoubts," Washington wrote. The soldiers also had barrels filled with rock and dirt, a device useful both as a shield and, when rolled downhill into tightly packed English ranks, a shock weapon. Knox's artillery bombarded Boston to cover the sounds of movement and construction. Engineers worked feverishly. Man and beast hauled ox cart after ox cart of material up the dark slopes. Officers cursed and cajoled. Marvelously, the jigsaw pieces all fit together. The weather cooperated; a bright moon illuminated the work site while a Boston mist concealed the bustle of activity from British sentries. When surprised English officers peered out of their windows at dawn, they saw a formidable fortress on what at dusk had been an undefended hill. Howe promptly tried to place artillery fire on the works to neutralize them as Gage had done to those on Ploughed Hill, but Dorchester Heights was too high; cannon could not be elevated sufficiently to hit the rebel positions. Howe had either to attack or evacuate Boston. He chose attack.

But, all along, Washington had been unhappy with so passive a plan, one that left the initiative entirely with the enemy. He had been thinking beyond the hoped-for event of Howe's advance against Dorchester Heights. The American commander reasoned thus: if the Briton committed a truly powerful force to the assault, which surely he must after having seen firsthand on Bunker Hill what defending Yankees could do, then Boston itself would be left weakly defended and vulnerable. It could fall to a swift and determined push while Howe's major force was separated by the waters of the bay and locked in battle on the steep flank of Dorchester Heights. Washington had planned a trap play. The occupation of the dominating ridge was "only preparatory," he said, to a greater stroke. He wanted a complete victory, not just another Bunker Hill; his aim was to destroy Howe, not merely to bleed him.

Once British forces were seen to be decisively engaged at Dorchester Heights, a signal from Roxbury would put in motion "a settled and concerted plan." Four thousand picked men commanded by Major General Israel Putnam waited in hidden positions along the Cambridge River. Boats to lift the entire body were snugged to nearby landings. Half the men, under Brigadier General John Sullivan, were to row directly toward a landing near the city's powder house and "gain possession of Bacon Hill and Mount Horam." Brigadier General Nathanael Greene, with the remaining two thousand troops, would swarm ashore at Barton's Point where he would link up with Sullivan and then take the enemy lines in rear, opening the city to troops standing by in Roxbury. Three floating batteries would support the daring amphibious operation.[13]

The snare was set to be sprung. American officers and men stood ready, were in fact eager now that the decision had been made. The British, too, were poised. Howe had put his troops aboard ship and was on the verge of landing. The hour of decision was at hand. The very elements seemed to hold their breath. It may be that the Revolution itself hung in the balance—and a most delicate balance it was. Washington's ambitious plan was extraordinarily complex for inexperienced officers and untrained troops to execute; his risk of receiving a crushing defeat was accordingly very high. On the other hand, Howe was fortuitously playing right into patriot hands; his position would be extremely precarious once he got ashore on the beach beneath Dorchester Heights and found Americans in Boston at his back. As historians ever since have observed, the outcome was wholly unpredictable. Perhaps Providence could not stand the suspense, for at that very moment a storm of near-hurricane force roared in from the sea. It lashed the area for two days, forcing postponement of Howe's landing at Dorchester Heights. It is not sure whether in those two days the English general learned of Washington's trap or whether he simply had second thoughts about leading another frontal attack against entrenched Americans. At any rate, he changed his mind. Swallowing his sorely injured pride, he decided to leave Boston for a safer and less confining base at Halifax, departing in great haste on 17 March. Washington stoically accepted the storm's interference as the unaccountable hand of God but refused to suppress his chagrin at having missed a chance to annihilate a hostile army. Regardless of the reason, he announced, he could "scarce forbear lamenting the disappointment."[14]

Unhappy as the commander-in-chief might have been, the rest of America rejoiced in the British departure. The thirteen colonies were free of royal troops for the first time, while the patriot tide had washed over the St. Lawrence to its high-water mark on the Plains of Abraham outside of Quebec. And all of that in less than a year. Harvard bestowed a doctorate of laws on the victorious Virginian and Congress ordered a gold medal to be struck in Paris in his honor.

Elsewhere that winter and spring, except in Canada, events continued to favor the revolutionaries. When General Gage had stripped the northern provinces of soldiers in order to concentrate at Boston, he had in effect removed any obstacle to a patriot takeover of those colonies north of Virginia. Rebels rather quickly did just that after the war erupted in April 1775, grabbing control of colony after colony. One governor, Jonathan Trumbull of Connecticut, actually led the revolutionary movement in his state; others, like popular Robert Eden of Maryland, were tolerated until the approach of independence in 1776, but possessed insufficient power to restrain events; still others were arrested or fled to evade imprisonment. Only in the South did insurgents have to overcome serious physical resistance. Lord Dunmore of Virginia gathered a mixed bag of soldiers sent up from Florida: Royal Marines borrowed from warships, local Loyalists, and blacks seeking escape from slavery. Aided by warships, he set about stamping out rebellion around the shores of Chesapeake Bay. However, unable to operate at any distance from the British ships, Dunmore exercised scant overall control in his colony. What little influence he had was much reduced when patriots soundly trounced him at the Battle of Great Bridge in December, and was entirely lost after he burned Norfolk on New Year's Day 1776. Similarly, South Carolina Loyalists were overwhelmed at Reedy River on 22 November 1775, and Governor Josiah Martin's efforts to organize resistance in North Carolina ended disastrously at the Battle of Moore's Creek on 27 February 1776. Shortly afterward, patriots chased Governor James Wright from Georgia in a sharp clash on Hutchinson's Island, and the South was in the hands of rebels. By the time William Howe sailed away from Boston there was no doubt as to the outcome of the first phase of the Revolutionary War: insurgents had successfully seized political and military control of all the thirteen colonies.

Heady with success, Americans were not content to stop there. They still wanted to expand. In March, an intrepid little fleet landed American marines at Nassau in the Bahamas, where they captured Fort Montagu, seized valuable military stores, including several score of artillery pieces, and made the royal governor a prisoner. Commerce raiders preyed on British shipping, which, in addition to being militarily rewarding, was a personally lucrative way of warring. The West competed for attention, as did the Floridas, but Canada continued to hold the preeminent place in American minds, more especially so after the British evacuated

Boston. Congress and commander-in-chief kept feeding reinforcements to that theater, but, despite their best efforts, disease,
desertion, and short enlistments held patriot strength too low to be
effective. When transports carrying fresh enemy soldiers arrived
from England in May, Continentals began a grudging withdrawal
that eventually stopped only at Lake Champlain. The number of
rebellious colonies would remain at thirteen. But not for lack of
will at high levels was Canada lost. On 24 May, Congress ordered
the field commanders to "contest every foot of the ground."
Benjamin Franklin made a personal journey to Montreal to appeal
for support from the Canadian inhabitants. The president of Congress summoned Washington to Philadelphia to confer on the best
way to hang onto gains already made in the North. They agreed to
try to raise a total of twenty thousand men to hold that distant land,
which, though quite more than could be raised, indicated how
strongly feelings ran. Clearly, succeeding in only thirteen colonies
was not success enough. Victory also meant spreading the flame of
revolution. Put another way, it meant expansion, and that had been
stopped, for the moment at least, at the borders of those provinces
represented by the Second Continental Congress.[15]

Although the goal of expansion proved elusive in the war's first
phase, that of independence took shape. Gradually over the
winter, the hope of reconciliation had hardened into the aim of
independence. As late as May 1776, Washington could detect that
several congressmen were "still feeding themselves upon the
dainty food of reconciliation." They were a rapidly dwindling rear
guard, however. Independence was much in the air in spring 1776.
By his stubborn refusal to negotiate, the king had thrown away
whatever chance he might have had to retain his colonies peacefully. His decision to use force to punish the Americans for their
military insubordination around Boston shoved many fence-sitters
over to the side of independence, while it confirmed the inclinations of those who had already committed themselves. "With
respect to myself," Washington wrote, "I have never entertained
an idea of accommodation since I heard of the measures which
were adopted in consequence of the Bunker's Hill fight." The

burning of Falmouth (now Portland) in Maine and Norfolk in Virginia made America ripe for pamphleteer Thomas Paine's rhetoric. Again, Washington recorded the mood of the people: "A few more such flaming arguments as were exhibited at Falmouth and Norfolk, added to the sound doctrine and unanswerable reasoning contained in the pamphlet *'Common Sense'*, will not leave numbers at a loss to decide upon the propriety of a separation." Many of those who remained unsure were convinced when English plans to employ Negroes, Indians, and Hessians came to light. Englishmen simply did not use slaves, savages, and foreigners to fight other Englishmen! It was evident in what light the British monarch viewed his American subjects. Washington urged Congress to proclaim independence "in words as clear as the sun in its meridian brightness."[16]

In June, the commander-in-chief worked energetically to defend New York State, where he had marched his army. He fully anticipated a British invasion of that province and was preparing to meet it. "We expect a very bloody summer of it at New York and Canada, as it is there I expect the grand efforts of the enemy will be aim'd," he told his brother. That assessment was correct, both in place and price. In June, also, patriots beat off a halfhearted English attempt to grab Charleston, South Carolina, adding one more victory to their lengthening list of laurels. All told, despite the cloud over Canada, Americans could look back with deep satisfaction on the past fourteen months. As Washington waited to do battle in New York, delegates prepared in Philadelphia to announce the birth of the United States of America, a republic free and independent. The rebellion had succeeded: insurgents had snatched control of the government, had consolidated power in thirteen colonies, had established a new nation. When men in Congress declared the independence of the United States, they were merely proclaiming on paper what men in arms had already established on the battlefields.

Washington's strategy had been simple in the extreme: take the offensive whenever and wherever possible. His single-minded intent had been to grapple with and defeat the British any place they could be reached. His forces had been pitifully weak, but the enemy had been even weaker. The commander-in-chief had taken grave risks, but the potential rewards had been commensurately great—and the alternative was eventual defeat through disillusion and dissolution. He had been prepared to "run all risques." It is hard to see the shade of Fabius in George Washington during this initial phase of the War of Independence.

8

A Choice of Difficulties:

July 1776-December 1777

Having won their independence, Americans were obliged immediately to defend it. That was the burden of the war's second phase, a period lasting a year and a half. It might appropriately be titled "defending the United States." Only twice did London assemble and send to America major expeditionary forces and both came during this phase—one in 1776, the other in 1777.

English generals viewed their mission as entering royal colonies to throw out a renegade regime in order to restore lawful government. Not surprisingly, patriot generals defined their own task in quite different terms; they saw it as the defense of national shores against a foreign invader. Each officer and soldier should now realize, Washington intoned solemnly in general orders announcing the Declaration of Independence, that the "peace and safety of his country depends (under God) solely on the success of our arms." Obviously, that was soldierly rhetoric meant to inspire the troops, but it was also true. The new nation had no allies, no central executive authority, no means to raise funds—in short, none of the trappings usually associated with national defense. Ultimate victory or defeat rested squarely on the performance of the thoroughly amateurish Continental army and the still-untried general at its head.

In the contest's first phase, rebels had possessed but little to lose; now, everything was at stake. William Pitt rose in the House of Lords in February 1777 to explain this. The patriots could no longer be viewed as "a wild and lawless banditti," he said, "who, having nothing to lose, might hope to snatch something from public convulsions; many of their leaders . . . have a great stake in this great contest." Earlier, a military defeat would have been bitter but hardly fatal; now it could signal the death of the infant republic. Previously, General Washington's primary thrust had been to defeat enemy forces; now his foremost imperative was to prevent a decisive defeat of his own army. Still and all, his mission was to defend the United States; he could not deliberately sacrifice any of the new states for the sake of saving the Continental army. He was clearly expected to stand and fight, but it would have to be in such a way that he could always disengage to fight another day. Audacity and boldness had to bow to tenacity and shrewdness. Washington quickly grasped the dilemma inherent in the new rules: if he fought, he could lose all, yet, if he refused to fight, he could lose all. "On every side there is a choice of difficulties," he moaned.[1]

As might be expected, none of the American leaders realized at once that the footlights had dimmed on the first act of the Revolutionary War. They recognized, of course, that the scene would shift, and they could assume changes of some sort were bound to occur. Washington apparently foresaw a more mobile role for himself. Before leaving Boston, he asked Congress to outfit him with a driver and "a pair of clever horses of the same color." He added prophetically, "After I have once got into a tent I shall not soon quit it." Still, the commander-in-chief was optimistic and eager for another opportunity to cross swords with Howe. Having beaten the Britisher once, he confidently believed he could do it again. He departed Boston for New York City in a buoyant spirit. Once there, he inspected the defenses begun by Charles Lee before that general had been sent on to command in the South. Washington saw nothing wrong with Lee's overall plan and consequently devoted his own energy to hastening the work already in train. Obstacles in the river and batteries along the shore appeared to his inexperienced eye sufficient to thwart enemy attempts to sail up either the Hudson or the East River. Satisfied with progress in New York, he rode to Philadelphia in late May to confer with Congress on a "plan of military operations for the ensuing campaign."[2]

Patriots fully anticipated some attempt by the crown to suppress the rebellion, but they were not at all prepared for the massive scale of London's reaction. Putting their heads together, a committee of congressmen and the commander-in-chief estimated that the king would send perhaps twenty-two thousand, five hundred men across the Atlantic: ten thousand to Canada and the balance to New York. Conceding the superiority of well-trained and completely equipped European regulars, the Americans decided that the Continental army would require at least a two-to-one ratio to be able to face the enemy on somewhat equal terms in battle. That meant fielding twenty thousand troops to fight in Canada, twenty-five thousand in New York, and ten thousand in a "flying camp," a strategic reserve to be held ready in the middle colonies. Militia could be relied upon to handle things in New England and the South. The men in Philadelphia missed the mark widely, both by underestimating the English and overestimating their own ability to raise soldiers. As events were soon to disclose, patriots would number barely half those hoped for, while the enemy total would more than double that expected. Instead of fifty-five thousand Americans fending off half that many invaders, forty-eight thousand British and Germans would confront twenty-five thousand patriots.[3]

Washington and the committee members had been more or less correct in guessing England would have trouble raising a large army of Englishmen; they had not counted, however, on so many foreign hirelings. Catherine the Great had haughtily refused Britain's bid for twenty thousand Russian soldiers, undiplomatically insulting the king as she turned him down, but several German principalities had jumped at the chance to help out George III—who was of German descent as well as being the Elector of Hanover—and incidentally to employ their idle and expensive regiments. While Washington had been waiting for ice to form around Boston so he could assail Howe, English negotiators in Europe had been signing contracts with the rapacious German princes to obtain the reinforcements needed to suppress the Virginian and his rabble of an army. Altogether, nearly thirty thousand

Germans were eventually shipped to America, the largest portion coming from Hesse-Cassel, giving the name of "Hessians" to all.

On 2 July 1776, the same day Congress voted for independence, the vanguard of General William Howe's army began streaming ashore on undefended Staten Island. Washington learned that the Englishman led about ten thousand soldiers and that a fleet commanded by his brother, Admiral Lord Richard Howe, was on its way with still more men. The Virginian was not unduly dismayed. He confidently expected the invaders to attack him in his fortifications as they had done before. If only the troops behave well, he informed Congress, the enemy "will have to wade through much blood and slaughter before they can carry any part of our works, if they can carry them at all; and at best be in possession of a melancholly and mournful victory."[4]

His cocksure attitude vanished rapidly. Sailing into New York harbor that fateful summer was the largest expeditionary force England had ever sent anywhere. By mid-August, William Howe commanded an army of thirty thousand British and German troops, with five thousand more Hessians yet to arrive. Richard Howe backed his brother with a fleet of several hundred vessels, including more than seventy warships. That armada, manned by thirteen thousand seamen, was nearly half of the entire British navy. One observer told how "onlookers gazed with awe on a pageant such as America had never seen before—five hundred dark hulls, forests of masts, a network of spars and ropes, and a gay display of flying pennants." Not only had Americans never seen such a sight, they had never in their most pessimistic moments imagined themselves facing such a host. Worse yet, hostile forces far to the north, rested and being reinforced to the strength of about thirteen thousand men, stood poised to push south on Lake Champlain against the reeling survivors of the ill-fated Canadian invasion. King and cabinet had galvanized the war office and the admiralty into making a major effort to achieve a decisive end to the war in 1776. Germain said the ministry was "exerting the utmost force of this kingdom to finish the rebellion in one campaign."

For the defense of New York, however, General Washington

could count in ranks fewer than ten thousand men, most of whom were relatively recent recruits. Only a scant few were veterans who had exchanged blows with redcoats in 1775. Frantic appeals to Congress and nearby states brought in enough reinforcements to double the numbers, if not the quality, of patriot forces in New York by the time the British finally attacked in August. It was to be the most numerous army Washington would ever have under his direct command, but, significantly, it was largely untrained and woefully inexperienced. Any novice could have walked through the ranks of the unseasoned American army and have foretold some difficult days ahead.

Moreover, New York City was a trap. The unopposed British fleet could have placed troops ashore anywhere on the American flanks or rear before defenders could withdraw. George Washington's one great strategic blunder of the war was his decision to defend there with his whole army. At a time when the loss of the Continental army might well have meant the loss of the Revolution, he put it into a position where it could be destroyed. Had Howe elected to land above the patriot lines to cut the defenders off from the mainland, it is hard to see how Washington and his troops could have escaped annihilation. However, Howe was a typical eighteenth-century soldier. He settled for a safer, more prosaic operation on Long Island rather than a deep, turning movement up the Hudson River.

A combination of three factors led Washington into taking a stand in New York: his own inexperience in high command; political pressure; and an overly optimistic assessment of the fighting qualities of his green troops. After all, Charles Lee, deemed at that time by many, including Washington, to be the most knowledgeable officer in the Continental army, had planned the defenses. Washington did not question Lee's military judg-ment. Politically speaking, to have surrendered New York City without some strong show of resistance could of itself have dealt a mortal blow to the cause. Revolutions, more so than other kinds of war, rest on political and psychological underpinnings as well as on the purely military leg. New York City was a center of Loyalist sentiment, it was a valuable seaport, and it was the first objective

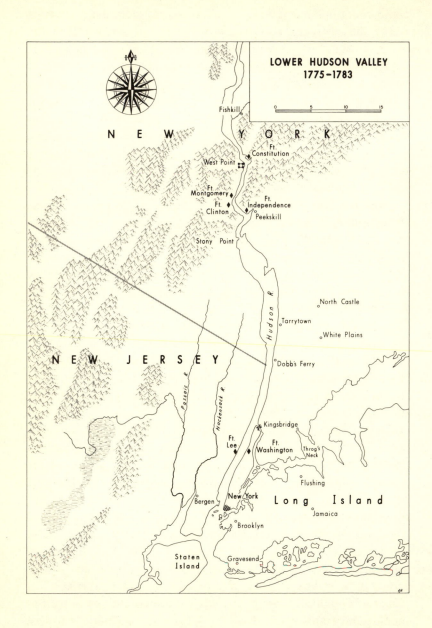

LOWER HUDSON VALLEY
1775-1783

0   5   10   15

Fishkill

N E W   Y O R K

Ft.
Constitution

West Point

Ft.
Montgomery
Ft.
Clinton

Ft.
Independence

Peekskill

Stony Point

North Castle

Hudson R.

Tarrytown

White Plains

N E W   J E R S E Y

Dobb's Ferry

Passaic R.

Hackensack R.

Kingsbridge

Ft.
Lee
Ft.
Washington

Throg's
Neck

Flushing

Bergen

New York

Long   Island

Jamaica

Brooklyn

Staten
Island

Gravesend

selected by the enemy. Declining to defend it might have been militarily wise, but it was politically and psychologically unthinkable. Moreover, control of the Hudson's mouth was strategically important, a fact Congressman John Adams had put clearly before Washington. The Hudson "is the nexus of the Northern and Southern colonies," he wrote. It is a "kind of key to the whole continent; as it is a passage to Canada, to the Great Lakes, and to all the Indian Nations, no effort to secure it ought to be omitted." As for the American fighting man, he had performed well enough when doing his work concealed in forest or fortification. Could he not be expected to stand as sturdily in the open? And besides, Washington intended to utilize fieldworks wherever possible. In short, historians who berate the commander-in-chief for defending New York City do so somewhat unjustly. Even had he been more experienced, the truth is that he could have taken no other course. He need not have endangered his *entire* army there, to be sure, but a good part of it had to run the risk of being cut off. The cause demanded it.[5]

As it turned out, the fighting along the lower Hudson that summer and fall comprised the capstone to George Washington's military education. He learned the value of a fleet when English ships ran unscathed up the Hudson past his gauntlet of artillery, effectively interdicting patriot communications with New Jersey. He learned the value of maneuver as Howe repeatedly turned American defenders out of their positions by simply marching around a flank. He learned the value of training when he witnessed patriot soldiers throw down muskets and flee in abject terror from the mere sight of a line of British or Hessian bayonets. Fortunately, the Howe brothers gave their American opponent time to assimilate all the lessons they were handing out so freely.

Richard and William Howe had come to America carrying a sword in one hand and an olive branch in the other. Besides commanding the expeditionary force, they were peace commissioners as well. They intended to be simultaneously coercive and conciliatory. The king was offering terms which a year earlier colonists would probably have welcomed. But this was 1776, not

1775. Americans were no longer interested in a redress of grievances; they were independent and wanted recognition of that fact.
When the brothers let it be known that they hoped to reach a
political agreement, they met a solid wall of resistance. The
Americans would not even talk. The olive branch being rejected,
the sword was drawn. On 22 August, William Howe crossed from
Staten Island to Long Island to begin a campaign which, in four
months' time, would carry the British banner to the banks of the
Delaware.

Washington's army, stationed on both Manhattan Island and
Long Island, was split by the East River, with a subordinate
commander in charge of each wing. Although they had strong
entrenchments atop Brooklyn Heights, the patriots on Long Island
chose to meet the enemy on high ground a couple of miles farther
south. Howe neatly outflanked and shattered that position in the
Battle of Long Island on 27 August, driving the Americans back
pellmell into their fortifications.

At that point Washington took personal command of the lines of
Brooklyn and, to the howls of historians ever since, brought
reinforcements over from Manhattan. Proof of his rank
amateurism! they have cried. Evidence of his poor generalship!
According to the often-repeated theory, the position on Brooklyn
Heights was untenable, was in fact a death trap, because the British
fleet could simply sail into the East River to cut off the defenders.
Not so. Whatever Washington was, he was not stupid. His risks,
always calculated, were never a gambler's throw. Unlike the broad
Hudson, the East River was cluttered with sunken hulks and other
obstacles, appearing to one British officer impassable to anything
larger than a row boat. So long as patriot cannon frowned from
Brooklyn Heights, warships, dependent on wind and current,
could enter the narrow, choked channel only at great hazard.
Despite appearances to the contrary, Washington had protected his
rear. He had also provided for a retreat by gathering enough boats
to ferry his men back to Manhattan. He stood confidently in his
entrenchments on Brooklyn Heights, fully intending to make his
foe "wade through much blood and slaughter" on the slopes
leading up to the American position. Redcoats could not outflank

him here. They would have to attack frontally. It would be another Bunker Hill.

But one Bunker Hill in a lifetime is enough. Howe still remembered the carnage there, could still see his men falling all about him on that bloody day. He began siege works. Spadework was slower, but it was surer and cheaper. Realizing the inevitability of that methodical process, Washington convened a council of war, which prudently voted to leave. The withdrawal itself was magnificently done, one of the finest maneuvers of the entire war. With his army safely reunited on Manhattan, Washington took steps to head off criticism. The voluntary departure from Brooklyn had been the first time American soil had been given up without a fight. At that time, there was still stigma to retreat. The general made the members of the council of war sign their earlier recommendation to evacuate, and he published in general orders on 31 August that the departure was decided upon only with "the unanimous advice of all the general officers." Now that the army was safe, he was covering his own rear.[6]

Washington had correctly assessed the damaging impact of defeat and retreat on patriot morale. Americans, accustomed for more than a year to victory, were stunned. In a single battle, more than a thousand of their countrymen had been captured, hundreds more slain or wounded. Then, strong works had been given up without a struggle. It looked bad. Desertions, particularly among the militia, soared. Those remaining in ranks muttered restlessly. They were frightened; their fear was not the normal fear of soldiers before battle but the fright of men on the edge of panic. Howe might have followed up with a rapid stroke against Manhattan and ended the rebellion then and there, but he and his brother, having wielded the sword so effectively, paused to wave the olive branch once again. On 11 September a committee of Congress— comprised of Benjamin Franklin, John Adams, and Edward Rutledge—met on Staten Island with Richard Howe to discuss a settlement. Their talks were fruitless, for the Americans would deal only on terms of independence, which the admiral could not grant. The meeting, however, did give General Washington a breathing spell to evaluate the military situation.

It was during those compressed, early days of September, when the Declaration of Independence was some two months old, that Washington came fully to grips with the fact that the war was in an entirely different phase requiring an entirely different strategy. He now admitted what he had not permitted himself to see before: there was no way he could defeat a force twice his size, better trained and equipped, and supported by a powerful fleet. He discussed the painful "choice of difficulties" with his officers: on one hand, they could not retreat lest the cause crumble psychologically; on the other, they could not fight lest the cause be lost militarily. What was to be done? Nathanael Greene put his thoughts into a cogent letter addressed to Washington on 5 September 1776. That message undoubtedly had a great impact on the commander-in-chief's thinking. Greene wanted to burn New York City and get away immediately. The outcome of the Revolution depended upon keeping an army in the field, the Rhode Islander argued:

> The City and Island of New York are no objects for us; we are not to bring them into competition with the general interests of America. Part of the army has already met with a defeat; the country is struck with a panick; any capital loss at this time may ruin the cause. *'Tis our business to study to avoid any considerable misfortune, and to take post where the enemy will be obliged to fight us, and not us them.*[7]

Two days later, Washington held a council of war to evaluate the patriot situation and to select a course of action. That gathering endorsed Greene's ideas. In a long letter on 8 September, the commander-in-chief reported the results to Congress, setting down the broad strategy he would follow for the rest of the year. He admitted it would be tough for Americans to understand or accept.

> In deliberating on this question it was impossible to forget that history, our own experience, the advice of our ablest friends in Europe, the fears of the enemy, and even the

declarations of Congress demonstrate that on our side the war should be defensive. It has even been called a war of posts. That we should on all occasions avoid a general action, or put anything to the risque, unless compelled by a necessity into which we ought never to be drawn, [is evident]. . . . when the fate of America may be at stake on the issue; when the wisdom of cooler moments and experienced men have decided that we should protract the war if possible; I cannot think it safe or wise to adopt a different system when the season for action draws so near a close.[8]

In that letter are the key precepts of American strategy for the second phase of the Revolution: ". . . the war should be defensive . . . a war of posts . . . avoid a general action . . . protract the war."

It was a masterpiece of strategic thought, a brilliant blueprint permitting a weak force to combat a powerful opponent. Indeed, there is a curiously modern ring to the ideas, even to the phraseology itself. Mao Tse-tung could have used Washington's letter in the twentieth century while preparing his thesis on the protracted war, the two concepts are so similar.[9]

Congress responded forthwith, approving the broad outline and specifically assuring Washington that he need not feel obligated to hold New York City "a moment longer than he shall think it proper." However, political leaders refused to let him burn the port in order to deny its use to the British as a base. A scorched-earth policy was an implied ingredient, or at least a logical outgrowth, of the new military strategy—a fact Washington fully appreciated. But it was politically inexpedient. Congress drew the line at burning an American city, much to the Virginian's disgust. Later, after nearly a quarter of the town had been destroyed by a mysterious fire anyway, Washington wrote, "Had I been left to the dictates of my own judgment, New York should have been laid in ashes before I quitted it . . . [this] may be set down among one of the capitol errors of Congress. . . . Providence, or some good honest fellow, had done more for us than we were disposed to do for ourselves."[10]

There followed throughout a dismal autumn a series of short, sharp encounters, first on Manhattan and then on the mainland above the island. None was decisive. Washington refused to fight in open country, and Howe declined to attack whenever the patriots held strong lines. The American was following his master plan, which amounted to a strategic retrograde. When the enemy advanced, he retreated; when they paused, he stopped and dug in; when they fell back, he followed cautiously. Contact between the two armies was constant but never entangling. Nathanael Greene was one of many who marveled at the skill General Washington displayed in managing "to skirmish with the enemy at all times and [yet] avoid a general engagement." An English officer, writing a personal letter, expressed his frustration with the Virginian's strategy. "As we go forward into the country the rebels fly before us, and when we come back they always follow us. 'Tis almost impossible to catch them. They will neither fight nor totally run away, but they keep at such a distance that we are always a day's march from them. We seem to be playing at bo peep." It was during this period that British officers began calling the rebel leader "the Old Fox," a derisive term when they were chasing him, an admiring one when he proved too slippery to catch.

Howe has been roundly criticized for not being more aggressive, for not trying harder to annihilate the struggling Continental army, but he was waging the war according to his own lights, which were those of a capable but unimaginative eighteenth-century professional soldier. He simply did not think in terms of annihilation. Victory would come from an accumulation of minor successes, not from a single decisive stroke. When the Americans escaped from Long Island, Howe then and there ceased considering an early end to hostilities. On 2 September, he sent a message to Germain warning him that the war could not be won in 1776, that it would carry over into the following year. So the Britisher was in no hurry to crush the insurgents. He wanted instead to carve out a base of operations where he could snugly winter his huge force and from which he could launch a campaign the next spring. He was jockeying for position.

Another reason for the English lethargy was Howe's understandable reluctance to absorb casualties. His troops, highly trained and at the end of a pipeline stretching all the way across the Atlantic, could not be replaced quickly, if at all. Besides, occupying all the territory they were uncovering dug deeply into the invaders' strength—and the final group of five thousand Hessians did not arrive until October. Still another factor was Howe's desire to create an impression of British invincibility. Nothing would fire patriot morale more, he knew, than a victory, even a small one, by the ragtag rebel army over his resplendent force. He dared not risk even a minor check. Englishmen had to win everywhere, could lose nowhere. Given his cautious concept for conducting the campaign, Howe performed admirably that summer and fall. He came to grief only when he grew uncharacteristically bold at the very close of the year.

Meanwhile, at opposite ends of Lake Champlain a kind of wilderness arms race was in progress. The British, commanded by Guy Carleton, were building an armada to transport their army southward; Americans, led by Benedict Arnold, were constructing a fleet to oppose them. The two sides finished the race in a dead heat. Both fleets set sail at about the same time, clashing near Valcour Island on 11 October. Arnold's outgunned flotilla lost the battle but managed to delay and discourage Carleton. It was a magnificent strategic victory, which Washington was quick to recognize. Upon hearing the results of Arnold's stand on the lake, the commander-in-chief lost most of his concern over British operations in the northern woods that year. On 22 October, he wrote to Major General Philip Schuyler, who was commanding the northern department, telling him to hold Fort Ticonderoga even if the foe should besiege it. "I should imagine you could keep Burgoyne and Carleton at bay till the rigour of the season would oblige them to raise the siege, not only for want of conveniences to lay in the field, but for fear the freezing of the lake should make their return impracticable in case of accident." The general was right. When the wind brought a touch of frost, Carleton ordered a withdrawal to Canada for the winter.[11]

November found the Continental army backed up beyond White Plains nearly to the Hudson Highlands. Morale was somewhat

higher in the American ranks, if only because the breast-beaters
and the weak-willed had already deserted. The position was
strong; safe retreat was assured. Washington decided to stand. But
Howe had gone as far as he wanted to. He turned suddenly away
and marched rapidly to invest Fort Washington, a Manhattan
stronghold the Americans had stubbornly continued to hold. Some
three thousand patriots occupied the fortress, high on the east bank
of the Hudson River where George Washington Bridge now enters
New York City. Leaving the men there had been in violation of the
new policy of putting nothing "to the risque," a lapse for which
the Americans were about to pay dearly. Washington, though he
had been uneasy over the isolated post, had all along assumed that
the garrison could resist for several days or more and that, in any
event, most of the troops could be evacuated by boat to the Jersey
shore of the river. Neither assumption was correct. Howe's swift
maneuver caught the Americans napping. He stormed the fortress
in a matter of hours, capturing or killing almost every defender. It
was a shocking defeat, causing the lantern of revolution to dim
perceptibly.

When he had seen the enemy marching away from White Plains,
Washington had crossed the Hudson with part of his army in order
to shield New Jersey, leaving the remainder in New York under
command of Major General Charles Lee, who had recently returned from the South. The commander-in-chief was too late.
After seizing Fort Washington, Howe sent a column led by General Charles Cornwallis to attack Fort Lee on the west bank of the
river. Nathanael Greene withdrew the garrison only in the nick of
time, in much disarray. Cornwallis, young and eager, scented
blood. He pushed boldly into New Jersey. Washington, with only
three thousand men, reeled back in considerable disorder. Howe's
deputy, Henry Clinton, also saw opportunity. He pleaded with
Howe for authority to land a force behind the Americans to crush
them. The fox could be bagged: But William Howe had already
decided to end the fighting for the year. He had done enough. It
was time to bed down. Besides, the enormous fleet needed a
second port for the winter. So, instead of finishing the Americans,
Howe sent Clinton off to capture Newport, Rhode Island, which

that unhappy officer did easily in December. English and Hessian columns could have—and should have—pursued the disorganized rebels relentlessly into the very laps of the Continental Congress, and beyond. But Howe was not that cut of soldier; it was not in his conventional mind to push the sword to the hilt if the blade were weighted with ice. A young German officer, commanding a *Yeager* company in the British advance guard, complained bitterly at the missed opportunities. "[It appeared the English] were always glad to see the enemy retire . . . we always built a golden bridge for our enemy. This is indeed acting in a Christian-like manner, but it is not doing justice to our King and country, for the principal duty of a general is to put an end to the war as soon as possible."[12]

Washington retreated rapidly through New Jersey with Cornwallis following hungrily at his heels. An observer described the Continentals as "half starved, half clothed, half armed, discontent, ungovernable, undisciplined wretches." The battered army stopped at Brunswick, but decamped quickly on the approach of the enemy. Washington told Congress that, since it was "impossible to oppose them with our present force with the least prospect of success," he would have to retire beyond the Delaware. Panic rocked Philadelphia when word of the British advance reached citizens there on 2 December. The city's Council of Safety had already warned inhabitants to leave or else brace for the "insults and oppressions of a licentious soldiery." Many did depart. Business all but ceased. Schools closed. Loyalists rejoiced (quietly, of course). Congress soon moved out to safer quarters. Americans could not believe that the British, with victory seemingly so near and winter thus far so mild, would stop short.[13]

But, as a matter of fact, Howe had not even intended to go as far as the Delaware, much less to Philadelphia. His original orders to Cornwallis had been to halt in the center of New Jersey, with Brunswick being the westernmost post. However, when patriot resistance turned out to be virtually nonexistent, the British commander gave in to the urgings of his more aggressive subordinates and authorized an advance to the Delaware. Probably Howe's major overall failing in 1776 had been his overcautiousness; ironi-

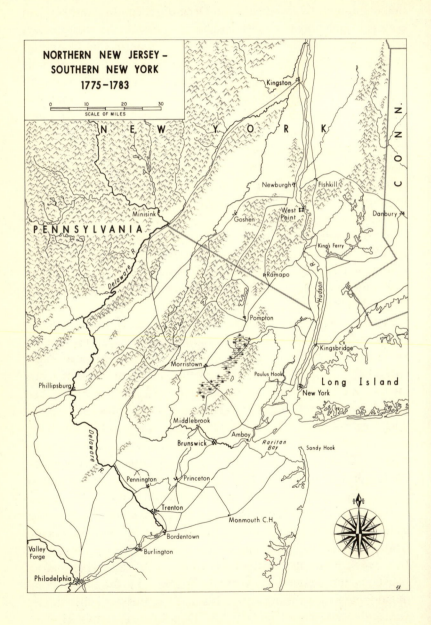

NORTHERN NEW JERSEY –
SOUTHERN NEW YORK
1775–1783

SCALE OF MILES
0   10   20   30

Kingston

N E W   Y O R K

C O N N.

Newburgh

Fishkill

Minisink

West
Point

Goshen

Danbury

PENNSYLVANIA

King's Ferry

Delaware R.

Ramapo

Hudson

Pompton

Kingsbridge

Morristown

Paulus Hook

Long Island

Phillipsburg

New York

Middlebrook

Delaware R.

Brunswick

Amboy

Raritan
Bay

Sandy Hook

Pennington

Princeton

Trenton

Monmouth C.H.

Valley
Forge

Bordentown

Burlington

Philadelphia

cally, his single greatest error was in not adhering to that prudent policy at the very last moment. He had insufficient strength to occupy bases at both Newport and New York and to hold all of New Jersey as well. Obviously overextended, he was risking the very reverse he had worked for months to avoid.

In late December, Sir William (he had been knighted for his campaign on Long Island) reported his dispositions to Germain. Taking all of New Jersey, he said, had freed and secured the Loyalists in that colony. But there was a danger: "The chain [of posts], I own, is rather too extensive." Nevertheless, he disavowed any uneasiness over the matter: "[Trusting] to the strength of the corps placed in the advanced posts, I conclude the troops will be in perfect security." European generals did not fight in winter, and they did not expect Americans to be any different. But even as Howe penned his assuring words, Washington, who perhaps did not know the European rules as well as he ought, was counterattacking.[14]

Just when the thought of turning on his pursuer first lodged in the General's mind is unknown, but it was quite early, perhaps shortly after he learned of the capitulation of Fort Washington on 16 November. That unqualified disaster was made even more lamentable, he believed, because it allowed Howe to report a major victory to cap all his maneuvering. Washington rightly saw that the English commander "would have had but a poor tale to have told without it" and would have been hard pressed "to have reconciled the people of England to the conquest of a few pitiful islands" at the mouth of the Hudson, which were indefensible in the first place. And, while the news of Fort Washington would surely buoy public spirit in England, it would have just the opposite effect in America. The general fully sensed the importance of the psychological factor in warfare. Every patriot was tired to the bone of retreat and loss—Washington more than any. Three days after redcoats stormed Fort Washington, the general confessed, "I am wearied almost to death with the retrograde motions of things." He definitely intended to turn on his tormentor: "I conceive it to be my duty, and it corresponds with my inclination, to make head against them as soon as there shall be the least probability of doing it with propriety." Nevertheless, he could do nothing just then but continue to fall back. Significantly, before leaving Brunswick, as British shells fell about his headquarters, he wrote to New Jersey Governor William Livingston, asking him to haul all river craft, especially those known as Durham boats, to the west side of the Delaware and to hold them in readiness there. During the next few weeks, he bent almost his every effort to mass the army, to consolidate all Continental units under his command on the Delaware's far shore. Without a larger force, he could not strike back—in truth, could scarcely defend even the broad Delaware. Reinforcements were coming in—Charles Lee was marching around the British through the hills in northern New Jersey,[15] Horatio Gates was bringing men from the northern department, William Heath had troops on the way from the Hudson, and Pennsylvania militia units were mustering—but not nearly fast enough. On 13 December, Washington made plans to retreat beyond Philadelphia should the enemy obtain a bridgehead over the Delaware. That very night, or maybe early the next morning, he learned of Howe's decision to stop at the river. The long retreat was over! The Virginian's plans switched immediately from retrograde to counterattack.[16]

Galloping couriers carried a spate of letters from American headquarters the next day, 14 December. To Lee, Gates, Heath, and others, Washington's message was clear and urgent: Come quick! The enemy has stopped, he is scattered, he feels secure. He is therefore ripe for a raid. "A lucky blow in this quarter would be fatal to them and would most certainly raise the spirits of the people, which are quite sunk by our late misfortunes." Washington ordered his officers to "weigh every circumstance of attack" on their way. The rather detailed instructions he sent indicated that an offensive was not a spur-of-the-moment idea but that he had been considering one for some time. Converge on Pitts Town, he directed, which may be a good position from which to strike the enemy at Trenton, twenty-five miles to the south. The rendezvous point was eleven miles from "Tinnicum Ferry," he added, where boats were already gathered to permit a crossing if necessary. To be sure his lieutenants fully understood that the Continental army was going to attack, not retreat, the commander-in-chief sent Major General William Alexander spurring off to brief them personally.[17]

Why the sudden switch? Why the abandonment of a policy of avoiding major engagement? Washington's strategic defensive had done well enough at limiting British conquests and had kept the flame of independence alight, but repeated reverses and withdrawals had irresistibly eroded spirit and will. Many erstwhile patriots in conquered territories had followed the example of Richard Stockton of New Jersey (who only five months earlier had signed the Declaration of Independence) in renouncing the Revolution and taking an oath of allegiance to the king. The Revolution balanced on the brink. To restore public confidence in the Continental army, it was absolutely necessary to lash back, to inflict a defeat on the enemy. The Continentals, too, needed a victory. They had been pushed far enough, emotionally and physically. "Pitiful" was a term often used to describe the men—and properly. Many had no shoes, all wore rags, few had retained such equipment as they had been issued. They were gangling tatterdemalions posing as soldiers. Despair prevailed, among officers as well as men. The specter of defeat lurked in their camps. Nor were they numerous. The Continental army was a mere fraction of its summer self, but those stout souls still in ranks were the ones who counted. They had been toughened in battle and had remained steadfastly loyal through all the dreary setbacks. They were the hard core, the winter patriots; not a sunshine soldier was among them. They wanted only to be led against the enemy with an even chance to beat him. Washington resolved to throw his whole weight immediately against the overconfident English and Hessians, no matter what. It was obvious to him that to save his army—and the Revolution—he had to risk it.

Even so, what he proposed doing was no blind gamble. Audacious it might have been, certainly daring, perhaps even desperate, but still calculated. By 20 December, Washington had assembled six thousand men, and more were straggling in every day. Across the river, Hessian Colonel Johann Rall had fifteen hundred men at Trenton, and Colonel Karl von Donop occupied Bordentown with another two thousand. Numbers alone for once favored the Continentals. Add to that the inestimable benefit of riding with surprise and initiative, and the American decision to attack hardly seems foolhardy. What's more, Washington now discerned something he had not noticed in his scrambling withdrawal from the Hudson to the Delaware—a way to wedge the British out of New Jersey by strategic maneuver alone. Charles Lee, in his march through the hills in northern New Jersey, had pointed out the value of holding a position there. The British would not dare advance toward Philadelphia, Lee wrote, ''with so formidable a body hanging on their flanks or rear.'' Lee wanted to stay there with the forces he had. He had been captured shortly after sending that message, but Washington carefully studied the proposition—and saw merit in it. Should the Continental army entrench itself in those hills, it could be supplied easily from broad valleys farther north, which ran from the Hudson nearly to Philadelphia. Further, the defenders would be impervious to attack, and, most importantly, Washington would sit in a commanding position on the flank of Howe's line of communications through New Jersey. The English general would then have little choice but to withdraw his outposts from most, if not all, of the province. In those grim days of December 1776, while others despaired, the commander-in-chief sought not only a tactical success but a strategic coup as well.

That winter, when Napoleon was a seven-year-old schoolboy and Frederick the Great basked in the twilight of his illustrious life, George Washington staged an astounding campaign ranking with the best of Frederick's past accomplishments or of Napoleon's future exploits. Had he achieved nothing before or afterward, Washington's actions during the ten days from 25 December 1776 to 4 January 1777 would alone assure him high mention in the annals of military history. What happened is history. The details need no repeating here. In the brief space of a week and a half, a demoralized army, which nearly everyone had expected shortly to disintegrate, won two splendid victories, eluded a superior force sent to chase it down, caused Howe to evacuate most of New Jersey, and renewed its own pride and sense of purpose. The crisis was over.[18] New life had been breathed into the Revolution. English historian George Trevelyan later wrote:

> From Trenton onward, Washington was recognized as a farsighted and able general all Europe over—by the great nobles in the Empress Catherine's court, by the French marshals and ministers, in the King's cabinet at Potsdam, at Madrid, at Vienna, and in London. He had shown himself . . . both a Fabius and a Camillus.[19]

Howe had sustained the severe setback which he had so carefully averted all year. In the final accounting, the king's mighty expeditionary force had accomplished precious little to crow about. Despite its awesome size and strength, regardless of all its tactical victories, Great Britain's great army found itself at the end of the campaign of 1776 with nothing more to show for all its efforts than bases around New York City and Newport. In London, an angry Lord Germain could not quite bring himself to call the crossing of the Delaware what it was—a smashing American victory. Resorting to euphemism, he managed to admit, "The disagreeable occurrence at Trenton is, I must own, extremely mortifying."

Finally the year's fighting was over. Both sides spent the remainder of the winter preparing for the next campaigning season. Howe considered ways to crush the rebellion; Washington girded himself to resist the onslaught.

Between Howe in New York and Germain in London, the British hatched an unbelievably muddled blueprint for operations in 1777. Knighthood had not made Sir William wise. Thinking was an activity at which he did not excel, a claim amply proven by his own correspondence that winter. He put his first plan on paper on 30 November 1776. Intending to continue the original 1776 strategy of first eliminating rebellion in New England, Howe figured he would need eight thousand men to pin down Washington in New Jersey, twelve thousand to garrison the bases in Newport and New York, ten thousand to go up the Hudson to meet a force heading south from Canada, and ten thousand to attack across country from Newport to Boston. Padding his current figures to reflect a larger number than he actually had, he told Germain he would need fifteen thousand replacements in order to execute that scheme. Three weeks later, after patriot resistance in New Jersey had evaporated, Howe sent a bolder plan to London. Now he reckoned he might gobble up Philadelphia with troops at hand while waiting for additional units to arrive from England. According to his newly optimistic calculations, he could lead ten thousand men overland to occupy the rebel capital while holding New York, New Jersey, and Rhode Island with the rest. Then, after the sobering ''disagreeable occurrence at Trenton,'' Sir William told Germain that he still planned to take both Boston and Philadelphia but would need twenty thousand troops first. After the herculean effort required to gather and send such a large force in 1776, Germain could not come close to reaching the preposterous new figure—which Howe probably knew. Besides, Germain ʹrecognized that Howe's strength count was misleading, that he had more men than he was reporting. Therefore, the minister decided, only three thousand troops could be spared to augment royal forces in New York. The others would go to Canada, from where John Burgoyne was scheduled to launch a powerful drive aimed at Albany.

A complete book could be written delving into nothing more than British command and control functions—or dysfunctions —during the 1777 campaign. Suffice it to say, the king's interests were abysmally poorly handled. Howe's flighty planning, Germain's faulty direction, and the ocean between the two stand out as the major reasons. The campaign opened with Germain and Howe having widely divergent views about manpower requirements, with Howe unsure of Burgoyne's precise instructions, and with everyone unaware of Howe's intentions. Germain wrote with great candor on 24 June, ''I cannot guess by Sir William Howe's letters when he will begin operations or where he proposes carrying them out.'' If ever a campaign bore the seeds of its own destruction it was this one.[20]

Meanwhile, at his lonely camp in Morristown, New Jersey,

Washington busied himself raising another army before spring blossoms signaled the end of his respite. This time around, it was a little easier in some ways. He had an encouraging leavening of veterans, men who had fought along the St. Lawrence, the Hudson, the Delaware, men who had tasted victory at Trenton and Princeton. And the officers knew their jobs better, if for no other reason than from having already had the opportunity of making nearly every mistake in the book. Also, taking advantage of emergency powers granted him by Congress to raise new regiments answering only to the United States, the commander-in-chief had laid the groundwork for an army not tied to the states. And enlistments were for three years. Long-range improvements, those, for an army is not just willed into being; it is built ever so slowly. Of more immediate benefit, however, was the secret help starting to arrive from Europe, mostly from Paris.

Early in 1777, eight ships laden with goods set sail from France. One was intercepted, but the other seven landed in March with scores of brass cannon, several hundred stands of firearms, tons of gunpowder, clothing for thirty thousand men, and a miscellany of other equipment. More followed, bringing money and advisors as well as materiel. From then on, the Americans, though often poorly fed and clothed and usually unpaid, would be the equal of their opponents in arms. The gap between the Old World regular and his New World counterpart was closing.

Probably no officer in the American army has ever enjoyed a more effective intelligence system than did George Washington. Rarely was he surprised. He learned early of English plans and took steps to counter them. First, hearing of Burgoyne's preparations in Canada, he strengthened the northern department, and, on 12 March 1777, shrewdly coached Schuyler to let the forest fight for him. Should the Englishman attempt to penetrate to Albany, which the Virginian thought would be foolish, patriots could foil him by stripping the countryside of cattle and wagons and by stoutly resisting at the various choke points. The commander-in-chief's advice was followed, almost to the letter, one of the major factors leading to Burgoyne's capitulation at Saratoga seven months later.[21]

Then the American leader turned his attention to the more dangerous threat—Howe's army in New York. He gathered as many units as he could under his own command to block a British move up the Hudson to Albany or overland to Philadelphia. Coiled in hills running from northern New Jersey to the rugged gorge where the Hudson Highlands intersect the Hudson River, patriots had the benefit of a central position between the hostile armies at Montreal and New York City. The ability to operate on interior lines—that is, the ability to march on the chord of a circle while the enemy has to travel around the circumference—was Washington's only counter to British seaborne mobility. Ordinarily, the English commander owned this advantage because he could move by water to any spot on the seaboard faster than his landbound American opponent could march to the same point. But not in this instance, not with British armies split between Canada and New York while Americans held the Hudson. No one explained it better than Washington himself:

It is of the greatest importance to the safety of a country involved in a defensive war to endeavor to draw their troops together at some post, at the opening of a campaign, so central to the theater of war that they may be sent to the support of any part of the country the enemy may direct their motions against. . . . Should the enemy's design be to penetrate the country up the Hudson River, we are well posted to oppose them; should they attempt to penetrate into New England, we are well stationed to cover them; if they move westward, we can easily intercept them; and besides, it will oblige the enemy to leave a much stronger garrison at New York.[22]

When the board of war attempted to intervene in order to station forces along the Delaware for the defense of Philadelphia, Washington angrily resisted their meddling. His posts in New Jersey, he insisted, "are so advantagiously situated that, if held, they effectually hinder the enemy from extending themselves." The British would not dare cross New Jersey without first destroying or dispersing the Continentals on their flank, and, should they go by sea, the general promised he could get to Philadelphia faster. He won the argument.[23]

Concluding by the end of May that Howe must be preparing to march to Philadelphia, Washington moved down from the hills to occupy a strongly entrenched position at Middlebrook. Howe responded quickly, drawing his army up before the patriot lines. But Washington would not leave his defenses and Howe would not attack them. The two armies looked at one another. Howe tried a ruse, pulling away rapidly as if to dash back to New York. Washington followed warily, and was not surprised when Howe suddenly wheeled around hoping to catch the Continentals in the open. The Americans scampered safely back to their fortifications at Middlebrook. "The Old Fox" was playing his game to perfection.

That was enough for Howe. He told Germain to forget hopes of ending the war in 1777. He then chose to go by sea to invade the middle colonies, deciding, for reasons which to this day remain unclear, against an operation up the Hudson to help Burgoyne. There are about as many explanations for that inexplicable decision as there are writers to espouse them. One looming factor, certainly, must have been Washington's strategic central position, his formidable station in New Jersey and the Hudson Highlands. Howe, in whose mind was indelibly etched that horrible scene on Bunker Hill, would not have found to his liking the prospect of attacking through craggy hills defended by a large patriot army. Whatever his reasons, he went to Chesapeake Bay, landing on 25 August after having wasted much of the year. Washington intercepted him south of Philadelphia as he had said he could.

Events that autumn turned the war around. Burgoyne, operating inland where the British fleet could not provide support, soon found himself over his head. Faced by a massive mobilization of militiamen who swarmed out of the northern districts to augment Horatio Gates' Continentals, the Britisher lost his entire army at Saratoga. The outcome of that campaign was to have far-reaching consequences. At the same time, Howe fought his way into Philadelphia, once again hammering Washington in a series of tactical clashes. But the surprisingly resilient Continental army emerged from each encounter more or less undaunted and ready to fight again.

Their first meeting was at Brandywine Creek on 11 September. The Continentals were still no match for British and German regulars, either in number or effectiveness; nevertheless, Americans could not yield Philadelphia without offering resistance. The second largest city in the British empire was too great a plum to be handed up free. Once again Washington had to cope with his disturbing "choice of difficulties." He picked Brandywine because the stream crossed the road to Philadelphia and afforded a naturally strong defensive position. The general planned to fight, but he also prepared to run; before the battle, he sent all the army's baggage far to the rear. Howe declined the offer to make a frontal attack, slipping instead around Washington's western flank. With some loss the patriots extricated themselves and withdrew.

Five days later, the opponents met at White Horse Tavern and squared off again for battle. Nature intervened, however, in the form of a day-long downpour. "It came down so hard that in a few moments we were drenched and sank in mud up to our calves," one German officer recorded. With much of his powder ruined, Washington quit the field. Skillfully, then, Howe maneuvered the Americans away from Philadelphia, entering that city in triumph on 26 September.

Still the patriots were not through. Washington watched for an opening as the British stopped to consolidate their gains. He redistributed ammunition, had all extra powder placed in wagons where it was ready to be moved rapidly should the army march, ordered the troops to discard all unnecessary impedimenta so they could react immediately, and hastened his quartermaster officers in their hunt for shoes that the men might "be able to move in a very short time." Scouts and spies searched for a soft spot in Sir William Howe's dispositions. At that moment, Washington received confirmation of the electrifying patriot victory over the British at Saratoga. His warrior's heart must have jumped. Here was inspiration! If the populace around Philadelphia would rally against Howe as their countrymen in the north had risen against

Burgoyne, a second great triumph might be won. At 4 P.M. on 28 September, Washington formed his army to announce the startling news of the capitulation of one entire wing of the invading forces. Thirteen cannons boomed out a joyous salute from the artillery park, the troops cheered with the fervor of men too long without word of victory, and all toasted success with an extra ration of rum. As the men returned excitedly to their tents, the commander summoned his senior officers to a council of war.[24]

The enemy, Washington told his lieutenants, occupied Philadelphia and Germantown with an estimated eight thousand men. So long as American defenses on the Delaware River held, General Howe would be separated from the support of his brother's fleet and would therefore be more vulnerable than after the two arms should be united. As for the Americans, their strength was growing. General McDougal had brought nine hundred men from the Hudson, General Smallwood had arrived with more than a thousand Maryland militia, and General Forman and six hundred troops from New Jersey were expected momentarily. All told, eleven thousand were in the American camp. Another two thousand men were enroute from Virginia and perhaps fifteen hundred more from New York. For the first time since the heady days at Boston, raw numbers seemed to give Washington a chance to attack Howe's main force. The Virginian asked the council of war to decide "whether with this force it was prudent to make a general and vigorous attack upon the enemy, or to wait further reinforcements." Of the fifteen members, five urged attack; the majority, however, voted to hold off until more reinforcements arrived. Everyone then agreed to move the encampment to a position closer to Germantown "to be in readiness to take advantage of any favorable opportunity that may offer for making an attack." The army shifted toward the enemy on 2 October.[25]

Perhaps it was the psychological effect of marching toward the foe, maybe the emotional lift of the victory over Burgoyne, possibly the offensive spirit emanating from George Washington —most likely it was the combination of all three. Whatever the reason, the result was soon evident. The patriots were overtaken by a compelling desire to assail the British. Washington kept that desire focused on the main body of the enemy. "It should be remembered always," he said, "that if we can destroy the enemy's grand army the branches of it will fall of course." At that point, intercepted messages revealed the location of the foe's "grand army." Howe had obligingly split his forces, giving the Americans the opportunity they sought. He had put some nine thousand men in Germantown, had occupied Philadelphia with three thousand, and had sent the remainder to open the Delaware. Washington at once convened another council of war.[26]

Although the enemy strength in Germantown and Philadelphia was greater than the Americans had at first estimated, other factors reinforced Washington's inclination to attack. Arrogantly, the forces at Germantown had erected no barricades. After all, no one would expect the patriots to throw themselves at a body of nine thousand of his majesty's regulars. Moreover, the nearest British reinforcements were seven miles away. Having the numerically superior force as well as the benefit of surprise, Washington calculated his odds for victory were a bit better than even. Most significantly, there was virtually no way he could lose his army even should he lose the battle. His arguments were persuasive. The council decided unanimously to attack the English and Hessians in Germantown. The army formed late on 3 October for a night march and a dawn assault.[27]

History has not generally been too kind to Washington for attempting to attack such a powerful foe with an army still largely untrained and untried in offensive action. But history, by definition, is hindsight, and more often than we would care to admit, brilliance is judged after the fact on the stark basis of success or failure. Had Germantown been the unqualified victory that Trenton was, we should likely hear fewer critical comments on the general's generalship in that instance. Be that as it may, Washington struck the unsuspecting British early on 4 October, failing to win a clear-cut decision, but scaring General Howe rather badly. As a matter of fact, the attack came surprisingly close to succeeding. "I really believe that few generals have ever been in a more critical situation, and owe more to fortune, than Sir William Howe," claimed a Hessian officer after the see-saw battle. The

Continentals blamed their repulse on a rotten break of luck —which was partially true—and considered themselves the real victors. American spirits rose, and that was the important result.[28]

Once the Delaware forts were reduced in early December, Howe marched to the American camp at Whitemarsh, only to be met there by Continentals glowering from behind entrenchments, a familiar sight by now. Predictably, Sir William neither attacked nor tried again to outmaneuver the patriots. He saw no way to pin down "the Old Fox." Besides, it was late in the year. The British moved into Philadelphia to pass the winter; Americans went to Valley Forge. The campaign of 1777 was over.

Howe tendered his resignation after Germantown. The king accepted it, appointing Henry Clinton to replace him. After two full campaigns, the vastly superior army and fleet George III had sent to America had carved out toeholds in New York, Newport, and Philadelphia. That was all. For such scant achievement, his majesty's forces had paid a dreadful price: Burgoyne's whole army at Saratoga and more than a third of the men who had marched with William Howe.

As the two armies bedded down in winter quarters that cheerless December, the curtain fell on the second phase of the War of Independence. If ever Washington could be called a Fabian general, it would be for his actions in 1776 and 1777. Even so, the description does not fit well, for, unlike the original Fabius, he offered battle time and again—only on his own terms, to be sure, which were usually from behind barricades, but he did fight. Twice he found the British guard down, once at Trenton and once at Germantown, and both times he swiftly launched a counterblow. When confronted with "a choice of difficulties," the aggressive Virginian had not sought solution in flight alone. Even when circumstances had dictated a defensive war, he had not excluded from his mind the spirit of the offensive.

9

One Great Vigorous Effort:
January 1778-October 1781

"His most Christian Majesty guarantees on his part to the United States their liberty, sovereignty and independence, absolute and unlimited." Those words were the ringing applause opening the third act of the American war. They came from the treaty of alliance between France and the United States, signed in Paris on 6 February 1778. Americans had been seeking such a treaty for some two years or more. The subject had first come up well before the signing of the Declaration of Independence. Proponents of proclaiming independence had in fact used the general desire for foreign assistance to bolster their arguments, saying that without a formal declaration no third nation would ever enter into an alliance with the rebels. There were other important reasons: merchants had yearned for a pact to protect trade; Congress had wanted one to open a door for economic assistance; military men had wished for armed assistance and naval support. And now it was a reality!

When news of the astounding patriot victory at Saratoga and reports of the encouraging performance of American arms outside Philadelphia reached Paris, the effect was electrifying. For years, France had been seeking revenge for the humiliating drubbing England had administered in the Seven Years War. Her military arm had been refurbished in anticipation of the day of *revanche*, and diplomats had eagerly read every sign to discern the right moment to strike. Agents had traveled through America looking for indications of rebellion as many as seven years before the outbreak of fighting in 1775. When a confrontation had appeared imminent, the foreign minister, Comte de Vergennes, rushed an emissary to London to sample the air. He reported back that the colonies were very likely to break free. Paris, with somewhat more hesitant assistance from Madrid, then plunged surreptitiously into support of the American rebels. Money and weapons from England's two old adversaries did much to keep General Washington's ragged legions in the field through the war's first three years. Now, with the colonials stronger than ever and England shocked by her unexpected reverses, Vergennes concluded that the time for open intervention was at hand. This looked like the long-awaited opportunity. London had never appeared more vulnerable. Louis XVI, whose own head would one day roll in the bottom of a rebel basket, overcame his scruples against revolutionaries; he decided to form an alliance with the upstart American republic. The war abruptly entered a new and ultimately decisive phase, which could bear the label "coalition victory."

Just as the second phase had presented Washington a set of conditions wholly different from the first, so was this third one completely unlike either of the previous two. France's entry into the war added international legitimacy to the revolutionary cause, assured a continuing source of supply, and held forth the promise of reinforcement by a French expeditionary army. But, important as those considerations were, they were surpassed in significance by one key factor: the introduction into the fray of the French navy. Henceforth, there would be a fleet to challenge British supremacy in North American waters. France had been energetically regenerating her naval arm ever since the last war while England had allowed her navy to atrophy. In weight of guns and number of warships, the French were stronger. Britannia would not rule the waves uncontested. No longer would English generals have the privilege of freely shifting units along the Atlantic seaboard; no longer would they enjoy the unopposed strategic advantage of interior lines. The only mobility edge they had ever held over the Americans was thus endangered—if not lost altogether.

The great impact of that fact was that now the entire thrust of

Washington's strategy could be reversed. Whereas he had been limited to acting on the strategic defensive so long as Great Britain had absolute superiority at sea, the arrival of a French fleet—or even the threat of arrival—would permit him once again to pass over to the offensive. Military victory became possible. The invaders could be decisively beaten, could be driven off American soil. Patriots could accept greater risks, for the loss now of a major portion of the Continental army would not necessarily be fatal; the revolution had taken too firm a hold in the country to be rooted out by an England at war also with France. This is not to say Americans could become foolhardy, just that they could operate with less constraint, more daring. Seizing the initiative was Washington's new imperative, defeating the British army his overriding goal. Historians have surprisingly failed to note it, but the predominant theme motivating American activities during the four years between Saratoga and Yorktown was the burning desire to smite the foe. In Washington's words, American actions were shaped by the need to make "one great vigorous effort at all hazards" to win the war.[1]

When Washington went into the miserable winter camp at Valley Forge, he could not foresee how drastically the war was slated to change. Nevertheless, certain alterations were already in evidence. Foreign aid had lately been a great boon to the cause, and a gaggle of foreign officers had imparted a cosmopolitan flavor to the Continental army. Lafayette, Kosciusko, DeKalb, Pulaski, Duportail, and Steuben were some of the more illustrious of Washington's new lieutenants. More of that sort of help the Americans fully expected they could count on, for a while at least. But not an outright alliance. That might be hoped for, hardly planned upon. In the dead of winter, struggling mainly to survive until spring, the patriots looked for warm weather to bring a campaign in 1778 not unlike that of the previous year. During January, in fact, Washington continued to speak emphatically of waging "a defensive war."

But, under whatever strategic cloak it fought, the American army had to be improved. One clear lesson Washington had learned was that his ragtag regiments required better training and organization if they were ever to have a decent chance of beating British and German formations. The somewhat amorphous mass with which he had previously fended off English parries had been none too responsive or dependable; Germantown had taught him that the Continental army was too dull a weapon to permit him to carry the war to the enemy with much expectation of success. Americans today tend to look back on the Valley Forge winter as an epic in suffering and survival. It was, in truth, a terrible time for the underfed, ill-clothed, poorly paid Continentals, but it was not the worst winter they would endure nor was mere survival their greatest accomplishment. Helped immeasurably by longer enlistments, which had provided a solid nucleus of veterans, and the influx of foreign officers, which had provided a professional base of knowledge, the Continental army came of age that winter. When it marched forth in the spring from its training camp at Valley Forge, it bore the stamp of Steuben, the Prussian drillmaster who had taught it to form line from column, to maneuver crisply on the battlefield, to wield the fearsome bayonet. For the first time, George Washington led an army not only rich in experience but one well trained and brimming with confidence, one the equal or better of its foe in many respects. Battles henceforth would be between British regulars and American regulars.

Floodlights illuminated the new phase in England much sooner than in America. The scene Londoners viewed was not a happy one. Word of the disaster at Saratoga stunned them. Germain could discuss nothing else for days. Lord North contemplated resigning. Opposition leaders in Parliament grew more vocal. The desire to press the war reached a low point. After but a little reflection, Germain concluded that chances of overrunning the colonies were gone, that reverting to a strategy of naval blockade was the only answer. Although a declaration of war on Britain did not immediately accompany Paris' alliance with the United States, the ministry in London knew that warfare between the two ancient enemies was inevitable and imminent. George III could also expect Spain to side with France. As a modern British scholar has noted, "England faced what she had always dreaded and averted: a coalition of maritime enemies undistracted by war in Europe."

Orders leaving London that winter made abundantly clear that king and cabinet realized a new phase in the fight was upon them.[2]

Henry Clinton was told to abandon Philadelphia in order to free forces for employment elsewhere. He was even, if need be, to give up New York and make Halifax the main British base in North America. With France in the conflict, London fully expected the Caribbean to become the new focus of fighting. Both France and England had bases there. And, though it may seem preposterous today, not a few Englishmen considered the sugar islands to be quite more valuable than the thirteen colonies. Once he had consolidated his scattered elements, Clinton was to detach five thousand men to the West Indies to attack the French island of St. Lucia. The new plans also directed him to send another three thousand troops to Florida where they would be in position either to defend Jamaica or attack New Orleans as the situation might dictate. In North America, except for naval actions in coastal waters, Great Britain's generals were told to adopt a strictly passive stance, thus forfeiting the initiative to the rebels.

Evacuating Philadelphia was not such a simple matter, Sir Henry soon discovered. The year before, upon hearing that General Howe had taken the city, Benjamin Franklin, who knew his town well, had quipped, "No, Philadelphia has taken Howe." The sage was right. Loyalists abounded in the area, and, believing the king's colors were there to stay, they had stepped forward in numbers to proclaim allegiance to the monarch. For the most part, they had been unwilling to take up arms against the patriots, but they had accepted the king's protection. The British stay in the city had been most pleasant, their idle hours filled with entertainment, the passage of winter weeks hastened by enjoyable companionship. Indeed, in some ways the natives might have been overly warm, for it seems the occupying army suffered more than was usual from intimate encounters. Apothecaries did a brisk business in such medicines as Dr. Yeldall's Anti-venereal Essence, which both prevented and cured, Hannay's Preventive, a London product, and Keyser's Pills, advertised as effective for "a certain disease." But the health of his command was not Clinton's primary problem as he prepared to depart. It was the Tories themselves.

They could not be left to the predictable fury of the patriots; on the other hand, he had insufficient shipping to transport both the army and the horde of Loyalists. After some soul-searching, the British commander finally decided to send noncombatants by sea while marching his army across New Jersey to the friendly lines around New York.

Not until 30 April did Washington learn of the treaty with France. A French frigate, *La Sensible*, had left Brest on 8 March, not reaching the United States until 13 April. From its landfall in Falmouth, a courier rode to York, Pennsylvania, to give word to Congress. Delegates hurried the message on to camp. The grand news found the general and many of his associates already in an aggressive mood. He promptly called a council of war to choose one of three courses of action. Should the Americans attack New York, strike at Philadelphia, or await developments? Nathanael Greene wanted to hold the enemy in Philadelphia while striking their New York sanctuary. Henry Knox, too, preferred to aim at the port on the Hudson, but he was more cautious than Greene. Anthony Wayne, as always, wanted to go immediately on the offensive, any offensive! Most of the others wanted to take some positive action to hit the British, but they could not see how or where. The army was not yet large enough and there was a shortage of heavy artillery needed to batter down fortifications. In the end, the council decided to wait a while longer to see what would develop.[3]

That new-found bellicose attitude had been growing for some time. Americans of that era were by nature activists, none more so than those involved in the rebellion. Patriots who thought about such matters could appreciate that General Washington's protracted war may have been necessary, but that did not make it palatable. By the middle of 1777, an obvious backlash had set in. All across the land, nearly everyone began more or less independently looking for some way to hit back at the royal invaders. On the very eve of being forced to flee from Philadelphia, Congress had worked up a plan for an assault against Pensacola. Many eyes also turned westward in 1777. Congress established a western department that year and sent Brigadier General Edward Hand out to command it. Washington's daring counterattack at German-town had itself fit into the nation's newly flowering pugnacious pattern. The year 1778 opened with some inventive patriots attempting to damage British vessels anchored at Philadelphia by floating mines down the Delaware—the so-called Battle of the Kegs—and with Congress enthusiastically plotting a new invasion of Canada. Washington, meanwhile, worked at organizing a mounted service, which would permit him to raid enemy outposts. These various enterprising efforts did not cease when Continentals took the field at winter's end. Virginia sent George Rogers Clark west in 1778; John Paul Jones conducted his first raid on the English homeland that same year, spiking the guns at two forts in the harbor of Whitehaven and setting several fires; Captain James Willing, with a courageous band of backwoodsmen, sailed down the Mississippi in an armed boat named *Rattlesnake*, raising havoc along the way; Major General Robert Howe led a venturesome, if unsuccessful, attempt to seize East Florida; and Congress planned yet another offensive to capture Canada. There was no mistaking the fact that Americans were eager for the war's new phase, that they were tired of defending, that they were ready to try snatching the initiative even had the British not decided to give it away.

Conclusive evidence of Clinton's pending departure from Philadelphia reached Valley Forge in late May. Washington made plans to hinder a march through New Jersey if the British should choose to go that way. ''The game,'' he wrote, ''seems now to be verging fast to a favorable issue and cannot, I think, be lost unless we throw it away by too much supineness on the one hand or impetuousity on the other.'' When the British started their trek from Philadelphia into New Jersey on 18 June, the Virginian eagerly set out in pursuit.[4]

At first patriots only harassed Clinton's long file of troops and wagons. Washington followed to the north and rear with the main body of the army, while Daniel Morgan, with six hundred rifle-men, hung on the southern flank. But Clinton moved slower than either he or Washington had anticipated. Rebels in New Jersey had burned bridges and otherwise impeded the route of march. En-cumbered with an excessive number of baggage wagons, the

English in seven days covered only forty miles. Washington was tempted by the opportunity. There was the enemy, struggling just to move and strung out in a long, vulnerable column. Americans stood poised on their flank with a slightly superior force, twelve thousand to the British ten thousand. The general convened a council of war on 24 June. Should the Continentals "hazard a general action?" If so, should it be a major assault, a partial one, or should they maneuver in such a way as to make the British attack?

Steuben, Lafayette, Wayne, Greene, and Duportail wanted to attack. But Charles Lee, who had recently been exchanged, argued against doing anything. Avoid all action and wait for the French to enter and win the war, he counseled. Lee was articulate and persuasive, and the aura of European professionalism still hung about him. The vote was close, but he carried the debate. Young Alexander Hamilton, who was taking notes, disgustedly labeled the timid council a "society of midwives." Anthony Wayne stalked out, refusing to put his name on the report. That night, Wayne, Lafayette, and Greene each wrote a note to Washington urging him to overrule the council and attack anyway. Realizing what a chance was slipping through his fingers—one that might never again be repeated—the general decided to take the bolder course. He gave Lafayette command of the advance detachment and set his entire army in motion on the road to Monmouth Court House.[5]

The battle of Monmouth was fought on 28 June 1778, three years to the month after the man from Mount Vernon had been appointed commander-in-chief. It was a landmark in the war, for Continentals that day performed in open battle as well as or better than the Europeans.

Lee, who had insisted that he, by virtue of seniority, should command the advance, replaced Lafayette. Upon reaching Monmouth, he found Clinton facing him with a small but vigorous covering force. Lee, the general who had not wanted to fight in the first place and who, despite his reputation, had never commanded men in battle, promptly lost control. A confused retreat of about three miles resulted. Washington, galloping to the sound of the guns, rode headlong into the midst of the reeling Continentals, at once assumed command, rallied the shaken troops, and stopped the British short. After reinforcing his stalled units, Clinton launched several attacks, only to be repulsed each time by disciplined and steady Americans. Washington then organized a counterattack, but the day was done. Nightfall ended the battle. Leaving his dead and wounded on the field, Clinton got away in the darkness, reaching the safety of the ocean at Sandy Hook. Counting desertions, he had lost some two thousand men. American casualties were put at two hundred and thirty dead and wounded. The Continental army had fought splendidly and, after Washington relieved Lee, it had been superbly led. Monmouth could not properly be called a victory for either side. Washington had won the day, but Clinton had escaped—not without being humbled and badly frightened, though. The Britisher had learned a jolting fact—the American ragamuffins could no longer be pushed about at will.

"It is not a little pleasing, nor less wonderful to contemplate, that after two years of maneuvering and undergoing the strangest vicissitudes that perhaps ever attended any one contest since creation, both armies are brought back to the very point they set out from." So wrote an elated George Washington from his new headquarters east of the Hudson and above New York City, where he had marched after Monmouth. The opponents occupied roughly the same ground they had held in 1776 before Howe had crossed the Hudson to invade New Jersey—the British owning Manhattan and the patriots entrenched south of the Hudson Highlands. But in 1778 there was one all-important difference: the roles of attacker and defender had been reversed. This time around, the Americans were on the offensive and the king's troops were hunkering behind barricades, wondering when and where the next blow would fall.

Chasing Clinton back to his lair was not the only event elevating patriot spirits. Paris and London had broken off diplomatic relations in March and had begun a shooting war in June. America had an active ally! Comte d'Estaing, a general appointed to serve as an admiral in the French navy, left Toulon in mid-April with a powerful fleet. His destination: the United States. Unfortunately, he loitered in crossing, taking nearly three months, thereby missing a grand coup at the Chesapeake by mere days. Admiral Richard Howe had left Philadelphia with his load of Loyalists barely in the nick of time. He scurried safely into New York just ahead of the French. D'Estaing promptly bottled the British up in the harbor. Howe had only nine ships of the line, his largest ones carrying but sixty-four guns. D'Estaing overwhelmingly outnumbered and outgunned the English, having six seventy-four-gun men-of-war, one behemoth of eighty guns, and another of ninety. General Washington learned of the French arrival on 13 July. Windows suddenly opened on new vistas of strategy. The means to annihilate the British garrisons were at hand. Washington sent his brilliant, French-speaking aide, Alexander Hamilton, to coordinate with d'Estaing, meanwhile maneuvering the American army to a position from where it could attack Henry Clinton's stronghold in New York.

But the story of d'Estaing in America was destined to be a story of dashed hopes. The general-turned-admiral looked at the treacherous bar he would have to cross to get into the harbor, glumly considered the restricted nature of the proposed battle site, and uneasily noticed Admiral Howe's readiness to fight. The Frenchman did not have the heart to try it. He claimed his deep-draft ships could not negotiate the channel. Without showing his great disappointment, Washington, ever the opportunist, quickly shifted sights to Rhode Island. D'Estaing agreed to support an attack there.

The isolated base at Newport was defended by only six thousand men, mostly Hessians. About four thousand marines were on board d'Estaing's ships, while John Sullivan, the American commander in Rhode Island, had another nine thousand, including last-minute reinforcements sent from the main army. The odds heavily favored an allied victory; Washington confidently reckoned the chances of winning stood at a hundred to one or better. To help smooth relations, he sent two of his more trusted generals —Nathanael Greene, a native of Rhode Island, and Lafayette, who was expected to coordinate actions with the French. At first all went well. Squeezed between d'Estaing's fleet and a combined French and American land force, the British garrison appeared doomed. Then English boldness, with an assist from lady luck, turned near victory into near disaster.[6]

Admiral Howe, though leading a much inferior fleet, sailed bravely from New York to the aid of his beleaguered compatriots in Newport. D'Estaing immediately picked up his marines and sailed out to meet Howe on 10 August, leaving the surprised Americans stranded in a rather awkward position. As the two admirals maneuvered for battle, a violent storm blew up, scattering and severely damaging their warships. Howe limped back to New York, and d'Estaing returned to Newport, but only to make temporary repairs. He had no stomach for further operations there. Oblivious to the entreaties of his allies, he sailed for Boston to refit. While there, he also decided to drop plans for amphibious raids against Halifax and Newfoundland. The season was late. He headed for the West Indies instead. Sullivan, meanwhile, had barely extricated his exposed forces in time to avert a crushing defeat. What had once looked like such a sure win had turned out to be a most frustrating loss. The new alliance was getting off to a rocky start.

Indians struck that year in the Wyoming valley, the first of a series of deadly raids into the frontier settlements of Pennsylvania and New York. General Hand, with few resources, had done little in the West in 1777. In what came to be known as the ''Squaw's Campaign,'' he could report nothing more decisive than killing four Indian women and one boy. General Lachlan McIntosh replaced Hand as commander of the western department. Given two Continental regiments in 1778, McIntosh pushed into the Ohio country, erecting Forts McIntosh and Laurens and planning to attack Detroit. But the Indian raids, hitting settlements much farther to the east, behind McIntosh's area of operations, effectively halted patriot expansion for the time being. The Indian terror had to be dealt with first. Arms and men bolstered the threatened sectors, and Washington began plans for a decisive campaign in 1779. ''The only certain way of preventing Indian ravages,'' he said, ''is to carry the war vigorously into their own country.''[7]

Still, the commander-in-chief's primary concern was with British units occupying American territory. So long as English forces remained behind their fortifications and the French fleet remained timid, there was no way the Americans could get at them. But what if English leaders tried some new scheme to regain the initiative? What if Clinton opened a front in a different area? Where could redcoats go? What could they do? Those and similar questions were asked at patriot headquarters in the autumn of 1778. As intelligence accumulated indicating a forthcoming British move of some sort, divining the correct answers became more important. Washington's analysis of what his opponent could and should do affords us a glimpse into the commander-in-chief's well-developed strategic grasp.

Admitting that he had no inside information to tell him what Clinton was up to, Washington reasoned that the Englishman could choose from a list of only three decisive objectives: the annihilation of the Continental army, the destruction of the French fleet, or the capture of fortress West Point. Without an army or a navy, the allies could not operate offensively; without the bastion at West Point, they would be hard pressed to thwart an enemy offensive. Therefore, the Virginian could hardly credit evidence saying Sir Henry was readying an expedition for the southern colonies, *away* from West Point and the Continental army. Surely the enemy must have learned by now, he said, "that the possession of our towns, while we have an army in the field, will avail them little. It involves *us* in difficulty, but does not, by any means, insure *them* conquest." To gain a victory, "it is our arms, not defenseless towns, they have to subdue." Then, quoting from Shakespeare, the Virginian stated that all British schemes would fade "like the baseless fabric of a vision" as long as an American army remained intact. What's worse, he continued, heading southward was not only illogical, it would be dangerous for the English. Before the entry of France into the war, a southern strategy would have been feasible, "but to attempt now to detach 10,000 men (which is, I suppose, half their army) and to divide their naval strength for the protection of it, would, in my judgment, be an act of insanity, and expose one part or the other of both land and sea force to inevitable ruin." The American leader was quite correct, of course—perhaps even prescient.[8]

Despite logic, though, Clinton had a southern campaign in mind. Savannah was his initial objective. It fell to an amphibious stroke on 29 December 1778, ending a year in which almost all the luck had dropped on the side of George III.

Uncharacteristically, right at year's end George Washington fought with all his might to prevent the launching of an offensive campaign. In October, the Continental Congress had proposed a grandiose French and American invasion of Canada. The congressmen instructed Benjamin Franklin to offer France a part of the Newfoundland fishing grounds in return for sending a naval squadron and five thousand troops up the St. Lawrence River to link up with an invading American army of twelve thousand men to be led by Lafayette. They thought Lafayette's name would tempt Paris to agree and might attract support from the thousands of French-speaking Canadians. Lafayette, naturally, was all for the scheme. But Washington, with one eye on the national goal of territorial expansion, was thoroughly shaken by the thought of the French flag flying once again over Quebec. He argued against the plan, publicly explaining that it was beyond patriot capabilities to launch such an invasion but privately expressing his fears of a French resurgence in the coveted lands. As an alternative, he suggested an American blow against Detroit and Niagara. The fact of the matter was that French officials had not the slightest interest in becoming involved again as a colonial power in North America, but Americans did not know that. If it was considered bad to have Britain remain in Canada after the war, it was unthinkable to have any semblance of French influence reasserted there. It would have been an embarrassing situation, indeed, had their allies claimed the very area the colonists desired so ardently. The mere thought, Washington wrote, "alarms all my feelings for the true and permanent interests of my country." He was looking into the future. With Frenchmen in Canada, Spaniards in New Orleans, and Indians along the western frontier, Paris would "have it in her power to give law to these states." Unsure of being persuasive enough by letter, the general went to Philadelphia in December to argue personally. That fact alone testifies compellingly to the seriousness with which he viewed the possibility of losing future claims to Canada. In the end, he persevered. The invasion was canceled. Americans turned their interests and hopes for 1779 back to the Atlantic coast. Lafayette returned to France for a visit.[9]

Another issue kept Washington in Philadelphia, away from his army, until well into February: the vexing problem of planning a campaign for the forthcoming season. The difficulties confronting him at that point in the war were as much political and economic as they were military. Decisions, therefore, could not be made in isolation at winter headquarters. And, for once, the Continental army was not on the verge of dissolving. It did not need General Washington's firm presence. The weather was mild and the men were tough. Most by now were immune to the diseases of camp life. Widely scattered cantonments in New York and New Jersey simplified the burden of transporting supplies, so the troops were relatively well fed. They were also warmer than was their usual winter lot—many sported shoes and blankets and uniforms made in France. No, the real threat of dissolution was not in the army, it was in the civilian sector. Hence, that is where Washington worked.

Affairs in America were tumbling sharply downward. Inflation was runaway, with money sometimes dipping 5 percent a day. Manipulators were growing rich while the country was sliding into financial ruin. Political factions were developing. Congress was practically impotent, for the "ablest and best men" had long since left it to serve elsewhere. Damning those seeking wealth from the woes of war, a bitter George Washington exclaimed, "Speculation, peculation, and an insatiable thirst for riches seem to have got the better of every other consideration and almost of every order of men." He railed against those "speculators, various tribes of money makers, and stock jobbers of all denominations" who were waging their own war for private profit. As for congressmen, the general noted sadly how "party disputes and personal quarrels are the great business of the day, whilst the momentous concerns of an empire . . . are but secondary considerations." Washington can be forgiven for overstating the case somewhat, for he was utterly dumbfounded by the contrast of "luxury and profusion" in Philadelphia with "want and misery" in camp. With much reason, he deeply feared for the future of the cause.[10]

Strategic discussions reflected that fear. "The question does not turn upon military principals only," the commander-in-chief stated. American poverty and European politics shaped military planning. The country's wracked economic condition would be the primary limiting factor in whatever was decided upon, while international developments would perhaps be the second most important consideration. Spain's open entry into the war, which was fully expected by all sides, would change the equation, as would the course adopted by other nations in Europe. Should England react to European events by evacuating its bases in the United States, Washington thought patriots ought to be in a posture to grab the opportunity to expand. As he phrased it, his army "should be ready to strike an important blow for the effectual security of our frontiers and for opening a door for a further progress into Canada." On the other hand, he continued, if the English stayed, the Continental army must be prepared to join with a French fleet in efforts to strike one of the enemy bases at Newport, New York, or Savannah. However, either of those eventualities—attacking westward or tackling an English enclave—required a large and expensive military establishment. The destitute nation, Washington felt, simply could not afford so heavy a burden just then. The standing army had no recourse but to stay small. If a French naval force arrived, the general would be obliged to depend on mobilizing militia units to swell his ranks to a size permitting offensive actions.[11]

In his analytical way, the Virginian next listed three options open to the Americans if the British kept their bases and a French fleet did not appear. First, and most desirable, was to attack in Rhode Island or New York, but the flattened state of finances would not support such an effort. Second was to conduct an offensive against Niagara. This, too, would be expensive because those forces containing the British in their coastal redoubts could be thinned out only at great risk, which meant Americans would be compelled to raise additional regiments. The last option was to remain on the defensive. "It is to be regretted," the general summarized, "that our prospect of any capital offensive operation is so slender that we seem in a manner to be driven to the necessity of adopting the third plan, that is, remaining entirely on the defensive." Economically, that was the best course, but it introduced dangerous psychological implications, he warned. Doing nothing might "serve to dispirit the people and give confidence to the disaffected." The paradox was that the country had insufficient funds to act, but lacked the spirit to sustain inaction. Washington pointed out that without the hope of a speedy end to the war, which had been provided earlier by France's entry, he would now command but "the shadow of an army." In a very real sense, regardless of its fiscal straits, the nation could not afford to do nothing. The sad fever of idleness could be fatal. That sobering consideration, he concluded, might require the making of "one great vigorous effort at all hazards."[12]

In the end, Congress and commander-in-chief decided to send a strong force into Iroquois country to punish the Indians, while standing on the defensive elsewhere—that is, unless a French squadron should put in an appearance. Then they would of necessity rely upon a surge of spirit to summon the needed manpower. That was bargain-basement war, at best, but the old cliché holding that beggars can't be choosers was certainly true of the impoverished rebels as they entered their fifth campaigning season.

The military tale of 1779 is quickly told. D'Estaing came again to American waters in September, but he wanted nothing to do with New York or Newport. Memories of the previous year's fiasco were too fresh. Instead, he sailed to Savannah where he joined Americans under Benjamin Lincoln in besieging the British. The English garrison was cut off from support when French warships took station, and should have been easy prey. However, d'Estaing was too impatient, insisting upon a premature attack which the defenders handily turned back. That single bloody repulse was all the combat the admiral wanted that year. He sailed away once more, leaving a fuming Lincoln to fend for himself. The name of d'Estaing is not a respected one in patriot chronicles of the war.

Elsewhere, results were better. Against the hostile tribes, John Sullivan and James Clinton led a highly successful punitive expedition, which was the beginning of the end of the power of eastern Indians. Colonel Daniel Brodhead, the new commander of the western department, also led a victorious march against savages near the Allegheny River headwaters. Washington was "in hopes these severe blows will effectually intimidate the Indians and secure the future peace of our frontier." Henry Clinton devised an involved scheme to grab West Point, which miscarried, giving Washington an opportunity to attack an exposed post at Stony Point. Anthony Wayne stormed it in darkness at bayonet point, gaining a splendid little victory and boosting patriot morale. In a similar stroke, "Light-Horse Harry" Lee, the father of Robert E. Lee, knocked off a key outpost at Paulus Hook, opposite New York City. Clinton, finding the Americans all too eager to fight and his own forces much too dispersed, was thoroughly frightened when he heard d'Estaing was operating along the coast. He shortened his lines around New York and withdrew completely from Rhode Island. John Paul Jones made his second raid on the British Isles, capturing the *Serapis* in September. George Rogers Clark completed his conquest of the Old Northwest, and the people of Boston, on their own, sent an ambitious if unsuccessful expedition off in forty vessels to capture Penobscot. Americans and Frenchmen were not doing all the fighting, however. After Spain entered the war, Bernardo de Galvez, governor of Louisiana, promptly seized British posts along the Mississippi. All in all, it was not a happy year for George III.

Americans had failed to dislodge the British from Georgia, but an indirect result of d'Estaing's short stay there had been the bloodless recovery of Newport. Nor had patriots been able to make a "great vigorous effort" anywhere, but the sum of all the minor victories was nearly as beneficial—maybe more so, because the cost could hardly have been lower. With Congress bankrupt, that was a significant point. Once again, it could be said that George Washington had employed American arms in perfect accord with American capabilities and needs.

Action on the diplomatic front heated up in 1779. Spain's entry required Congress to decide upon its minimum war aims, sparking a debate lasting several months. Pointedly, the French ambassador told the president of Congress that his country would not support United States claims to lands outside the thirteen states unless Americans were in possession of them at the beginning of peace talks. For that matter, he cautioned, it might not be possible to prevent England from retaining any territory its army might occupy—including parts of the United States. That stance served as a sharp spur to invigorate the Americans, as well as a warning that, while Paris would back the patriot goal of independence, it would not be bound to support the aim of territorial aggrandizement.[13]

Already the maneuvering for postwar position had begun, although, since neither side was yet willing to terminate hostilities, fighting remained paramount. A nation at war normally seeks peace only when it has gained all it can expect to achieve, or when it anticipates greater losses by continuing, or when it has absorbed its limit of punishment. The American war was obviously not near its end, for any of those reasons, but all participants would henceforth be judging military actions more for their political impact than had heretofore been the case. That was an aspect of the war Americans were unsure of. In international politics, the patriots were, in John Adams' colorful phrase, "militia diplomats." When playing the tricky game of state with practiced European statesmen, they would surely have to hold the strongest hand possible, which was a solid military position.[14]

For Americans, the low point of the war came in 1780, appropriately known ever since as "the Black Year." The year opened forebodingly enough with the worst blizzard in memory and a mutiny in the Massachusetts line stationed at West Point. Soon came word of staggering patriot setbacks in the South—including the costliest loss of the war (Charleston) and the bloodiest defeat (at Camden). Continental dollars became so inflated that they were practically worthless, giving rise to the phrase "not worth a Continental." English and German units swiftly overran Georgia, South Carolina, much of North Carolina, and threatened Virginia. Benedict Arnold, the most renowned combat leader in patriot ranks during the war's early years, shocked his countrymen by turning traitor, only narrowly failing to sell West Point to the British. French agents made secret overtures to London, suggesting George III might keep the American South. Spain obstinately refused to sign an alliance with the rebels. At year's end, a British force opened a new front in Virginia. In truth, it was a black, black year for the United States.

In all that adversity, however, were lodged the seeds of victory that would sprout in full glory just a year later. George Washington strove mightily to get an offensive operation off the ground in 1780; he was unable to do it, but his prodigious efforts set the stage for a decisive campaign in 1781.

As had been the case the year before, internal problems in the United States severely limited Washington's strategic choices in 1780. From the start, things were bad. Survival itself was no small feat, as the army found itself caught in the icy grip of a terrible winter made worse by a paralyzed economy. The general could hardly contemplate a summer campaign when he was unsure if he would have even the skeleton of any army when spring came. Desertions outstripped enlistments. "I assure you," the Virginian told the president of Congress, "every idea you can form of our distresses will fall short of reality." There could be seen "in every line of the army the most serious features of mutiny and sedition." Winter's end brought warmth to the frozen wretches in Continental rags, but not an end to misery. An army surgeon wrote, "Our poor soldiers are reduced to the very verge of famine; their patience is exhausted by complicated suffering, and their spirits are almost broken." Mutiny struck again in May, this time in the Connecticut line. Pennsylvanians, who themselves would revolt a few months later, suppressed the uprising. George III gloated over the appallingly low state of patriot morale. If no great disaster befell Britain, the monarch opined, the United States would sue for peace that summer. For once, he was not far wrong in guessing the mood of his erstwhile subjects.[15]

Washington's efforts to inspirit his countrymen in that gloomy spring of 1780 were utterly unavailing. The nation was sunk in a torpor. After five years of war, it seemed absolutely unable to rouse itself for a sixth. Alexander Hamilton caught the mood of abject despair in one terse paragraph:

> . . . our countrymen have all the folly of the ass and all the passiveness of the sheep in their compositions. They are determined not to be free and they can neither be frightened, discouraged nor persuaded to change their resolution. If we are to be saved France and Spain must save us. I have the most Pigmy-feeling at the idea, and I almost wish to hide my disgrace in universal ruin.[16]

The first good news of the year came in May. Lafayette returned to America carrying word of a French expeditionary force which, at that very moment, he said, should be in passage across the Atlantic. Louis XVI was sending not only a naval squadron but a land component as well. The Comte de Rochambeau, leading an army of several thousand French regulars, had orders to place himself under Washington's command. Those foreign troops would fill the gap Americans no longer seemed willing or able to fill—the gap in numbers of fighting men between Washington's army and one large enough to beat the British. That news galvanized the general to action. Never mind that his army was weak, that his country was lethargic, that his supply system was in a shambles—here was the way to win the war, the means of inflicting a decisive defeat on the British! With the cause standing so dangerously close to the edge of the abyss and with what amounted almost to a miracle about to arrive in the form of French regulars, patriots had no choice but to gird themselves for that one great, vigorous effort.

Meeting with a committee from Congress at his headquarters in late May, Washington bluntly told the lawmakers what must be done. He tried to rekindle in the delegates some of the fire and spirit of 1775 and 1776. Americans would march with the French, he stated unequivocally: "Offensive operations, on our part, are doubtless expected . . . we have not, nor ought we to wish, an alternative." America must exert to the utmost to permit the army to make "a decisive effort," even if that required drafting men to fill Continental units. "Our arrangements should be made on the principle of the greatest enterprise we can undertake," which meant fielding a total of forty thousand men, he added. The congressmen rode back to Philadelphia, awed by the new opportunity, dubious of their ability to raise the necessary forces, but convinced that the commander-in-chief fully intended to fight regardless of what else happened.[17]

Indeed he did. He had begun making his plans before the congressional committee had reached camp. Immediately upon hearing of Rochambeau's approach, the general had urged Lafayette to try to get word to him to steer directly for New York. Henry Clinton, with a large part of his army, was away just then, tied up in the siege of Charleston. New York was very vulnerable. Knowing how difficult it would be to intercept a convoy at sea and unsure of Rochambeau's precise plans, Washington also alerted his lieutenants elsewhere, exhorting them to be ready to take advantage of the French force wherever it made land. He told Heath in New England to examine the methods of attacking Halifax. To Lincoln at Charleston he sent word of the possibility of French succor. But New York was his dream. Gather equipment for a strike at Manhattan, he directed Greene, but, while doing it, spread rumors of a pending raid along the Canadian coast. Lafayette, as part of the deception plan, prepared a proclamation to the Canadians, asking them to cooperate with a French fleet sailing up the St. Lawrence to join an American corps invading from northern New York. "It will get out," Washington said confidently.[18] France also had a powerful fleet afloat in the Caribbean commanded by the Comte de Guichen. Could Lafayette relay word to him of New York's inviting vulnerability? The eager American was overlooking no bets in attempting to mass a superior allied force for a supreme effort.[19]

Charleston fell on 12 May, a loss opening South Carolina to the enemy. The end of the siege also freed Clinton to rush reinforcements back to New York. Washington learned of the grievous setback on 31 May, but not even that news dimmed his determination. He even found some good in it: "The enemy, by attempting to hold conquests so remote, must dissipate their force, and of

course afford opportunities of striking one or the other extremity.''
On 6 June he assembled a council of war at Morristown. Best
intelligence estimates set British strength at about thirty thousand
men, but they were scattered beyond mutually supporting distance. Some eight thousand troops, bolstered by four thousand or
more Tories, held New York; perhaps nine thousand were in
Charleston, twenty-five hundred were in Halifax; five hundred
manned the works at St. Augustine; and four hundred garrisoned
Penobscot. Patriots, Washington reported, could count on maybe
eight thousand around New York (twenty-four thousand if a second miracle should fill all requisitions) and twenty-five hundred in
the South. When Rochambeau arrived, with seven thousand to ten
thousand men, the allies would clearly be stronger at any point
where they chose to mass. The general asked his council not
whether there should be an offensive; he directed the members
only to select an objective for an attack, specifically mentioning
New York City, Halifax, Canada, and St. Augustine. The council
chose New York with little argument. That was what Washington
wanted. For the next five weeks, he worked on plans for the
assault, worried about the sluggish response of the states to his
appeals for men, and scanned the horizon for French sail. Unhap-
pily, the first vessels to appear off Sandy Hook were those of
Admiral Marriot Arbuthnot, bringing Sir Henry Clinton and several thousand men back from their victory at Charleston. New
York was no longer open to a swift coup. Taking the city would
require heavy fighting.[20]

Rochambeau, escorted by the Chevalier de Ternay with twelve
ships of the line, made land in Rhode Island on 10 July 1780. He
put more than five thousand men ashore.

As soon as he learned of the French landfall, Washington sent
Lafayette galloping to Newport with a memorandum for concert-
ing a plan of action. Pointedly, he first explained the prerequisite
of attaining naval superiority before a land campaign could be
launched. ''In any operation, and under all circumstances, a decisive naval superiority is to be considered as a fundamental principle, and the basis upon which every hope of success must ultimately depend.'' Next, he carefully described the strategic signifi-

cance of the port of New York and explained the urgency of launching an allied attempt soonest. Any delay in seizing the city, he said, ''may defeat all our projects and render the campaign inactive and inglorious.'' To begin with, Washington's outline stated, French vessels would be required to take the harbor and open the Hudson. ''To render our operations nervous and rapid, it is essential for us to be masters of the navigation of the Hudson River and of the sound.'' Once that was done, the combined French and American armies would attack Manhattan from Morrisania, near Kingsbridge. Washington set 5 August as the tentative rendezvous date. Finally, remembering d'Estaing's abrupt departures from battles at Newport in 1778 and Savannah in 1779, the general tactfully but forcefully informed Rochambeau that the French would have to agree beforehand not to abandon the operation suddenly.[21]

Washington's soaring aspirations were dealt a severe blow when Admiral Thomas Graves brought six more British ships of the line into New York harbor. The English then had a clear naval superiority. Nevertheless, the patriot leader flatly refused to relinquish his desire to open an offensive. Maybe not in New York, but somewhere, anywhere. One had to consider the possibility of help from the French and Spanish fleets cruising in the West Indies, he reported wistfully. Furthermore, having seen American citizen-soldiers rally before to swell Continental ranks in a time of need, the Virginian hoped it might happen again. Rochambeau's arrival ought ''to excite in us a determination to be prepared at all events,'' he told Congress. But he was grasping at straws. The time had passed when Americans would spontaneously spring to arms in the numbers needed; the war had been long, casualties had exacted a heavy toll of the spirited, and enthusiasm had waned among the others. There would never again be a massive uprising. Whatever was done had to be accomplished with the understrength Continental army and a sprinkling of staunch militia units. However, Washington stubbornly told Greene to continue preparations for the assault on New York. To facilitate those plans, the commander-in-chief sent three harbor pilots familiar with approaches to New York to serve Admiral Ternay, ordering them to stick with the Frenchman no matter what. Not for lack of drive at the top would the plan of attack be abandoned.[22]

Late in July, Henry Clinton decided to test his new French opponent. British warships sealed the harbor at Newport, and Clinton began transporting a large land force toward Rhode Island. Although he could assemble on such short notice barely three thousand men fit for duty, General Washington boldly maneuvered them toward New York. Clinton, believing Washington led at least twelve thousand troops, scampered back to protect his base.

For his part, Rochambeau had no intention of leaving his haven in Newport until he had a stronger naval arm to support him. He had expected to be joined in Rhode Island by another increment of the navy, but that was not to be. British warships had bottled the reinforcing squadron in Cadiz, on the wrong side of the Atlantic. Being deprived of the better part of his fleet was enough in itself to make the Frenchman cautious—and patriot spirit he found to be something less than reassuring. Americans had not flocked enthusiastically to arms upon his arrival. He was not impressed with the Continental army. "Do not depend upon these people, nor upon their means," he bluntly told Paris. A chagrined Washington finally brought himself to admit the unlikelihood of masses of aroused recruits mushrooming his army. "We may expect soon to be reduced to the humiliating condition of seeing the cause of America, in America, upheld by foreign arms," he lamented. Then he learned of the blockade of the needed French shipping in Cadiz, sad indication that foreigners were unlikely to uphold the cause either. A successful offensive depended upon a French fleet and American militiamen—the fleet could not come and the citizen-soldiers would not. "The flattering prospect which seemed to be opening to our view in the month of May," he wrote, "is vanishing like the morning dew."[23]

Washington and Rochambeau met for the first time in September. The Frenchman, steeped in European ways of warring, thought establishing a base at Newport was achievement enough for one campaign. He planned to winter right where he was. The American came away from the conference understanding that

Rochambeau's loudly proclaimed subordination to him was so much window dressing, that it would apply only when French ends were served. He noted wryly, "My command of the French troops stands upon a very limited scale." The two commanders could agree only to concert their efforts for a conclusive campaign in 1781.[24]

A less-determined officer than Washington might have accepted what appeared to be the inevitable and have taken steps to shelter his men for the winter, but the commander-in-chief was not of that sort. Study as he might, he kept coming to one conclusion: "The affairs of this country absolutely require activity on whatever side they are viewed." Balked in the North, Washington began glancing hopefully southward. Following the fiasco at Camden, a subdued Congress meekly withdrew its finger from the strategic pie and turned all authority in the South over to the commander-in-chief. Washington lost no time in appointing a general who thought and fought like himself: Nathanael Greene. He also sought naval support, appealing in September directly to Admiral de Guichen, the commander of the French West Indies fleet. Having expected aid from France in 1780, he pointedly told the admiral, "great exertions have been made on our part for offensive operations." It was too late to strike New York, but might not a campaign farther south be productive? There was no response. On 31 October, after hearing the heartening news from North Carolina of the unexpected victory at King's Mountain, Washington called a council of war. He ordered the group of officers to respond to three questions: Should more reinforcements be sent south? Where should the Continental army spend the winter? When should it go into winter quarters? The council advised the general to send no more men to Greene, to take a winter position that would protect West Point, and to settle down immediately. On that third point he overrode the council's judgment. The tenacious commander intended to end the year with an attempt on New York—without the French.[25]

Everything Washington needed for an assault was at hand. Greene had collected it all for the proposed August attack. Initially, the general set the night of 5 December as the target date, but later apparently moved the time forward about ten days to a date in late November. After a feint at Staten Island, he planned to storm the defenses at Kingsbridge under cover of darkness. As at Trenton four years before, surprise and boldness would be his allies. Moving as inconspicuously as possible, the army shifted into position during the cold, wet November days. Then, at the very last moment, with all in readiness, word passed down from echelon to echelon suspending the operation. The attack would not take place. Purely by coincidence some British warships had come to anchor in a position that would have interfered with the American crossing. Fearing the loss of surprise, which had been his only trump card, Washington canceled the affair. Later he wrote:

> An earnest desire . . . of closing the campaign with some degree of eclat led me to investigate the means most thoroughly of doing it; and my wishes had so far got the better of my judgment that I had actually made some pretty considerable advances in the prosecution of a plan for this purpose when, alas! I found the means inadequate to the end.

Finally, even he recognized that history would record no great offensive that year in the North. Perhaps the depth of his disappointment is told by a gap in his voluminous correspondence, a break stretching from 30 November to 7 December. He put his army into quarters in an arc around West Point, deeply concerned lest weather as harsh as that of the preceding winter should destroy the spirit and health of his remaining veterans. "It would be well for the troops if, like chameleons, they could live upon air, or, like the bear, suck their paws for sustenance during the rigour of the approaching season."[26]

Still he was not ready to quit trying to get something started somewhere. Might not the winter provide a chance to bring pressure to bear on the foe in the South? Hearing that the Spanish were planning an expedition against Florida, the general eagerly suggested to Rochambeau that American and French troops could join the Spaniards and recover Georgia and South Carolina as well as Florida. More and more, disappointed with the stalemate in the

North, he was looking southward. Under escort of a Spanish fleet, the Virginian told the Frenchman, the allies could embark safely from Newport and Philadelphia. Rochambeau said no. Well, then, if he could not end the year on a grand high note, he would end it on a small high one. In the last days of December, he slipped special agents into New York in an attempt to kidnap Henry Clinton. Like all his other plans that year, the final one failed, too.[27]

Except for the turning of the calendar, there was hardly a break between 1780 and 1781. Benedict Arnold, wearing the bright red coat of a British brigadier, rode at the head of an invasion of Virginia in December, just three months after his treason had been discovered. Washington was furious when he learned what was happening—the detested traitor ravaging the Old Dominion, perhaps even burning Mount Vernon! He sent Lafayette and twelve hundred troops pounding overland to Virginia while he himself galloped to Newport to plead with Rochambeau to send warships to support Lafayette's operations against Arnold. A winter gale had scattered the British fleet blockading Newport, giving the French a temporary edge. They had sailed, Washington learned to his great joy, but soon lost heart en route and turned back. After some confusion, they headed out to sea again, but Admiral Arbuthnot, having regained his station, beat them back into Newport. The try to trap Arnold failed, but the snare was thereby baited for even larger game. The British had established a base in Virginia, which, like all English enclaves on the coast, could be isolated at any time by a French fleet, but, unlike bases farther south, this one was close enough to be reached by a swift move of the Continental army.

Arnold, after establishing a stronghold at Portsmouth, raided as far as Richmond, nearly capturing Governor Thomas Jefferson and successfully paralyzing the state. Jefferson and remnants of his government fled to Charlottesville, where Arnold's hard-riding detachments pursued and scattered them again. Jefferson escaped over the mountains, but his term expired and there was no government left to elect a new governor. Virginia lay prostrate and leaderless in the enemy's grip.

Reinforcing Lafayette, Washington sent more men under

Steuben and another contingent led by "Mad" Anthony Wayne. The Continental build-up in Virginia had begun.[28]

Meanwhile, unrelated events in Europe and the Carolinas were setting the stage for George Washington's long-sought, but long-elusive, grand effort.

Congress had sent Colonel John Laurens as a special emissary to Paris to press the American argument for the need of a superior fleet to operate against the British in North American waters. Benjamin Franklin introduced Laurens at court, where he forthrightly presented his case. As it happened, the French were interested in increasing their exertions anyway. The time was right. Holland was now a belligerent against Britain, the League of Armed Neutrality was hurting London, and the English seemed to be tiring of the war. The moment for a major effort had never been more propitious. Separate messages had also reached Paris from Rochambeau and Lafayette. Both of them urged sending the fleet Laurens was requesting. Louis XVI agreed to do it. In March, Admiral François Joseph Paul Comte de Grasse set out from Brest with 20 ships of the line, 3 frigates, and 150 other vessels. His orders were to sail for the Caribbean, from where he was to cooperate with Rochambeau and Washington. De Grasse was no d'Estaing. He would fight if he had the chance. The king also opened his purse, sending six million livres to permit the Continental army to take the field, the first of some sixteen million livres France would provide the United States that year.

Nathanael Greene, meanwhile, in a superb campaign which is itself a strategic classic, was shrewdly pushing Cornwallis out of the South. "Few generals," Greene reported, "[have] run oftener or more lustily than I have done. But I have taken care not to run too far, and commonly have run as fast forward as backward to convince our enemy that we were like a crab that could run either way." The Rhode Islander had been among the original proponents of a protracted war, and he had closely observed Washington's astute manipulation of the reins in 1776 and 1777. Now, with some modifications to adapt that strategy to conditions peculiar to the South, he demonstrated that he had learned well from watching the Virginian. Unlike most strategic operations of the Revolutionary War, Greene's southern campaign has been thoroughly documented by historians—and deservedly. It was magnificently done. Curiously, he never won a battle, but his defeats always cost the British more than they could afford to pay. Superior strategy led ultimately to victory despite tactical setbacks. Like Washington, Greene accepted battle willingly enough but, also like his mentor, never in situations where he could not withdraw from the fray. English officers who had fought in New York and New Jersey four years earlier might well have experienced an eerie sensation of having lived through all of this before. Perhaps they recognized in the exasperating Nathanael Greene a younger version of "the Old Fox"—especially as they watched the bleeding ulcer of attrition ruin their once strong and vigorous army. For a change, it was the British who were naked and starving as Cornwallis limped out of the Carolinas in April to join forces with those Arnold had brought to Virginia. Greene let him go and turned his attention to clearing South Carolina and Georgia, where partisan fighters were already making life miserable for British posts and patrols.

Cornwallis, receiving conflicting and confusing orders from both Henry Clinton in New York and Lord Germain in London, achieved very little in a series of clashes with Lafayette. The English general had neither a strategy for operations in Virginia nor even a good reason for being there. By August, he had withdrawn to a fortified base at Yorktown. When Henry Clinton had sailed from Charleston for New York in 1780, he had been optimistic but not unaware of a serious risk he was running: "I leave Lord Cornwallis here in sufficient force to keep [the South] against the world, without a superior fleet shews itself, in which case I despair of ever seeing peace restored to this miserable country." Cornwallis had squandered much of his "sufficient force" by August 1781, and "a superior fleet" was about to show itself.[29]

In the spring, of course, Washington could know neither that a powerful French fleet would arrive nor that Cornwallis would get himself bottled up in Virginia. The commander-in-chief warned Lafayette in April, as a matter of fact, that chances of his coming from New York to operate in the Virginia area were quite remote. In May, the general rode to Wethersfield, Connecticut, for a strategy session with Rochambeau, believing that New York would become the allied objective.

Rochambeau, in memoirs published after his death, recalled how Washington was so obsessed with New York that he could see no other objective. Washington, also trying to recollect events years later, said that was not so. He and Rochambeau had agreed, the Virginian remembered, to attack wherever success beckoned—be it New York or Virginia or Charleston. He did not plan to attack New York without a certainty of success, he claimed, but he was going to attack somewhere. A victory, "whether upon a larger or smaller scale," was absolutely necessary. The evidence tends to support the American.[30]

At Wethersfield, Rochambeau did not tell Washington about de Grasse. Their talks, then, were in the context of *possible* naval support, not *probable* assistance. Washington, disappointed so often, refused to build plans predicated on a fleet that might never show up. He and the French commander agreed on an offensive, with the target being either New York City or enemy forces in the South. At the end of May, a message from Laurens informed Washington of the departure of de Grasse. From then on, with some assurance of cooperation from a fleet, the commander-in-chief looked with more favor on a strike southward. He ordered supplies held in Virginia in preparation for possible operations there. Nevertheless, he continued to keep both options open, preparing also for the storming of New York.

Trying to follow the progression of Washington's thoughts that summer is to walk a maze. There is no doubt that he wanted to attack New York if it were feasible, but keeping that goal a secret was neither possible nor necessary. So he did not try. His intention of marching to Virginia as an alternative is also clear, but an operation of that sort would require strict secrecy lest the prey be frightened away. So he concealed all mention of the subject. He went to surprising lengths to convince everyone concerned of his single-minded determination to assault Manhattan, believing the British certainly would not fall for a deception plan unless the

Americans themselves were convinced of it. Obviously, the French had to be convinced, too. Unfortunately, historians have no certain method for screening spurious messages from the real, of discerning between plan and coverplan. About all that can be said, without much fear of contradiction, is that the American leader fully intended to attack *somewhere* in 1781.

Washington urged Rochambeau to shift his army secretly from Newport to New York for a surprise attempt to make a lodgement on Manhattan. While Continentals executed a feint from the west, French soldiers could grab a beachhead on the east of the island, the general reckoned. Rochambeau was slow in marching and the British were not surprised, so the scheme had to be abandoned after the armies were in motion. But the maneuver had left the allied forces in a position to attack New York—or, alternatively, to race to Virginia. It might be that both Washington and Rochambeau were playing the same game, that each had his eyes set more on Virginia than New York but dared not level with the other.

Washington's flexible intentions are perhaps best revealed in his messages to Lafayette. He wrote to the commander in Virginia on 13 July, telling him to gather as large a body of troops as possible, especially cavalry, and prepare for operations in either Virginia or South Carolina. Cornwallis, according to Washington's calculations, might occupy a strong position on the coast and send regiments to reinforce either New York or Charleston. Lafayette was also to establish a secure route of express communications between Virginia and Philadelphia. In a private letter sent on 30 July, Washington mentioned a complete change in previous plans should Cornwallis ship troops to New York. If New York should become too strongly defended, he wanted "to expel [the British] totally" from the South. Lafayette was to gather his forces wherever the British set up a base and to harass them if they tried to march to the Carolinas. On 14 August, Washington heard from de Grasse. The admiral announced his intention of being at the Chesapeake on 3 September and of remaining until mid-October. That settled matters. The decision was made. The South would be the scene of the great vigorous effort. Immediately, Washington sent a courier to de Grasse to let him know the Americans intended to fight. Should they find the English still in Virginia when they arrived, Washington wrote purposefully, the allies "ought, without loss of time, to attack the enemy with our united force." At the same time, he ordered Lafayette to prevent Cornwallis from leaving Yorktown in an attempt to escape to South Carolina. The Englishman was not to be permitted to slip out of the trap. Washington wanted a victory—a big victory.[31]

The very speed with which the combined armies moved indicates something less than a blind fixation on New York. The maneuver was not simple. Half the American forces would have to remain on the Hudson to keep pressure on Clinton in New York and to protect West Point, while the other half and all of the French would be required to shift nearly four hundred miles south to link up with other Continentals in Virginia for a rendezvous with a French fleet, which was then somewhere at sea. The coordination was inordinately complex. Within a week, the allied regiments were in motion. A well-executed feint at Staten Island sufficed to keep Clinton in the dark until Washington and Rochambeau reached Philadelphia. By then it was too late.

Because the troops had not been paid for some time, Washington did not know how they would behave around Congress. He rushed them through Philadelphia. Rochambeau, though, paused to march his men in a parade past the State House. Unsure just how an executiveless body fit into protocol arrangements, he instructed his officers "to salute Congress as a crowned head and the President as a first prince of the blood."[32]

No incident marred the involved move to the Chesapeake. De Grasse arrived right on schedule, bringing still more soldiers to add to those already with Washington and Rochambeau. Cornwallis was doomed. Benjamin Franklin later expressed the general astonishment that allied forces "should with such perfect concord be assembled from different places by land and water, form their junction punctually without the least regard for cross accidents of wind or weather or interruption from the enemy; and that the army which was their object should in the meantime have had the

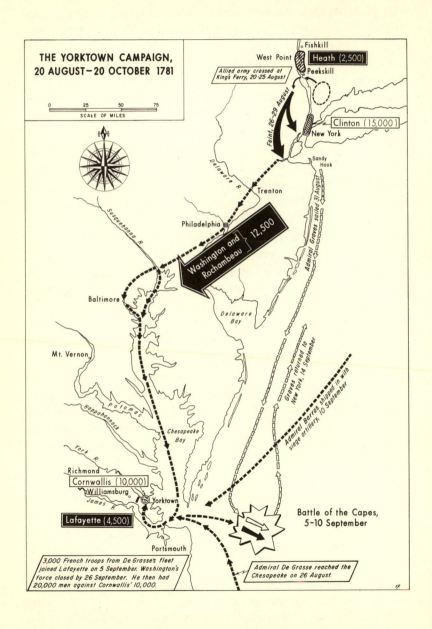

THE YORKTOWN CAMPAIGN,
20 AUGUST–20 OCTOBER 1781

SCALE OF MILES
0   25   50   75

Fishkill

West Point   Heath (2,500)

Allied army crossed at
King's Ferry, 20-25 August

Peekskill

Clinton (15,000)

New York

Sandy
Hook

Delaware R.

Trenton

Philadelphia

Washington and
Rochambeau   12,500

Admiral Graves sailed 31 August

Susquehanna R.

Baltimore

Delaware
Bay

Mt. Vernon

Graves returned to
New York, 14 September

Admiral Barras shipped in with
siege artillery, 10 September

Potomac

Rappahannock

Chesapeake
Bay

York R.

Richmond

Cornwallis (10,000)

Williamsburg

James R.

Yorktown

Lafayette (4,500)

Battle of the Capes,
5-10 September

Portsmouth

3,000 French troops from De Grasse's fleet
joined Lafayette on 5 September. Washington's
force closed by 26 September. He then had
20,000 men against Cornwallis' 10,000.

Admiral De Grasse reached the
Chesapeake on 26 August.

goodness to quit a situation from whence it might have escaped, and place itself in another from whence an escape was impossible."[33]

Yorktown was won at sea. French Admiral de Barras dashed from Newport with the necessary siege artillery and equipment stowed in his ships. The British set out in pursuit from New York. De Grasse, on learning of the approach of the English fleet, eagerly sortied to meet it. Although he ordinarily stood six feet two inches tall, it is said that de Grasse grew to six feet six inches at the prospect of a slugfest. While the two fleets were inconclusively pounding one another in the Battle of the Capes, from 5 to 10 September, de Barras slipped into Chesapeake Bay, sealing Cornwallis' fate. British warships returned helplessly to New York.

Nevertheless, Washington had no intention of leaving himself at the mercy of the whims or fears of the admiral of the French fleet. He carefully wrote out a series of questions for the commander of the foreign armada. The very first one asked de Grasse to specify the precise date he would be obliged to depart. And would he consider continuing the campaign to include the capture of Wilmington and Charleston? On 17 September, when Washington and Rochambeau met de Grasse for the first time, the American leader politely but pointedly handed over his list. The Frenchman promptly answered each query in writing. He committed himself to stay until the end of October, but he said further operations after Yorktown were probably out of the question. Satisfied that he would not be deserted, Washington initiated the investment of Yorktown, opening formal siege approaches on 6 October.[34]

It was well that the Virginian had been so prudent, for only one problem threatened to disrupt the otherwise splendid campaign. De Grasse, hoping for another crack at the opposing fleet and growing restless as preparations for the siege were in progress, suggested on 23 September that he might do more good off New York than as "an idle spectator" at Yorktown. Washington had a horrible vision of being left in the lurch again. He received the French recommendation with "painful anxiety." Yorktown was a sure thing only so long as the fleet maintained the blockade,

Washington cried. De Grasse simply must stay in order "to secure an important general good." The admiral acquiesced.[35]

Inexorably, the siege works squeezed the British defenses tighter and tighter. On 17 October, in celebration of the fourth anniversary of Burgoyne's surrender at Saratoga, American and French batteries delivered the heaviest cannonade yet. That night the British asked for terms. Cornwallis had been "Burgoyne'd." Allied casualties were in the neighborhood of three hundred, England's nearly ten thousand.

Yorktown stands high on the list of history's most decisive campaigns. It ended British attempts to subdue her thirteen rebellious colonies, assuring the independence of the United States of America. For four successive years, ever since marching out of Valley Forge, George Washington had been laboring with dogged persistence to put everything together in order to make one great vigorous effort to win the war. At long last he had done it. The result was precisely as decisive as he had predicted all along.

10

The Arts of Negotiation:

November 1781-

December 1783

In many ways, the two years between Yorktown and the official end of the war were more fraught with danger for the young American republic than any of the previous six. Having for all intents and purposes won their revolution, patriots came perilously close to throwing it all away.

Euphoria flooded the countryside following the capture of Cornwallis. The nation relaxed. Although the war had by no means ended, the major scenes of confrontation shifted away from the United States. The opening of negotiations in Paris added to the widespread sense of security by raising heady expectations of imminent peace. Relaxation was a natural reaction. After all, the bitter struggle had been interminably drawn out. Soldiers wanted to go home. State political leaders hoped to turn their attention to long-neglected local problems. People hungered for normalcy. The citizenry was manifestly tired of the prolonged conflict. Pressures for the dissolution of the nation's military establishment were all but irresistible. It took every bit of Washington's power and influence just to keep his army intact during the extended peace talks. What English generals had never been able to do

—destroy the Continental army—Americans very nearly let happen by default. It was true, as nearly everyone sensed, that the conflict had turned a decisive corner: Britain could probably not have won the American war in the years after Yorktown. The king's external foes were too numerous and his internal opposition too powerful. But Americans could well have forfeited the fruits of their victory—which they almost did. Some contend that George Washington's greatest achievement was holding everything together during that final trying period. They may be right.

Peace, like war, can be won or lost. The war was due to end, but the final form of peace would be molded by military actions in far-flung theaters ranging from the West Indies all the way around the globe to India. The thirteen colonies were fated to become a backwater of the contest, though not an unimportant theater at all. What happened in North America affected what happened elsewhere, and vice versa. Events everywhere were interrelated. Despite the virtual absence of fighting in the United States, the war had not gone away, and the goals for which patriots had sacrificed so much for so long, although at last within sight, were not yet attained. The future of the United States depended upon the activities of the Continental army. Washington's task was to bring patriot military power to bear in such a manner as to maintain and, if possible, to strengthen American bargaining power. Patriots, having won their war, set out to win their peace. Thus, the fourth phase of the Revolutionary War can be captioned "shaping the peace."

Immediately after Cornwallis surrendered, George Washington was not thinking of peace; the warrior instinct in him cried for more war. He had torn one arm from the enemy at Yorktown; now he wanted to go for another. On 6 October, the very day he opened the Yorktown siege, Washington gave Lieutenant Colonel Lewis Morris a message to memorize. To be spoken only into the ear of Nathanael Greene, the words were too sensitive to be written down. The commander-in-chief was already anticipating another blow. He intended to send the Pennsylvania, Maryland, and Virginia lines to Greene right after Yorktown fell. All the cavalry he could mount would go as well. He would try to get the French fleet to assist, but he cautioned Greene not to count on it. Further, if Rochambeau could be talked into joining him, Washington would personally lead the combined armies to South Carolina. He was after greater game than the single enclave at Yorktown.[1]

When beaten British and German units marched out of York-town on 20 October to stack arms in surrender, Washington wasted no time in savoring one victory at the expense of the next. He wrote that same day to de Grasse, urging the admiral to support an operation against Charleston. "It rarely happens that such a com-bination of means as are in our hands at present can be seasonably obtained by the most strenuous of human exertions," he correctly observed. Having waited so long for the chance to work with a fleet, the general could not bear the idea of failing to exploit the marvelous opportunity. If not Charleston, then how about Wilmington? Or, at the very least, would de Grasse just ferry American troops and equipment southward? Next day, Washing-ton visited the admiral aboard his mammoth 110-gun flagship, *Ville de Paris*, where he personally pursued his request. However, the old salt had found no excitement in besieging fortifications. He had his eye cocked on the West Indies where a British squadron roamed. Prospects of battle at sea made him deaf to American entreaties for another campaign on land. He agreed only to trans-port two thousand Continentals to Wilmington, if they could be ready to depart on 1 November. But the eager admiral could not contain himself even that long. A few days later he told Lafayette to try to explain to Washington as best he could—and left. The American, biting his tongue, sent a diplomatic note thanking the Frenchman for his help during the Yorktown campaign and im-ploring him to return the next year for a similar purpose. Neverthe-less, he was angered. If de Grasse had cooperated, he lectured Lafayette, there was not a doubt "upon any man's mind of the total extirpation of the British force in the Carolinas and Georgia."[2]

With the campaign closed by the departure of the French fleet, as well as by Rochambeau's subsequent decision to go into winter quarters in Virginia, Washington turned his mind to the next year. He sent southward the reinforcements he had promised Nathanael Greene and started the long journey north to rejoin those forces he had left guarding the Hudson. New York was still the strategic center of operations, so his place was there. Stopping at Mount Vernon—his stepson had just died—the general briefed Lafayette in preparation for the young Frenchman's return to Paris. Lafayette would be listened to by the court. "A constant naval force would terminate the war speedily," Washington told his close friend, emphasizing the word "constant." It could operate from June to September in the North and during all other months in the South. The success of the next campaign, the American emphasized, "must depend *absolutely* upon the naval force which is employed in these seas, and the time of its appearance next year. No land force can act decisively unless it is accompanied by a maritime superiority." The British had been sorely weakened by their loss at Yorktown, and Washington clearly wanted to take advantage of the opportunity to annihilate the remaining garrisons.[3]

Already, though, the commander-in-chief was detecting worrisome signs abroad in the land. All too many of his countrymen were talking as if the war were at an end, an end he could not see at all. If pursued vigorously, he admonished in mid-November, the victory at Yorktown could "be productive of much good . . . but if it should be the means of relaxation and sink us into supineness and security it had better not have happened." He was going to Philadelphia, he told Nathanael Greene, where he would "attempt to stimulate Congress to [capitalize on Yorktown] by taking the most vigorous and effectual measures to be ready for an early and decisive campaign the next year. My greatest fear is that Congress, viewing this stroke in too important a point of light, may think our work too nearly closed and will fall into a state of langour and relaxation." When he reached Philadelphia, he learned that his worst fears were true. Ecstatic citizens were celebrating the end of the war—two years prematurely.[4]

In retrospect, it is rather too easy to criticize Washington for not recognizing straightway that Yorktown had finally given the English a bellyful of the American war. We now know what was to be the eventual outcome—king and cabinet agreeing to write off their thirteen former colonies. To have a better view of events, however, one needs inquire not into the final but the initial reaction in London. Washington, it turns out, was quite justified in believing the war would continue, for decision makers in the enemy capital thought so, too.

When word of Yorktown reached England, Lord North, predictably enough, tried to resign. Even Germain, whose incredibly bad management had led to both Saratoga and Yorktown, saw that chances for military victory in the colonies had disappeared. George III, however, reacted with that tenacity which makes the bulldog a more recognized symbol of England than the lion. The war would continue, he stubbornly insisted, "though the mode of it may require alteration." Dutifully, Germain drafted new instructions for his majesty's forces in America. They were to remain strictly on the defensive ashore, with no inland operations permitted. The navy would carry the burden of the new effort by closing American ports and interdicting trade. Redcoats and Tories would assist the navy in distressing the patriots by conducting raids along the coast. In the end, Great Britain turned to the first strategy proposed back in 1775—naval blockade—but it was too late. While those revised instructions were crossing the Atlantic, Lord North was struggling vainly against a rising tide of resistance in Parliament.[5]

Perhaps the king could have pulled it off if Yorktown had been the only dark news. Although his support had been dwindling for some time, he could still muster a majority of forty-one in the House of Commons in December. Then came the deluge. Operating boldly in the West Indies, French seaborne forces captured a string of valuable islands, including St. Eustatius, Nevis, Montserrat, and St. Kitts. They threatened Jamaica. De Grasse had found his excitement. Elsewhere, the fall of Minorca and West Florida deepened the gloom in London. The North ministry could not withstand the mounting pressure. Its support dropped to a margin of just nineteen votes early in January. George III accepted Germain's resignation on 11 February, but even by ridding himself of the albatross of the "ghost of Minden" the king could not stall his opposition. A motion to abandon all attempts to coerce the colonists failed by a single vote on 22 February; the same resolution passed easily just days later. For the first time, Parliament had acted to stop the war against the colonists. The ministry resigned, and the king himself considered abdication.

Upon more sober reflection, George III did not take that drastic step, but he was compelled to accept an opposition ministry led by the Marquis of Rockingham. The new government was dedicated to reconciliation with America. Rockingham's policy was to pursue the war against Britain's European enemies while striving somehow to persuade Americans to accept a union with Britain somewhere short of full independence. Accordingly, revised orders went out to English generals in America.

Henry Clinton returned to England under a cheerless cloud after a stay in America that had begun with Bunker Hill. Guy Carleton came down from Canada to replace him as commander of all British forces. Carleton's instructions were the kind to make a professional soldier choke; they prohibited him from engaging the patriots in any fashion, even from defending himself in event of a major attack. He was to capitulate rather than resist. If he could work out an arrangement with Washington, he was to withdraw the bulk of his men from the United States for duty in other theaters. Carleton's conciliatory action at the front paralleled a similar diplomatic offensive in Paris. British agents contacted rebel representatives there, ostensibly opening peace negotiations but really trying to foster better Anglo-American relations while attempting to split the patriots away from their French allies. The English had some success in Paris but none at all in America where a suspicious George Washington stubbornly refused to ease the military pressure on Carleton one bit.

Nothing was further from the Virginian's mind than an under-the-table deal with his foe. The war, so far as he was concerned, could not terminate until its goals were achieved, and England had in no way indicated a willingness to accept either the territorial claims or the independence of the United States. At first he was convinced that "the enemy intend to prosecute the war vigorously," especially in the West, which would "serve to establish and secure their claim to the extended limits of Canada." To counter that threat, he contemplated sending an expedition to seize

Detroit, or, at the very least, throwing a sufficient force beyond the mountains to stop hostile advances. Those were his thoughts in February. Later, learning of the change of government in England, he paused in his planning. The nature of American operations, he said, "must depend greatly on the views of the enemy and the particular mode of war which they shall in future adopt." His opinion of what the British would do was precisely on the mark —he guessed they would cease all operations in the South, hold one or more bases, and "take up the desultory naval war." The contemplative American leader told Nathanael Greene, still in the South, to content himself for the time being with "confining the enemy to their lines, and preventing them from carrying their ravages into the country." Although he was waiting to see what path the conflict would take, Washington forecast no early end to it. "I confess to you candidly," he wrote his wife's brother, "that I see very little prospect of the war ending with this campaign."[6]

As it gradually became evident that royal forces meant only to sit tight, that they would likely neither attack nor depart, Washington began to analyze his chances of striking them somewhere. Fortunately for Carleton, the American never learned of London's instructions to surrender if attacked. New York City, the general informed the secretary at war, could be cracked only if a French fleet participated, if Rochambeau could send some five or six thousand soldiers, and if the Continental army could be augmented by another ten thousand men. A campaign in the South also required a fleet, "without which it is folly even to think of one." Bermuda was a candidate for a raid, and Halifax was a possibility, if no other objective appeared feasible. But it was the old magnet Canada that drew Washington's attention most strongly. All other objectives would require support from a fleet, which patriots could not control. The northern province could be won, Washington thought, in just two campaigns, with an invasion force marching either by way of the Great Lakes or straight north over the well-trod Lake Champlain route. Besides expanding the limits of the United States, the Virginian reckoned, the proposed expedition would subdue "all the Northern and Western Indians," restoring peace on the frontier all the way from the Bay of Fundy to the backwoods of North Carolina. Moreover, invading Canada would cost no more than protecting the extensive frontier against Indian depredations over a prolonged period of time. Defense was an annual expense, the commander-in-chief explained, while attack would put "the axe to the root, would remove the cause, and make a radical cure." That, of course, would also mean an end to any worry over British "intriguing after peace shall be established." Furthermore, it "would at once develop the mysterious conduct of the people of Vermont," who were threatening to align themselves with the Canadians. Last, there was the matter of money: Canada's business, especially the lucrative fur trade, would be a boon to the economy of the United States. Washington figured he could take Canada by starting in September with only eight thousand men.[7]

It was just as well that the general was thinking again of operating without assistance from a fleet. Admiral de Grasse, after a series of victories, went down to defeat in a climactic encounter off Saints Passage in April 1782. De Grasse himself was captured. That defeat ended the period of French naval predominance in American waters and virtually eliminated any hope of another combined campaign like Yorktown. Washington's reaction to the loss is evidence of his keen awareness of the variegated shadings of this phase of the war. Militarily, of course, it robbed the allies of flexibility. Rochambeau had been holding his army in Virginia, a central location from which he could march quickly either to New York or Charleston, wherever de Grasse might show. Now there was no chance of an allied assault against either base, Washington informed his subordinates. But all was not black. To the secretary of foreign affairs he wrote, with remarkable insight, that the British victory at sea might even draw peace nearer! For the first time in a long while, he said, England had a distinct advantage. The king could bargain now from a position of relative strength. If Americans remained strong and ready, London might see this as the moment for opening serious negotiations.[8]

Throughout summer 1782, the American commander walked gingerly through the confusing maze that he termed "concilitary war." Carleton tried in every way he could think of to convince his opponent that, so far as the British were concerned, "all hostilities stand suspended." But Washington remained skeptical. When he asked Carleton to provide passage for the return to Charleston of several South Carolina refugees—a normal humanitarian act typical of eighteenth-century warfare—the Englishman responded with an alacrity serving only to raise American eyebrows. His rapid and full agreement, the commander-in-chief puzzled, "strikes me in a very disagreeable light." When the Englishman suggested exchanging captured American seamen for British soldiers, the doubting Virginian saw behind the plan a veiled attempt to strengthen royal units fighting in the West Indies, which, he cautioned Congress, would be nearly the same as employing the returned soldiers in America itself. Besides, English warships under Admiral Robert Digby were aggressively blockading American ports, and General Frederick Haldimand, in Canada, was energetically stirring up strife on the American frontiers. Both actions bothered Washington. He was so concerned with Haldimand's operations, in fact, that he took a hurried trip north in July to examine the upper Hudson and the Mohawk River areas, thinking that theater might once again become a scene of active war. The patriot leader insisted on holding Carleton responsible for all warlike acts, on land or sea, by regulars or Tories or Indians.[9]

At midsummer Washington still read duplicity into Britain's pacific overtures. "Sir Guy Carleton is using every art to soothe and lull our people into a state of security," he claimed, quite correctly, of course. Of the "line of conduct pursued by the different commanders," he wrote sarcastically:

> Sir Guy gives strong assurances of the pacific disposition of his most gracious Majesty, by land. Sir (that is to be) Digby gives proofs . . . of his most gracious Majesty's good intention of capturing everything that floats on the face of the waters. . . . To an American, whose genius is not susceptable of refined ideas, there would appear some little inconsistency in all this; but, to the enlarged and comprehensive mind of a Briton, these things are perfectly reconcilable.

Nevertheless, the general did cancel an expedition against Indians in western Pennsylvania on grounds that they were relatively quiet and that he believed Carleton was actually trying to restrain them. Nor could he refrain from gloating over the discomfiture caused New York Tories by Carleton's persistence in talking of peace. "[They] are little better than a medley of confused, enraged, and dejected people. Some are swearing and some crying; while the greater part of them are almost speechless."[10]

On 2 August, Carleton sent his American counterpart a message reporting on the favorable progress of peace talks in Paris, adding his own belief that prospects for an armistice were good. Washington, informing Nathanael Greene of developments, remained unconvinced. "I confess I am induced to doubt everything, to suspect everything." He could not rid his mind of the former "duplicity and perverse system of British policy." However, he could not deny the mounting evidence, such as the British evacuation of all bases in the South except Charleston. Unless the English were blatantly lying, he wrote James McHenry, "we are now advanced to that critical and awful period when our hands are to be tried at the arts of Negotiation."[11]

Caution should be the American watchword, Washington warned. Even if the British were sincere, peace talks could still fail. What is more, he said, if the Rockingham ministry meant to offer no more than the "independence" given to Ireland, the war would definitely continue. Regardless, the Continental army would have to remain ready: "Nothing will hasten peace more than to be in a condition for war."

Then, a thunderclap! With even the ever-pessimistic Virginian talking guardedly of peace, shocking news crossed the ocean. The Marquis of Rockingham had died suddenly on 1 July, being replaced by the Earl of Shelburne. Shelburne was known to be no friend of Americans, no supporter of independence. Making matters worse was a resurgence of British fortune. After trouncing de Grasse in April, the Royal Navy had won several other key clashes, putting England in a powerful bargaining position. Worst of all, perhaps, was painful evidence of double-dealing on the part of France and Spain. The two Bourbon kingdoms were combining to thwart patriot aspirations to expansion. England was once more in a position—and in a mood—to be less generous in responding to colonial demands for territory and independence, while America's recent allies were becoming, at the very best, friendly foes. It was fortunate that George Washington had not relaxed his guard.

"Our prospect of peace is vanishing," the commander-in-chief concluded glumly. "That the king will push the war as long as the nation will find men or money admits not of a doubt in my mind. . . . If we are wise, let us prepare for the worst; there is nothing which will so soon produce a speedy and honorable peace as a state of preparation for war, and we must either do this or lay our account for a patched up, inglorious peace after all the toil, blood, and treasure we have spent." Writing to the secretary of foreign affairs, Washington predicted the negotiations would be "spun out to a considerable length" or else they might be broken off altogether. "In the meantime it will be our policy to proceed as if no negotiations were on foot." Writing to Greene in September, the general quoted Benjamin Franklin: the British were "unable to carry on the war and too proud to make peace." Then he penned a letter to Franklin, telling him how the year that had opened with such high hopes was closing with a question mark. "We are now beginning again to reflect upon the persevering obstinacy of the King, the wickedness of his Ministry, and the haughty pride of the nation, which ideas recall to our minds very disagreeable prospects, and a probable continuance of our present trouble."[12]

Once again, the commander-in-chief took stock of his military options. It was too late that year to do anything effective, but he put events in train for 1783. As always in the past, his primary aim was to drive the enemy out of New York. He ordered Greene to start troops on the long trek north from the Carolinas because he expected the British soon to evacuate Charleston, their only remaining base on American soil outside New York, and also because there would be no more foreign help. The French fleet had been removed from the scene, and the army was removing itself. Rochambeau marched his troops from Virginia to Boston that fall, where he embarked for the West Indies. The patriots were on their own again. Washington, standing at West Point with an army small but more efficient than ever, watched New York like a spider watching a fly; if Carleton sent reinforcements to the Caribbean and should leave too weak a garrison, he planned to descend swiftly upon the city. And, in the event none of his New York schemes panned out, there was always Canada. He instructed Brigadier General William Irving, commander of the western department, to lay in provisions for a campaign by way of Lake Erie, and he took other steps to insure a passage beyond Fort Ticonderoga.[13]

But there were to be no more campaigns. Despite Shelburne's staunch anti-American sentiments, the very momentum of events made a peace of some description inevitable. England was weary to the bone of the long, unpopular, and largely unsuccessful war. The time to quit was at hand. Thomas Paine, pondering those strange days that seemed suspended in some never-never land between war and peace, concluded correctly that the conflict was drawing to a close. Since a growing number of modern scholars have turned to plumbing the reasons why nations terminate wars, Paine's unusual but very perceptive thoughts merit repeating.

I fully believe we have seen our worst days over. . . . I draw this opinion from the peculiar effect which certain periods of time have more or less on all men. The British have accustomed themselves to think of the term of seven years in a manner different to other periods of time. They acquire this partly by habit, by religion, by reason, and by superstition. They serve seven years apprenticeship; they elect their Parliament for seven years; they punish by seven years transportation, or the duplicate or triplicate of that term; their leases run in the same manner; and they read that Jacob served seven years for one wife and seven years for another; and the same term likewise extinguishes all obligations (in certain areas) of debt or matrimony; and thus, this particular period, by a variety of concurrences, has obtained an influence in their minds superior to that of any other number.

They have now had seven years war, and are not an inch farther on the Continent than when they began. The superstitious and the populous part will conclude that it is *not to be*; and the reasonable part will think they have tried an unsuccessful scheme long enough, and that it is in vain to try it any longer.

Paine might also have mentioned the interesting coincidence of the date of the formation of a new ministry bent on peace—seven years to the month after the clash between redcoat and minuteman on Lexington Green.[14]

Whether weary of war or not, though, king and cabinet were not about to cut everything loose and run. Fortunes, reputations, and sometimes even kingdoms stood to be gained or sacrificed in the give and take of the negotiating table. It was not unusual for skilled diplomats to win in bargaining what generals had been unable to win in battle. That did not mean military actions diminished in importance as nations negotiated—contrarily, they often became more significant. Thus, those battles fought after Yorktown were in many ways far more important than earlier and better known engagements. All of the European antagonists accepted this fact; not every American leader even understood it. Fortunately, Washington was one of the handful who did.

In the end, the patriots emerged victorious from the prolonged negotiations. Of all the belligerents in the war, only the United States had held firm objectives from which it had steadfastly refused to budge. And, in one of the conflict's supreme ironies, America's "militia diplomats," with aged Benjamin Franklin spearheading the attack, turned the duplicity of European politicians to advantage, brilliantly playing one off against the other. On 30 November 1782, while Washington was looking for an opening to attack New York, American and British representatives in Paris signed a preliminary treaty of peace. When Parliament heard the terms granted to the revolutionaries, it was shocked—independence *and* generous territorial concessions! Shelburne was voted out of office for conceding too much, but events had progressed too far to be retrieved by the successor government. On 20 January 1783, faced with the surprising American diplomatic fait accompli, the other powers agreed to a general armistice. The fighting was over, barring an unlikely breakdown in the final negotiations. Nothing remained now but to await an agreement on the wording for a definitive treaty.

Nothing indeed! How curious those words might sound to a Continental soldier brought back to life to hear how most military histories treat his war. His ordeal had by no means ended. On 23 December 1782, Congress learned of England's willingness to treat on the basis of American independence. It would be a full year before Washington could safely resign his commission, twelve agonizing months in which the revolution, having triumphed, had to be prevented from consuming itself. In a frightening way, the war's final year was the one that came closest to seeing the failure of the revolution.

Mount Vernon was never far from Washington's thoughts. Throughout the war, he dreamed of the beauty and tranquillity of his plantation on the Potomac. Now, for the first time in nearly eight years, the international situation seemed calm enough to permit him to spend some of the winter months there. He bubbled joyously as he contemplated relaxing at his own hearth rather than in some borrowed house near a dreary Continental encampment. But it was not to be. When time came to leave headquarters, he could not, he dared not.

"The temper of the Army is much soured," he wrote on 14 December 1782, "and has become more irritable than at any period since the commencement of the war." It was not just the men who so worried the commander-in-chief; they were usually restless, and mutinous flare-ups from time to time were more or less expected. This time it was different—and more dangerous. The new, ugly mood of the Continental army originated with "combinations among the officers," who always before had "stood between the lower order of the soldiery and the public."[15]

The rebellion within a rebellion had been building ever since the great victory at Yorktown. Its causes were part economic, part political, and part psychological.

The first is easily explained: Congress was broke. Members had been obliged to assess themselves a dollar each just to pay the expenses of the rider bearing the news of Yorktown. France, after sending such generous aid in 1781, announced a sudden end to her largesse, forcing Americans to raise their own funds. Congress, though, had no way to tax. Under the Articles of Confederation, that was a right belonging to the states. Congress could only levy assessments against the various state governments and hope they would meet them. But the states, never reliable to begin with, simply stopped trying after Yorktown. By 1 June 1782, their total contributions for the year amounted to about $20,000, which was enough for just one day's operation of the Continental establishment. By September, even after impassioned pleas for support, Congress had gathered but $125,000 of a required $6 million. Soldiers went unpaid. So did congressmen, for that matter, but they were able to get along. Many delegates simply went home—a privilege called desertion in the army—leaving Congress often unable to do business for lack of a quorum. Some found sponsors. Haym Salomon, a Polish Jew who had emigrated to America shortly before the outbreak of war, personally paid the bills of several congressmen, including James Madison. Fortunately, though Americans seemed perversely unwilling to finance their own ship of state, the fledgling nation was not set completely adrift by European statesmen. Loans from Holland helped, and Benjamin Franklin wheedled yet another advance from Louis XVI. "Our people certainly ought to do more for themselves," the sage wrote acidly as he forwarded the money. "It is absurd the pretending to be lovers of liberty while they grudge paying for the defense of it." But those foreign gifts merely postponed the moment of crisis. The financial crunch came to a head when the paymaster of the Continental army ceased to function for lack of funds. Congress could afford neither to maintain the army nor to reduce it. There was no money to pay forces that were not needed, nor was there any to pay up what was owed to those who would be leaving. The men could not in conscience be turned out destitute, could not with safety be released without being given their back pay. They would rebel. Fielding an army without money had been difficult; disbanding one without it would be dangerous.

Politically, the story is rather more sordid. Economic agonies could be traced to excess demands on short dollars or, at worst, to ineptness and indifference; political problems, on the other hand, sprang from raw maneuvering for personal power quite to the detriment of the ideals of liberty and democracy for which the revolution had been waged. There were those, justifiably upset with the demonstrated impotence of Congress, who wanted to establish a stronger form of government. Their goal was hardly improper; in truth, it was quite valid. The Constitutional Convention of a few years later was called for that very purpose. It was in the means selected to achieve that desirable end where many of them skirted the precipice of disaster, threatening to plunge the United States into internal war. Some saw the army as a useful instrument for oppressing civil government. Not a few believed a military dictatorship would be an appropriate antidote to the ills of the United States, while still others actually contemplated the establishment of an American monarchy. Such ominous talk was rife in officers' huts during the winter of 1782-1783, much of it planted and encouraged by outsiders, including some congressmen.

Perhaps the saddest reason for unrest, and in several respects the most difficult to combat, was the psychological. The average American had not been so well off in years. Farms were producing bountifully, trade was increasing, business beginning to boom, armies no longer ravaged the countryside, militiamen heard fewer calls to arms to take them away from their work. The people had plenty—which made the poverty of the army hard to comprehend, impossible to accept. Men who had given many of their most productive years, who had risked their lives, who had endured terrible conditions, were men not likely to appreciate the success and ease of those who seemingly had sacrificed nothing. As the officers stated it in a petition to Congress, "Shadows have been offered to us while the substance has been gleaned by others." The way the army saw things, the country was acting most ungratefully. For all their blood and sweat, Continental veterans were receiving neither recognition nor reward. That hurt—deeply.

Who can say what would have followed had the Continental army turned upon the Continental Congress? The very thought is too painful to contemplate. And yet it could easily have happened;

a body of soldiers acting without officer leadership did in fact chase Congress from Philadelphia in 1783. The War of Independence certainly would not have passed into history as the only revolution to devour itself. At the very least, the ground would have been cut from under American negotiators in Paris, with devastating results. However Americans might have sorted out their differences, the geographical limits of the United States would very likely have been curtailed drastically, and the ideal of independence would surely have been lost altogether for all too many patriots.

Only George Washington had the prestige and influence to keep the restive army in hand. His successful suppression of the budding rebellion among the officers is well chronicled. His actions, culminating in the dramatic Newburgh address, may have kept the Revolutionary War from degenerating into a civil war. In a marvelous display of personal leadership, he prevented penury, intrigue, and self-pity from destroying the army—which is probably to say, the nation itself. Having been rudder and keel and mainsail through the long, rough voyage, he was a firm anchor in the final storm.[16]

With that last, dangerous winter safely behind him, Washington received heartwarming news in the spring. It came first in a polite dispatch from the British. Carleton told him in early April of the general armistice signed in January. Pending official word from Congress, the general promptly ordered his outposts "to suspend all acts of hostilities." On 14 April, he let a British messenger pass through Continental lines to carry word to General Haldimand in Canada. On his own, to speed communications, the American commander sent word by Indian runner directly to the English officer commanding at Niagara, telling him of the cease-fire and urging him to keep Indians off the warpath. Recent events had indicated the likelihood of another round of brutal warfare on the frontier. Still Washington did not announce the treaty to his own men. He wanted to hear it from Congress first. Then, when official word finally arrived, he waited a little longer for the most appropriate day he could think of. With a fine flair for the dramatic, he had the announcement "publicly proclaimed" right at noon on 19

April 1783, the eighth anniversary of Lexington and Concord. Every man received an extra ration of liquor to join the general in a toast wishing "perpetual peace, independence, and happiness to the United States of America."

Although victory loosed in the nation a sincere wave of elation and relief, the next months were not necessarily easy ones for soldiers. Until Carleton evacuated New York, which would not be until completion of the definitive treaty, the army's job would not be done. A small, ready force would have to remain to prevent English or Loyalist opportunism and to hedge against a possible resurgence of the war. That presented Americans a most difficult dilemma. The military establishment was much too large and Congress much too poor. The government still could afford neither to retain nor reduce its army. As the secretary of the board of war told Steuben, "The difficulty which heretofore oppressed us was how to raise an army. The one which now embarrasses us is how to dissolve it." Yet the moment could be delayed no longer. The army had to be disbanded. An unhappy but pragmatic Washington found the answer. He released most of his men on furloughs, which ostensibly permitted him to recall them in event fighting flared again but which was really a way to reduce the army without having to produce severance pay. Washington preferred to see injustice done to his faithful followers if the alternative were to trample the civil government. Perhaps he had learned that Cromwell's New Model Army had become disloyal only after Parliament had tried to dismiss it without pay. From first to last, he was not a Cromwell. Most of the Continentals marched home, never to receive the money due them. Their homecoming was not particularly joyful; many citizens looked upon the returning veterans with resentment rather than the respect the soldiers had expected. A few were even mobbed. Later the country would express gratitude, but not then. The war had been too long and too bitter. Those who remained in ranks were consolidated at West Point to await the British departure.

Washington was too active a person to sit around idly and too responsible an officer to leave his men before their work was done. He looked for a way to use his diminished forces. Eight years of constantly searching for a course to achieve his nation's goals had left the habit imprinted on his mind; the war's final year was no different in that regard. Before learning of the armistice, he had recommended making "one great and decisive effort to expel the enemy from their remaining possessions in the United States." After the cease-fire, he shifted his thinking westward. In July, he journeyed to Albany for a closer look at frontier events.[17] Concerned by some of the reports he heard, he sent Steuben on an inspection tour of posts in the West and ordered Robert Howe to be ready to take four hundred to five hundred men to occupy the British forts as soon as they were evacuated.[18]

As a matter of fact, the general had never let his attention stray for very long from the beckoning land over the mountains. Even in the midst of the crucial events of 1781, he had continued to push campaigns aimed at reducing the threat posed by hostile tribes. Preparing for an offensive into the West, he had begun cutting a road early in 1782 from Fort Pitt to Niagara. Although George Rogers Clark's destruction of Chillicothe in Ohio on 10 November 1782 was the war's final clash beyond the mountains, Washington asked Congress to authorize one last campaign against the Indian nations in 1783. Right up until the moment peace was actually declared, the future shape of the new nation held the Virginian's abiding interest. As it turned out, few of the commander-in-chief's aggressive plans made during those final two years ever came to fruition. It was for want of means, though—not desire.

After Yorktown, preserving the Continental army had once again become more important than defeating the enemy army. Offensive operations would be undertaken, Washington had informed his lieutenants, only when patriots had a "moral certainty of succeeding." Nonetheless, it would be inaccurate to picture him acting defensively, incorrect to portray him behaving passively. Achieving the national goals, particularly territorial aggrandizement, obliged him to keep pressure on the enemy in New York while trying to extend American sway wherever he could. The arts of negotiation, as the commander-in-chief well understood, do not permit one to break stride near the finish line. For the most part, the military weakness of a small nation, tired of war and weak of purse, frustrated his efforts in this final phase. But, by keeping an army together and exerting constant, albeit light, pressure on the enemy, he helped assure a favorable settlement.[19]

The final treaty was signed in Paris on 3 September 1783. Its first article stated: "His Britannic Majesty acknowledges the said United States . . . to be free, sovereign and independent." The goal of independence had been attained. The second article specified the new nation's boundaries, the third acknowledged American rights to the Great Banks fishing grounds, and the eighth guaranteed free navigation of the Mississippi. In all the accords on territory, the United States fell short in only two areas of getting everything it had ever hoped for: Florida went to Spain while Canada remained in English hands. Florida was no great loss, in American eyes, but the failure to win Canada represented less than complete achievement of the second patriot war aim, territorial expansion. That was a galling disappointment, especially because the preliminary treaty had ceded much of Ontario to the United States while the final agreement did not. Even so, Americans emerged with more than they could have reasonably expected. They had not occupied Canada, so they could make no valid claim to it. On the other hand, much of the land between the Appalachians and the Mississippi was still contested at war's end. Both London and Madrid had claims there—which were neither frivolous nor indifferently pressed. Spain, in particular, had worked to exclude the patriots from the Mississippi valley. That all of the West went to the United States was by no means a foreordained result of the negotiations. Beyond question, the patriots came out ahead. Firmness after Yorktown, at both the fighting front and the truce table, had won much for America.[20]

Not until a ship traversed the Atlantic could Washington and Carleton learn that they had been at peace for weeks. The Englishman lost no time in folding his tents, sailing in late November. Washington promptly rode into New York, the city he had been forced from in 1776 and which he had striven ever since to retake, signifying the completeness of his victory. After a tearful farewell party at Fraunces' Tavern, he left the Continental army. Stopping at Annapolis, where Congress was meeting, the general surrendered his commission. Only one of the members then in attendance had been present when it had been given to him in June 1775. Nothing the Continental Congress had ever done had been more fortunate than bestowing the rank of commander-in-chief on the Virginian—unless it would be the keeping of him in that position. That final duty done, George Washington, esquire, spurred away for Mount Vernon, reaching his home on the Potomac in time for Christmas.

Conclusion

A modern biographer has said Washington's "strategy was a Darwinian achievement of adaptation to environment; it was evolved to overcome the specific problems with which he was faced." In a sense, that is a very incisive observation—but it is also quite misleading. Darwinian adaptation implies a more-or-less unreasoning, malleable reaction to outside forces and pressures in order to survive, a process leading to a higher, more developed stage. Certainly Washington was malleable; that he learned from his encounters is well known. And he obviously responded to pressures exerted by his opponents. War is, after all, a violent dialogue wherein neither actor can ignore the lines of the other. But he did not merely react; he was an innovator as well.[1]

A general always has two aims: to defeat the enemy and to avoid his own defeat. Sometimes the two are synonymous, sometimes not. Winning is not the same as not losing. At first glance, that distinction may seem contrived, but it is not. It is very real and very significant. A skilled strategist derives his primary purpose from an analysis of whatever situation prevails at any given moment and the integration of that analysis with long-range or national goals. In the Revolutionary War, there were times crying for victory and others demanding avoidance of defeat. The watchword some days was audacity; on others it was take care. Washington seemed always to know the difference.

Consider the conflict's four phases. Each was unique, providing its own special array of forces, objectives, terrain, and political considerations, its own logic and grammar. One might even venture to say that each was almost a separate war. America's two national aims—independence and expansion—never varied, but the strategy required to achieve them changed radically from phase to phase.

During the initial period, when the revolutionaries stood outside the law and only a handful of English troops supported royal governments in the colonies, winning was all-important. Patriots were impelled by opportunity to "run all risques" to beat the enemy. Victory was everything, defeat of little consequence because the rebels had so little to lose. Washington attacked at every conceivable turn, taking the strategic offensive to the full extent of his limited powers.

With the advent of the next phase, however, a wholly different situation confronted Americans. Overnight, enemy strength became overwhelming, virtually precluding any patriot hopes of winning an encounter. What was more, revolutionary governments held sway in thirteen colonies, all responding to a Continental Congress which had boldly declared the birth of the United States of America. The rebellion itself was over. Now there were shores to defend, a foreign aggressor to repel, a nation to keep or lose. However, with winning all but impossible and defeat a distinct likelihood, not losing became the foremost goal of the Continental army. Yet, if the revolution were not to be forfeited, the new nation had no alternative but to defend itself. Presented with that painful "choice of difficulties," Washington turned cautious, not refusing battle altogether, and occasionally even precipitating one, but always fighting with his wagons hitched and facing the rear. The strategic defense chosen by "the Old Fox" was designed to defend the United States, to be sure, but its primary purpose was to avoid a decisive defeat of the Continental army.

The third act was totally unlike either of the first two. No longer was the conflict a family spat between the thirteen colonies and the mother country. It became a worldwide war. With the entry of France—and later Spain and Holland—Britain's previously awesome military superiority was at once whittled down to size. The allies even had a slight advantage. Victory once more became possible, while a setback would not necessarily prove fatal. Although Washington could not throw caution to the winds—for the British were not about to concede defeat—serious domestic difficulties compelled him to try to bring the war to a speedy conclusion. Winning was more important than not losing. He strove mightily to coordinate allied arms in "one great vigorous effort." His strategic offensive, though greatly prolonged because of problems inherent in cooperating with a foreign fleet operating from a base thousands of miles away, resulted finally in victory at Yorktown.

For the final two years, the war was fought mainly in theaters other than the United States, including the negotiating arenas in Europe. With independence all but assured, Americans shifted their interest to furthering the aim of expanding their national borders. Washington's strategic stance remained an offensive one, but with the significant if subtle difference that once again avoiding a defeat was more important than winning a victory. Patriots had achieved much—and consequently had much to lose. They wanted more, of course, but not at the expense of ground already gained. Among "the arts of negotiation" is the rule of dealing from strength. Keeping the Continental army ready and responsive was itself an imperative of the war's final phase. It could neither be squandered in futile offensives, suffered to dissolve through inactivity, nor permitted to turn against the very nation it had created. Washington steered a successful course through the uncharted and dangerous reefs separating war from peace. One cannot imagine any other helmsman at the wheel without also envisioning the revolution in wreckage.

Through all four phases, Washington recognized what had to be done, and he did it. This is the crucial point most historians have missed and why writers have had so much difficulty in getting a handle on his generalship. Unless one recognizes the fact that the War of Independence wore four faces, it is all but impossible to comprehend the genius of General Washington. In the first period, which called for audacity, he was audacious; when the second cried caution, he turned cautious; as decisive victory became feasible, he thirsted for a decision; when events after Yorktown required steadfastness, he became the nation's solid anchor.

The researcher scratches in vain for a single instance in all the years of the war when Washington ever lost sight of the objectives for which he was fighting. From first to last, he never added to or subtracted from the vision of a United States free of Europe and supreme in North America. Achieving that was victory. In those terms, and those alone, he unfalteringly devised his strategy. No one has ever summed it up better in one sentence than Marcus Cunliffe: "Victory was the goal he kept in sight; unlike the British commanders, he never hopelessly confused the secondary advantage with the primary aim."[2]

Having examined the war in the light of its strategic subdivisions and after having witnessed George Washington's precise reading of requirements and his correct planning of campaigns, it is hard to credit those who espouse the theme of inevitability. The war provided high drama, but it was not a Greek tragedy. The British did not have to lose; the patriots were not fated to triumph. Had English leadership been better, or that of the Americans less astute, the war could well have ended differently. Who can guess what would have happened? Possibly only a few of the states would have become independent. Perhaps England would have held onto chunks of the provinces. Maybe rebel diehards, defeated in the colonies, would have carved out a redoubt in the forest fastness beyond the Appalachians. One can rather easily see the colonies accepting some sort of semi-independent dominion status. It is even quite feasible that the provinces might have lost their unity, producing in North America a Balkanized area of numerous small countries, squabbling among themselves and unable to resist European meddling. It is entirely possible that patriots might not have achieved either of their two goals. Indeed, an honest reading of the situation at any of several points in the struggle would have indicated the probability of their emerging with far less than they did.

The ultimate outcome was the result of many contributing factors, but at the head of any list must stand the strategic acumen of the American commander-in-chief. Overall, he was completely successful in achieving the goal of independence and partially successful in gaining the objective of territorial aggrandizement.

Given what he had to work with, more could hardly have been hoped for, much less anticipated. He won for a variety of reasons, not the least of which was the fact that he out-generalled all his opponents.

Washington's place in history is secure. He needs no defender. Even had he possessed no strategic ability whatsoever but, as some claim, had still somehow muddled through to victory despite so severe a shortcoming, his other outstanding traits and deeds would have been enough to mark him as a great historical figure. Nevertheless, in order to understand him more fully, one cannot avoid studying Washington the general, which is to say, Washington the strategist.

That he possesed an unusual degree of strategic scope and grasp appears almost certain. The evidence is compelling. On balance, we must conclude that, even before the word was coined, George Washington had become this nation's preeminent strategist. He was, indeed, first in war.

Notes

INTRODUCTION

[1]John R. Alden, *A History of the American Revolution* (New York, 1969), 258. Raymond G. O'Connor, ed., *American Defense Policy in Perspective* (New York, 1965), 18. The selection used for the Revolution is from Matthew Forney Steele's *American Campaigns*, published in 1907, which may be indicative of O'Connor's judgment of the value of more recent works touching on military policy. Douglas Southall Freeman, *George Washington* (New York, 1948-1957), V: 481. Freeman did not live to complete his seven-volume monumental work, but he did evaluate Washington's generalship. North Callahan, *George Washington, Soldier and Man* (New York, 1972), 279. James Thomas Flexner, *George Washington in the American Revolution, 1775-1783* (Boston, 1967), 544-47. Russell Weigley, *History of the United States Army* (New York, 1967), 65. See also Weigley's *The American Way of War* (New York, 1973), 15. Thomas G. Frothingham, *Washington, Commander in Chief* (Boston, 1930). 109.

[2]The comments of Jefferson and Marshall are reproduced in Morton Borden, ed., *Great Lives Observed: George Washington* (New Jersey, 1969), 105, 113-14. Jefferson's are from a letter written in 1814 and Marshall's are from his biography of Washington, vol V, 773-779. Charles Stedman, a Loyalist, published his *History of the Origin, Progress, and Termination of the American War* in Dublin in 1794. Weigley, *History of the United States Army*, 43. Freeman, *George Washington*, V: 480-81. Don Higginbotham, *The War of American Independence* (New York, 1971), 88. Marcus Cunliffe, *George Washington: Man and Monument* (Boston, 1958), 127. Richard M. Ketchum, *The Winter Soldiers* (New York, 1973), 36. Alden, *A History of the American Revolution*, 185. R. Ernest and Trevor N. Dupuy, *The Compact History of the Revolutionary War* (New York, 1963), 474.

Chapter 1

STRATEGY BEFORE CLAUSEWITZ

[1]Many of the ideas put forth in this chapter, and even some of the phrases, were gleaned from a series of conversations with Professor Theodore Ropp at the Army War College, where he was a visiting professor of military history in 1972-1973. The influence of Professor Jay Luvaas is also heavy in this chapter.

[2]V. D. Sokolovsky, ed., *Military Strategy* (Moscow, 1968), 10. The version quoted here is from the third edition, translated by Harriet Fast Scott. For a brief summary of the impact of Guibert, see Edward Mead Earle, ed., *Makers of Modern Strategy* (Princeton, 1943), 62-66.

[3]Carl von Clausewitz, *On War*, ed. Anatol Rapoport (Baltimore, 1969), 179, 241, 264.

[4]B. H. Liddell Hard, *Strategy*, 2d rev. ed. (New York, 1972), 333-336. John M. Collins, *Grand Strategy* (Annapolis, 1973), 15. Collins' book fills a long ignored void.

[5]Clausewitz, *On War*, 243.

Chapter 2

THE PRUSSIAN SHADOW

[1]Works on weaponry abound, catering mostly to the tastes of collectors or antiquarians. Bernard and Fawn Brodie, *From Crossbow to H-Bomb* (New York, 1962), is an excellent study of the evolution of arms. A fine book dealing more specifically with those weapons employed in North America is Harold L. Peterson, *Arms and Armor in Colonial America, 1526-1783* (Harrisburg, 1956).

[2]A good discussion of the accuracy and rate of fire of the musket is in Peterson, *Arms and Armor*, 159-163.

[3]For a concise account of the role of the rifle, see ibid., 192-204. The quote from Washington is from John C. Fitzpatrick, ed., *The Writings of George Washington* (Washington, D.C., 1931-1944), VIII: 236.

[4]Fitzpatrick, ed., *Writings of Washington*, X: 368.

[5]Winston S. Churchill, *Marlborough, His Life and Times* (New York, 1935), III: 112-113.

[6]Quoted in Edward Earle, ed., *Makers of Modern Strategy* (Princeton,

1943), 55. A concise study of Frederick's writings is Jay Luvaas, *Frederick the Great on the Art of War* (New York, 1966). For an excellent brief description of Frederick's system, see Peter Paret, *Yorck and the Era of Prussian Reform* (Princeton, 1966), 7-21.

[7]The discussion on limited warfare follows largely that of Thomas E. Griess, ed., *The Art of Warfare in the 17th and 18th Centuries* (West Point, 1969).

[8]This incident is from *Candide*, chap. 2, as quoted by Theodore Ropp, *War in the Modern World* (New York, 1962), 54.

[9]Peter Paret, *Yorck and the Era of Prussian Reform* (Princeton, 1966) 21.

[10]A good contemporary account describing some of the experimentation with light troops in the Revolution is Colonel von Ehwald, *A Treatise Upon the Duties of Light Troops*, trans. A. Maimburg (London, 1803). Perhaps the best short defense of the old system is George A. Rothrock's introduction to his translation of Vauban, *Manual of Siegecraft and Fortifications* (Ann Arbor, 1968). A concise discussion of the use of light troops—called "little war"—in the last half of the eighteenth century is in Peter Paret, *Yorck and the Era of Prussian Reform* (Princeton, 1966), 21-46.

[11]Frederick the Great kept his instructions to his generals closely guarded state secrets. Consequently, few of his many writings were published until after his death. However, not all soldiers were so secretive. Americans had a wide choice of works by Turenne, de Saxe, and others of the formal school, many of whom described Prussian methods. Debates on the Articles of War are printed in Worthington C. Ford, ed., *Journals of the Continental Congress* (Washington, D.C., 1904-1937), V: 670-671, 788-807.

[12]Quoted in William B. Willcox, *Portrait of a General* (New York, 1964), 48.

Chapter 3

THE MEAGER SETTING

[1]Colonial population estimates are just that—estimates. J. Franklin Jameson in his *The American Revolution Considered as a Social Movement* (Princeton, 1940), calculated a figure of 2.5 million, which is generally accepted, although some historians reckon the total may have

been as much as 3 million. A population chart of the United States in 1790, which wouldn't have been markedly different from one drawn in 1780, is in Francis A. Walker, comp., *Statistical Atlas of the United States at the Ninth Census, 1870* (Washington, 1874), plate XVI.

[2]John Alden, *The American Revolution, 1775-1783* (New York, 1954), 165.

[3]*Public Records of the Colony of Connecticut, October 1772-April 1775* (Hartford, 1887), XIV: 495-501.

[4]Ibid. See also: Victor L. Johnson, *The Administration of the American Commissariat During the Revolutionary War* (Philadelphia, 1941); Robert A. East, *Business Enterprise in the American Revolutionary Era* (New York, 1938); Albert L. Olsen, "Agricultural Economy and the Population in Eighteenth-Century Connecticut," *Tercentary Commission of the State of Connecticut* 40 (1935): 3-5.

Chapter 4

THE VIEW FROM LONDON

[1]Biographies of George III abound. Stanley Ayling, *George the Third* (New York, 1972), and John Brooke, *King George III* (New York, 1972), are among the most recent. Sir John Fortescue, ed., *The Correspondence of King George the Third* (London, 1928) provides indispensable material for both an insight into the personality of the king and an understanding of the American war.

[2]J. W. Fortescue, *A History of the British Army* (London, 1911), III: 174-175.

[3]William Howe, *Narrative in a Committee of the House of Commons* (London, 1780), 19.

[4]Harvey to General Irwin, 30 June 1775, quoted by Fortescue, *A History of the British Army* III: 169. Basil H. Liddell Hart, *The British Way of Warfare* (London, 1932), 16, 35-36.

[5]Fortescue, *A History of the British Army*, III: 169. Piers Mackesy, *The War for America, 1775-1783* (Cambridge, 1964), 143. For a book-length treatment of the line of the Hudson strategy, see Dave R. Palmer, *The River and the Rock* (New York, 1969).

[6]An early strategic survey can be seen in collections of the New York Historical Society, *The Letters and Papers of Cadwallader Colden,*

1765-1775 ("The Cadwallader Colden Papers" [New York, 1923]), VII: 197-198. See also Dartmouth to Gage, 15 April 1775, Whitehall, in Public Record Office, *America and the West Indies and Military Correspondence, 1773-1783*, C.O. 5/92, 103.

[7]Gage to Dartmouth, 1 October 1775, in Peter Force, ed., *American Archives*, Fourth Series, III: 927-928.

[8]Sir Henry Clinton, *The American Rebellion*, ed. William B. Willcox (New Haven, 1954), 11-12. Fortescue, *A History of the British Army*, III: 168. Sir George Otto Trevelyan, *The American Revolution* (London, 1928), II: 69.

[9]Quoted in Fortescue, *A History of the British Army*, III: 338-39.

[10]An admirably concise discussion of the British command and control system is in Don Higginbotham, *The War of American Independence* (New York, 1971), 139-143.

[11]A disparaging analysis of London's faith in a Loyalist uprising is in Fortescue, *A History of the British Army*, III: 170-171. But Fortescue also overestimates the Tory sentiment in America. Howe is quoted by Lynn Montross in *The Reluctant Rebels* (New York, 1950), 177. A good summary of the role and fate of Loyalists is in John Alden, *A History of the American Revolution* (New York, 1969), 443-456, 493-506.

[12]Liddel Hart's discussion of the naval strategy is in his *The British Way of Warfare*, 35-36.

Chapter 5

THE ETERNAL QUESTION

[1]Don Higginbotham, *The War of American Independence* (New York, 1971), 91.

[2]Lynn Montross, *The Reluctant Rebels* (New York, 1950), 136.

[3]Peter Force, *American Archives*, Fourth Series, II: 621.

[4]Worthington C. Ford, ed., *Journals of the Continental Congress* (Washington, D.C., 1904-1937), II: 52.

[5]Ibid., 59-61, 64.

[6]Ibid., 96.

[7]Ibid., 100-101. John C. Fitzpatrick, ed., *The Writings of George Washington* (Washington, D.C., 1931-1944), III: 297.

[8]Ford, ed., *Journals*, II: 97.

[9]Charles Francis Adams, ed., *Familiar Letters of John Adams and His Wife Abigail Adams* (Boston, 1875), 70. The desire to help the army by direct participation persisted at least as late as mid-1779. On 14 July that year, John Dickinson, seconded by William Henry Drayton, moved that Congress adjourn and fight with the army. Ford, ed., *Journals*, XIV: 835-836.

[10]Ford, ed., *Journals*, V: 602.

[11]Ibid., 434-435.

[12]Montross, *The Reluctant Rebels*, 190-192. Fitzpatrick, ed., *Writings of Washington*, VI: 402.

[13]Ford, ed., *Journals*, II: 111-112, V: 670-671, 788-807.

[14]Edmund C. Burnett, ed., *Letters of Members of the Continental Congress* (Washington, D.C., 1921-1936), II: 263.

[15]Adams, *Familiar Letters*, 276; Ford, ed., *Journals*, VII: 180; Fitzpatrick, ed., *Writings of Washington*, VII: 285-286.

[16]Fitzpatrick, ed., *Writings of Washington*, VII: 221-226. Extracts from Morris' letter, dated 27 February 1777, are on p. 222.

[17]Burnett, ed., *Letters*, II: 446-447; Ford, ed., *Journals*, VII: 649, 659; Fitzpatrick, ed., *Writings of Washington*, VII: 433-438, VIII: 34-35.

[18]Ford, ed., *Journals*, IX: 818-820, 976.

[19]Adams, *Familiar Letters*, 292, 322-323.

[20]Ford, ed., *Journals*, X: 84, 87. General Stark received eight votes, Lafayette and Conway six each, while McDougall and Glover got one each. Nevertheless, Congress designated Lafayette as commander with Conway as deputy. DeKalb later replaced Conway as deputy, but none of the officers ever served because the invasion could not be mounted.

[21]A current and good account of the Conway cabal is in James Flexner, *George Washington in the American Revolution* (Boston, 1967), 241-277.

[22]Ford, ed., *Journals*, X: 329, 354-355, 362, 364, 368-369, 384; Fitzpatrick, ed., *Writings of Washington*, XI: 290-291.

[23]These comments and many others are printed in Morton Borden, ed., *Great Lives Observed: George Washington* (New Jersey, 1969), 87, 95.

[24]Fitzpatrick, ed., *Writings of Washington*, XXVI: 213-216, 276-277, 291-293. Burnett, *Letters*, VI: 15, 83.

[25]Fitzpatrick, ed., *Writings of Washington*, XXVI: 213-216, 276-277, 291-293. Several documents pertaining to the Newburgh crisis are printed in Ford, ed., *Journals*, XXIV: 291-311.

Chapter 6

BEYOND THE HORIZON

[1]B. H. Liddell Hart, *Strategy*, 2d rev. ed. (New York, 1972), 336.

[2]Worthington C. Ford, ed., *Journals of the Continental Congress* (Washington, D.C., 1904-1937), II: 56.

[3]Ibid., II: 109-110. Raymond Aron, *The Imperial Republic* (New Jersey, 1974), xxv.

[4]Ford, ed., *Journals*, VI: 1055-1057.

[5]East and West Florida were the lands south of the thirty-first parallel and extending from the Mississippi River to the Atlantic. West Florida encompassed much of modern Alabama and Mississippi and the western parts of Florida. The Apalachicola River was the boundary between the two; Pensacola and St. Augustine were the only sizable settlements.

[6]For a succinct account of the debate triggered and later influenced by Gerard, see William C. Stinchcombe, *The American Revolution and the French Alliance* (Syracuse, 1969), 62-76. See also Ford, ed., *Journals*, XIII: 239-244, 263-265, 329-331, 339-341, 345-352, 369-373, XV: 1103-1121.

[7]Albert H. Smyth, ed., *The Writings of Benjamin Franklin* (New York, 1905-1907), VIII: 144. An excellent recent work on the entire panorama of negotiations is Richard B. Morris, *The Peacemakers* (New York, 1965).

[8]Knox is so quoted in North Callahan, *George Washington's General, Henry Knox* (New York, 1958), 39. The study referenced is *The Sullivan-Clinton Campaign in 1779*, prepared by the Division of Archives and History of the University of the State of New York (Albany, 1929), 10.

[9]The fear of encirclement never left Washington. It was one of the concerns that troubled him throughout his Presidency as well as during the Revolution itself. On 27 August 1790, for example, he sent a secret letter to the Vice President, the Chief Justice, and the three primary cabinet members asking their advice should England and Spain come to blows along the Mississippi River, as it looked like they might. English forces could march from Detroit, the President thought, and easily overrun the weakly garrisoned Spanish posts along the Mississippi, including perhaps even New Orleans. He wanted his advisors to tell him if they saw anything the United States could do to prevent such an

eventuality, for he dreaded the "consequences of having so formidable and enterprising a people as the British on both our flanks and rear, with their navy in front."

¹⁰Ford, ed., *Journals*, I: 98, 114, 369; John C. Fitzpatrick, ed., *The Writings of George Washington* (Washington, D.C., 1931-1944), IV: 494, V: 102-162.

¹¹See John Alden, *A History of the American Revolution* (New York, 1969), 55, for a brief elaboration of prewar English thoughts on American expansion.

¹²Peter Force, ed., *American Archives*, Fourth Series, I, 216-220. The parenthetical inclusion of two clauses purporting to preserve old boundaries and grants seems to have had little soothing effect on the colonists. See also Ford, ed., *Journals*, I: 9-13, 22.

Chapter 7

RUN ALL RISQUES: APRIL 1775-JUNE 1776

¹Worthington C. Ford, ed., *Journals of the Continental Congress* (Washington, D.C., 1904-1937), II: 56. John C. Fitzpatrick, ed., *The Writings of George Washington* (Washington, D.C., 1931-1944), III: 320*n*, 415-416.

²Fitzpatrick, ed., *Writings of Washington*, III: 386-387.

³Ibid., 302-303, 374, 386-387, 415, 347-348, 475-476, 478*n*, 511, IV: 112, 172. Naval History Division, *Naval Documents of the American Revolution* (Washington, D.C., 1964-1970), II: 1-2.

⁴Fitzpatrick, ed., *Writings of Washington*, III: 436-439, 510.

⁵Ibid., 394, 405, 453-454, 462, 488.

⁶Peter Force, ed., *American Archives*, Fourth Series, III: 768. Fitzpatrick, ed., *Writings of Washington*, III: 483-485, 488, 511.

⁷Fitzpatrick, ed., *Writings of Washington*, III: 511.

⁸Force, ed., *American Archives*, Fourth Series, III: 1153. Congress chose Knox to be "Colonel of the Regiment of Artillery" on 17 November 1775, but the regiment itself did not come into service until 1 January 1776, and it had no artillery of any note until its young colonel returned from Ticonderoga with the captured pieces.

⁹Ford, ed., *Journals*, III: 444-445. Fitzpatrick, ed., *Writings of Washington*, IV: 208, 321. James Flexner, *George Washington in the American Revolution* (Boston, 1967), 65.

[10]Force, ed., *American Archives*, Fourth Series, IV: 604. Fitzpatrick, ed., *Writings of Washington*, IV: 217-219, 259-260.

[11]Force, ed., *American Archives*, Fourth Series, IV: 1193. Fitzpatrick, ed., *Writings of Washington*, IV: 335-337.

[12]Fitzpatrick, ed., *Writings of Washington*, IV: 359-366.

[13]Ibid., 371, 373-374.

[14]Ibid., 434.

[15]Ford, ed., *Journals*, IV: 383-384, 388, 399-401. Force, ed., *American Archives*, Fourth Series, VI: 472-473.

[16]Fitzpatrick, ed., *Writings of Washington*, IV: 297, 321, V: 92-93.

Chapter 8

A CHOICE OF DIFFICULTIES: JULY 1776-DECEMBER 1777

[1]John C. Fitzpatrick, ed., *The Writings of George Washington* (Washington, D.C., 1931-1944), VI: 28. Pitt as quoted in Marcus Cunliffe, *George Washington: Man and Monument* (Boston, 1958), 124.

[2]For a good description of Washington's outlook in spring 1776, see Douglas Freeman, *George Washington* (New York, 1948-1957), IV: 76.

[3]Worthington C. Ford, *Journals of the Continental Congress* (Washington, D.C., 1905-1937), IV: 399-401.

[4]Fitzpatrick, ed., *Writings of Washington*, V: 247-250.

[5]Adams to Washington, 8 January 1776, in Peter Force, ed., *American Archives*, Fourth Series, IV: 604.

[6]Fitzpatrick, ed., *Writings of Washington*, V: 502, 506-507.

[7]Greene to Washington, 5 September 1776, in Force, ed., *American Archives*, Fifth Series, II: 182-183.

[8]Fitzpatrick, ed., *Writings of Washington*, VI: 27-33.

[9]Interestingly, Washington and Mao were both concerned, after they had become victorious, that outside impurities might spoil the gains of their respective revolutions. Though the Virginian would never have dreamed of visiting on his countrymen anything like Mao's brutal "Cultural Revolution," he did see the need to fight the spread of cosmopolitan licentiousness. As he prepared his first inaugural address, his mind wandered over possible strategies for such a campaign. Not surprisingly, he drew from his Revolutionary War experiences. He had then used the very size and wilderness of the thirteen colonies to help defeat the British; he now believed the same geographical realities of a frontier nation would

help Americans "maintain something like a war of posts against the invasion of luxury, dissipation, and corruption." (See Fitzpatrick, ed., *Writings of Washington*, XXX: 307.)

[10]Ibid., XXXVII: 531-533. Ford, ed., *Journals*, V: 749.

[11]Fitzpatrick, ed., *Writings of Washington*, VI: 223-225.

[12]Colonel von Ehwald, *A Treatise upon the Duties of Light Troops*, trans. A. Maimburg (London, 1803), 232.

[13]Fitzpatrick, ed., *Writings of Washington*, VI: 321-322.

[14]Howe to Germain, 29 December 1776, in ibid., VI: 341*n*.

[15]Lee was approaching slowly and reluctantly. Heavy in his mind was the notion that Washington should be removed, to be replaced, naturally, by Lee himself. Lee's capture by a British cavalry patrol took him out of the play for the rest of the war's second phase, a most fortunate stroke for the cause of the Revolution.

[16]Fitzpatrick, ed., *Writings of Washington*, VI: 243-247, 330, 373.

[17]See Freeman, *George Washington*, IV: 306*n*15, for a discussion of Washington's decision to attack. Many of Washington's instructions are reproduced in Fitzpatrick, ed., *Writings of Washington*, VI: 365-373.

[18]Thomas Paine, whose *Common Sense* had moved the nation a notch toward independence, had been serving as a military secretary during the retreat through New Jersey. Once again his pen came to the aid of the cause at a crucial moment, this time in the form of a pamphlet titled *The American Crisis*. "These are the times that try men's souls," he wrote. "The summer soldier and the sunshine patriot will, in this crisis, shrink from the service of his country; but he that stands it *now* deserves the love and thanks of man and woman." Washington had Paine's stirring words read to the troops before they crossed the Delaware.

[19]George Trevelyan, *The American Revolution* (London, 1928), III: 143. Camillus was a Roman hero (c. 447-365 B.C.) who, through offensive campaigns, extended Rome's domain by the conquest of Veii, the rout of Brennu's Gauls, and victories in Latium.

[20]Germain to William Knox, in Historical Manuscripts Commission, *Various Collections* (London, 1901-1904), VI: 131. A good, concise summary of the situation at the beginning of the campaign is in Don Higginbotham, *The War of American Independence* (New York, 1971), 181.

[21]Fitzpatrick, ed., *Writings of Washington*, VII: 274.

[22]Ibid., 272-276.

[23]Ibid., 400-401, 436-437.

[24]Ibid., IX: 273, 275-277.

[25]Ibid., 277-279.

[26]Ibid., 293-294, 308-309.

[27]As he had done before Trenton, General Washington assembled all his men and had an inspirational message read to each regiment. Alexander Hamilton had written the words, but, for all his wit, the young aide was no Thomas Paine. Whereas Paine had moved the Continentals before Trenton (was that only nine months ago?) with his penetrating call to patriotism, Hamilton challenged their spirit of competition. Reminding the men of the recent victory over Burgoyne, the message implored them to equal that feat. "This army, the main American Army, will certainly not suffer itself to be outdone by their northern brethren; they will never endure such disgrace. . . . Covet! My countrymen and fellow soldiers! Covet! A shadow of the glory due to their heroic deeds!"

[28]Ehwald, *A Treatise*, 65.

Chapter 9

ONE GREAT VIGOROUS EFFORT: JANUARY 1778-OCTOBER 1781

[1]John C. Fitzpatrick, ed., *The Writings of George Washington* (Washington, D.C., 1931-1944), XIII: 11.

[2]Piers Mackesy, *The War for America* (Cambridge, 1964), xiv. Richard B. Morris has suggested that the war might have ended sooner without French entry. His conclusion is that Paris' action saved the British government from collapse after 1777, rallied the British, and undercut the peace party in London. Much of that might well be true, but, even so, Morris makes the mistake of confusing not losing with winning. An American victory meant independence and territorial expansion. That both were within reach in 1777 is most doubtful. Alone, the Americans might not have lost the war, but they almost surely would not have won it without French help. See Morris, *The American Revolution Reconsidered* (New York, 1967), 98-105.

[3]Fitzpatrick, ed., *Writings of Washington*, XI: 363-366. Douglas Freeman, *George Washington* (New York, 1948-1957), IV: 630-631. The composition of that council of war amply demonstrates the reach of foreign influence in the rejuvenated Continental army. Of ten officers comprising it, four were Europeans: Lafayette, DeKalb, Steuben, and Duportail.

[4]Fitzpatrick, ed., *Writings of Washington*, XI: 453.

[5]Harold C. Syrett, *The Papers of Alexander Hamilton* (New York, 1961-1972), I: 510-513. Fitzpatrick, ed., *Writings of Washington*, III: 115-117, 140-141.

[6]Fitzpatrick, ed., *Writings of Washington*, XII: 488.

[7]Ibid., XIV: 387.

[8]Ibid., XII: 488, XIII: 15-16. William Shakespeare, *The Tempest*, act iv, scene 1.

[9]Lynn Montross, *The Reluctant Rebels* (New York, 1950), 257-264. Fitzpatrick, ed., *Writings of Washington*, XIII: 223-244, 254-257.

[10]For an excellent account of Washington's stay in Philadelphia, see James T. Flexner, *George Washington in the American Revolution* (Boston, 1967), chapter 37.

[11]Fitzpatrick, ed., *Writings of Washington*, XIII: 485-502, XIV: 3-11, 382.

[12]Ibid., XIV: 3-11.

[13]At the same time, though, the ambassador told his superiors in Paris that since Americans thirsted so strongly for Canada, it would not hurt relations between the two countries to insist that France would not assist in operations there.

[14]Worthington C. Ford, ed., *Journals of the Continental Congress* (Washington, D.C., 1904-1937), XV: 1103-1121; Gerard to President of Congress, 22 May 1779, in Francis Wharton, ed., *The Revolutionary Diplomatic Correspondence of the United States* (Washington, D.C., 1889), III: 177. William C. Stinchcombe, *The American Revolution and the French Alliance* (Syracuse, N.Y., 1969), chapter 5.

[15]Sir John Fortescue, ed., *The Correspondence of King George the Third* (London, 1928), V: 57. James Thacher, *Military Journal of the American Revolution* (Hartford, Conn., 1862), 197. Fitzpatrick, ed., *Writings of Washington*, XVIII: 413.

[16]Syrett, *Hamilton Papers*, II: 347-348.

[17]Fitzpatrick, ed., *Writings of Washington*, XVIII: 416-419, 455-499.

[18]He did not know how right he was. For printing, the proclamation went to Benedict Arnold in Philadelphia. Arnold promptly sent a copy to Henry Clinton.

[19]Fitzpatrick, ed., *Writings of Washington*, XVIII: 360-363, 369-373, 386-388, 459-461, 476.

[20]Ibid., 454, 482-485, 509-510, XIX: 27, 107-109.

[21]Ibid., XIX: 174-176.

[22]Ibid., 169-170, 180, 211-213, 236-237.

[23]Ibid., 407, 419-423, 443-445, 481-483.

[24]Ibid., XX: 374.

[25]Ford, ed., *Journals*, XVII: 699. Fitzpatrick, ed., *Writings of Washington*, XX: 15-16, 39-42, 272-273.

[26]Fitzpatrick, ed., *Writings of Washington*, XX: 351, 379-396, 425-434, 459.

[27]Ibid., 480-484.

[28]For an interesting firsthand account of the British raids in Virginia, see Colonel von Ehwald, *A Treatise upon the Duties of the Light Infantry*, trans. A. Maimburg (London, 1803), 50-62.

[29]Greene as cited by Don Higginbotham, *The War of American Independence* (New York, 1971), 375. Clinton to William Eden, 30 May 1780, Sir Henry Clinton Papers, William L. Clements Library, University of Michigan.

[30]Fitzpatrick, ed., *Writings of Washington*, XXX: 26-28.

[31]Ibid., XXII: 367-369, 431-434, 501-502, XXIII: 8.

[32]See Lynn Montross, *The Reluctant Rebels* (New York, 1950), 321-322, for a description of the French parade.

[33]Albert H. Smyth, ed., *The Writings of Benjamin Franklin* (New York, 1905-1907), VIII: 333.

[34]*Correspondence of General Washington and Comte de Grasse*, ed. L'Institute Française de Washington (Washington, D.C., 1931), 35-41.

[35]Ibid., 45-51. Fitzpatrick, ed., *Writings of Washington*, XXIII: 136-139.

Chapter 10

THE ARTS OF NEGOTIATION: NOVEMBER 1781-DECEMBER 1783

[1]John C. Fitzpatrick, ed., *The Writings of George Washington* (Washington, D.C., 1931-1944), XXIII: 193-195.

[2]Ibid., XXIII: 250, 286, 298, 340-342. De Grasse's mental anguish and vacillation is revealed in his letters in *Correspondence of General Washington and Comte de Grasse*, 128-141.

[3]Ibid., 340-342.

[4]Ibid., 346-347, 351-352.

[5]Sir John Fortescue, ed., *The Correspondence of King George the Third* (London, 1928), V: 304.

[6]Fitzpatrick, ed., *Writings of Washington*, XXIV: 16-17, 115-116, 139, 152-153.

[7]Ibid., 164-171, 194-215.

[8]See Richard Morris, *The Peacemakers* (New York, 1965), for a full dress account of the strange paths taken by the negotiations.

[9]Fitzpatrick, ed., *Writings of Washington*, XXIV: 270-296, 405-406, XXV: 136-138.

[10]Ibid., XXIV: 421-423, XXV: 17, 198-199.

[11]Ibid., XXIV: 471, XXV: 21-23.

[12]Ibid., XXV: 150-152, 180-181, 192-195, 272-273.

[13]Ibid., XXV: 192-195, 420-421, 446-449.

[14]Thomas Paine to George Washington, 18 September 1782, quoted in part in ibid., XXV: 176*n*.

[15]Fitzpatrick, ed., *Writings of Washington*, XXV: 430-431.

[16]An excellent account of "the nation's most dangerous hour" is in James Thomas Flexner, *George Washington in the American Revolution, 1775-1783* (Boston, 1967), 467-508. Some recent scholars believe the threat of military dictatorship may have been exaggerated. Perhaps. But the danger was undoubtedly there, and the weight of historical evidence clearly demonstrates that it is not unusual for dictators to ride to power through revolution.

[17]Washington had always wanted to see northern New York. "The present irksome interval, while we are waiting for the definitive treaty," he decided, was a good time to go there. He was also tired of "troublesome applications and fruitless demands, which I have neither the means nor the power of satisfying."

[18]Fitzpatrick, ed., *Writings of Washington*, XXVI: 76-78, 85, XXVII: 100.

[19]Ibid., XXIV: 124.

[20]A sketch depicting various boundary proposals between 1779 and 1783 is in Morris, *The Peacemakers*.

CONCLUSION

[1]James Thomas Flexner, *George Washington in the American Revolution, 1775-1783* (Boston, 1967), 536.

[2]Marcus Cunliffe, *George Washington, Man and Monument* (Boston, 1958), 126.

Selected Bibliography

For a work of this sort, ranging the whole length and depth of the Revolutionary War, a complete bibliography would be too exhaustive to print. So, too, would one considered to be even close to definitive. The dilemma is that anything less is rather unsatisfactory. At the very least, though, one ought to provide the reader a convenient listing of those references cited in the book. This selected bibliography does that.

Adams, Charles F., ed. *Familiar Letters of John Adams and his Wife Abigail Adams*. Boston, 1875.

Alden, John R. *The American Revolution, 1775-1783*. New York, 1954.

————. *A History of the American Revolution*. New York, 1969.

Aron, Raymond. *The Imperial Republic*. New Jersey, 1974.

Ayling, Stanley. *George the Third*. New York, 1972.

Borden, Morton, ed. *Great Lives Observed: George Washington*. New Jersey, 1969.

Brodie, Bernard and Fawn. *From Crossbow to H-Bomb*. New York, 1962.

Brooke, John. *King George III*. New York, 1972.

Burnett, Edmund C., ed. *Letters of Members of the Continental Congress*. Washington, D.C., 1921-1936. 8 vols.

Callahan, North. *George Washington's General, Henry Knox*. New York, 1958.

————. *George Washington, Soldier and Man*. New York, 1972.

Churchill, Winston S. *Marlborough, His Life and Times*. New York, 1935. 6 vols.

Clausewitz, Carl von. *On War*. Edited by Anatol Rapoport. Baltimore, 1969.

Clinton, Sir Henry. *The American Rebellion*. Edited by William B. Willcox. New Haven, 1954.

Collins, John M. *Grand Strategy*. Annapolis, 1973.

Correspondence of General Washington and Count de Grasse. Edited by L'Institute Francaise de Washington. Washington, 1931.

Cunliffe, Marcus. *George Washington, Man and Monument*. Boston, 1958.

Division of Archives and History of the University of the State of New York. *The Sullivan-Clinton Campaign of 1779*. Albany, 1929.

Dupuy, R. Ernest and Trevor N. *The Compact History of the Revolutionary War*. New York, 1963.

Earle, Edward M., ed. *Makers of Modern Strategy*. Princeton, 1943.

East, Robert A. *Business Enterprise in the American Revolutionary Era*. New York, 1938.

Ehwald, Colonel von. *A Treatise upon the Duties of Light Troops*. Translated by A. Maimburg. London, 1803. A copy of this quite rare work is in the Military History Research Collection, Carlisle Barracks, Pennsylvania.

Fitzpatrick, John C., ed. *The Writings of George Washington*. Washington, D.C. 1931-1944. 39 vols.

Flexner, James Thomas. *George Washington in the American Revolution, 1775-1783*. Boston, 1967. The second of Flexner's fine four-volume biography.

Force, Peter, ed. *American Archives*. Fourth and Fifth Series. Washington, D.C. 1837-1853.

Ford, Worthington C., ed. *Journals of the Continental Congress*. Washington, D.C., 1904-1937. 34 vols.

Fortescue, Sir John, ed. *The Correspondence of King George the Third*. London, 1928. 6 vols.

————. *A History of the British Army*. London, 1911. 13 vols.

Freeman, Douglas Southall. *George Washington*. New York, 1948-1957. 7 vols.

Frothingham, Thomas G. *Washington, Commander in Chief*. Boston, 1930.

Griess, Thomas E., ed. *The Art of Warfare in the 17th and 18th Centuries*. West Point, 1969.

Higginbotham, Don. *The War of American Independence*. New York, 1971.

Historical Manuscripts Commission, *Various Collections*. London, 1901-1904.

Howe, William. *Narrative in a Committee of the House of Commons*. London, 1780.

Jameson, J. Franklin. *The American Revolution Considered as a Social*

Movement. Princeton, 1940.

Johnson, Victor L. *The Administration of the American Commissariat During the Revolutionary War*. Philadelphia, 1941.

Ketchum, Richard M. *The Winter Soldiers*. New York, 1973.

Liddell Hart, Basil H. *The British Way of Warfare*. London, 1932.

————. *Strategy*. Second revised edition. New York, 1972.

Luvaas, Jay. *Frederick the Great on the Art of War*. New York, 1966.

Mackesy, Piers. *The War for America, 1775-1783*. Cambridge, Mass., 1964.

Montross, Lynn. *The Reluctant Rebels*. New York, 1950.

Morris, Richard B. *The American Revolution Reconsidered*. New York, 1967.

————. *The Peacemakers*. New York, 1965.

Naval History Division. *Naval Documents of the American Revolution*. Washington, D.C., 1964-1970. 4 vols.

New-York Historical Society. *The Letters and Papers of Cadwallader Colden, 1765-1775*. (From The Cadwallader Colden Papers.) New York, 1923.

O'Conner, Raymond G., ed. *American Defense Policy in Perspective*. New York, 1965.

Olsen, Albert L. "Agricultural Economy and the Population in Eighteenth-Century Connecticut." *Tercentenary Commission of the State of Connecticut*. Hartford, 1935.

Palmer, Dave R. *The River and the Rock*. New York, 1969.

Paret, Peter. *Yorck and the Era of Prussian Reform*. Princeton, 1966.

Peterson, Harold L. *Arms and Armor in Colonial America, 1526-1783*. Harrisburg, 1956.

Public Record Office. *America and the West Indies and Military Correspondence, 1775-1783*. London. Much of this voluminous file is on microfilm.

Public Records of the Colony of Connecticut, October 1772-April 1775. Hartford, 1887.

Ropp, Theodore. *War in the Modern World*. New York, 1962.

Smythe, Albert H. ed. *The Writings of Benjamin Franklin*. New York, 1905-1907. 10 vols.

Sokolovsky, V. D., ed. *Military Strategy*. Translated by Harriet Fast Scott. Moscow, 1968.

Stedman, Charles. *History of the Origin, Progress, and Termination of the American War*. Dublin, 1794. A reprint of this work, combined with a rebuttal by Sir Henry Clinton and with a preface by Dave R.

Palmer, is scheduled to be released soon by Greenwood Press, Westport, Connecticut.

Stinchcombe, William C. *The American Revolution and the French Alliance*. Syracuse, 1969.

Syrett, Harold C., ed. *The Papers of Alexander Hamilton*. New York, 1961-1972. 17 vols. to date.

Thacher, James. *Military Journal of the American Revolution*. Hartford, 1862.

Trevelyan, Sir George Otto. *The American Revolution*. London, 1928. 6 vols.

Vauban, Sebastien. *Manual of Siegecraft and Fortifications*. Translated by George A. Rothrock. Ann Arbor, 1968.

Walker, Francis A., comp. *Statistical Atlas of the United States at the Ninth Census, 1870*. Washington, D.C., 1874.

Weigley, Russell. *The American Way of War*. New York, 1973.

————. *History of the United States Army*. New York, 1967.

Wharton, Francis, ed. *The Revolutionary Diplomatic Correspondence of the United States*. Washington, D.C., 1889. 6 vols.

Willcox, William B. *Portrait of a General*. New York, 1964.

Index